**North Dakota State University Libraries**

GIFT FROM

Allen Osmundson
2008

The Norwegian-American Historical Association

# Norwegian-American Studies

## *Volume 32*

1989

The Norwegian-American Historical Association

NORTHFIELD, MINNESOTA

*In Memory of Carlton C. Qualey*

# Preface

The present volume of *Studies*, the thirty-second in the series, again makes apparent the need to pursue the story of immigration on both sides of the Atlantic. Immigration was a two-sided phenomenon that involved circumstances in the old as well as in the new society. The forces that sent people overseas to begin life anew in America are the subject of discussion in the article by Aage Engesæter. He considers the early and extensive emigration from the district of Sogn on Norway's west coast and questions traditional causal explanations relating to population increase and the resulting strain on limited resources, but leaves the question open for further research and scholarly debate. B. Lindsay Lowell reviews sociological theories of migration and tests the accuracy of the different hypotheses with statistical methodology, citing several local Norwegian studies of the movement to Amercia.

Information spread through personal correspondence influenced mobility, as has been evidenced in studies of immigrant letters from America; letters sent in the opposite direction simultaneously affected immigrant perception of the homeland. For the first time, the series offers examples of the latter. They are communications from the district of Telemark to immigrants in the Midwest — or "Norway letters," as these exhibits may well be designated — collected and translated by

Øyvind T. Gulliksen. They represent a largely untapped historical source which few students of immigration have hitherto considered. Letters exchanged, circulated, or printed in Norwegian-language newspapers in America have fared only slightly better, though their role in encouraging the westward movement of Norwegian settlers has long been recognized. Both types await the interested scholar for a more thorough treatment. The twelve Civil War letters from Col. Hans Christian Heg to his son, edited by E. Biddle Heg, reveal the value of such documents to the social historian; furthermore, the letters at hand give an intimate and touching glimpse of this Norwegian-American war hero within the family circle. Researchers have not nearly exhausted the potential of the better known "America letters" in the study of emigration and the image of America they created in Norway. J.R. Christianson introduces a letter written in the 1850s from the Eldorado settlement in northeastern Iowa, whose very name conveyed a favorable impression.

The lead essay, based on ethnographic field work by Robert A. Ibarra and Arnold Strickon, is an incisive analysis of farm production strategy in Norwegian farming communities in southwestern Wisconsin. The authors demonstrate how a combination of tobacco cultivation and dairying represented a logical production plan that also reflected ethnic values connected with Norwegian-American rural culture.

Norwegian values are likewise at the base of the interpretive illustrated article on the Jacobson farmstead by Steven L. Johnson and Marion J. Nelson. The farmstead, which was donated to Vesterheim, the Norwegian-American Museum in Decorah, Iowa, by the Jacobson family, is located seven miles southeast of Decorah. As the family grew, it was physically modified to satisfy changing needs and is thus typical of general developments, as is much of the family life depicted, with its tensions and conflicting influences. Reidar Bakken details the mixture of Norwegian and American features in two immigrant log houses built in the pioneer era in the Midwest, both of which have been moved to the grounds of the Norwegian Emigrant Museum at Hamar, Norway. Pictorial evidence and scale drawings illustrate how familiar building techniques were altered in the American environment.

The article by Janet E. Rasmussen deals with the intriguing issue of choosing a mate by Scandinavian women and the part played by ethnic loyalty in their selection. To a high degree the women interviewed for this study preferred Scandinavian husbands even though life in America brought about marked changes in attitude and courting behavior. Gracia Grindal, focusing on a drawing, enters the world of pastors' wives in the Norwegian Synod with its aristocratic traditions during the early period in its history and shows the blend of Norwegian and American household practices that prevailed.

Einar Haugen relates the plot and places in context Ole E. Rølvaag's apprentice work titled "Nils og Astri," a novel which has received little notice in considerations of Rølvaag's growth as a literary artist. Paul Benson directs the reader's attention to another neglected area: the emergence and flourishing of a cappella choirs of high merit and reputation at Lutheran colleges founded by Scandinavian immigrants.

Rolf H. Erickson, assisted for Norwegian titles by Johanna Barstad, lists recent publications of both general and specialized interest. Charlotte Jacobson contributes yet another installment of archival acquisitions; the potential obviously exists for an even greater effort in securing documentation of the Norwegian-American experience.

This volume is fittingly dedicated to the memory of Carlton C. Qualey, who as a young scholar collected valuable materials for the Association's archives, and who at the time of his death at age eighty-three in March, 1988, had served on its publications board for fifty-five years. By precept and by friendly advice and constructive criticism he encouraged high professional standards in the Association's program.

C.A. Clausen translated the two articles originally written in Norwegian; the Association thereby, as on many past occasions during Clausen's long service, again benefits from his skill as a translator, knowledge of the subject matter, and dedication to its mission. It is a privilege to acknowledge with

much personal gratitude the work of my untiring and competent editorial assistant, Mary R. Hove; her assistance in
preparing volume thirty-two for publication greatly eased the
editorial burden and as in earlier volumes substantially en-
hanced its quality.

Odd S. Lovoll
*St. Olaf College*

# Contents

# Norwegian-American Studies

*Volume 32*

# 1

# The Norwegian-American Dairy-Tobacco Strategy in Southwestern Wisconsin*

## by Robert A. Ibarra and Arnold Strickon

Southwestern Wisconsin is among the oldest and most successful locations of Norwegian agricultural settlement in the United States. Among its unique characteristics is the established relationship between Norwegian — and, afterwards Norwegian-American — farmers and the growing of tobacco.[1] This association between Norwegian-American identity and tobacco has received some academic attention by Karl B. Raitz in 1970 and more recently by the present authors.[2] Both studies concentrated upon the history and dynamics of the relationship between Norwegians and tobacco. Further, they recognized tobacco as but a single element in a set of farm production strategies. Neither work, however, concentrated upon the larger interrelationships among Norwegian-American ethnic identity, tobacco cultivation, and the goals and purposes of agricultural production, on the one hand, and the strategies developed and followed to achieve those goals,

*Research for this article was supported by the award to Arnold Strickon of HEW Grant MH 24587. Pilot projects leading to this research were funded by grants from the Research Committee of the University of Wisconsin-Madison awarded to Strickon and Herbert S. Lewis. The authors wish to express their sincere gratitude to Professor Lewis for his assistance throughout this project.

on the other. It is the purpose of this essay to focus upon the question of farm production strategy relating to tobacco and the Norwegian-American farm community in southwestern Wisconsin.

The article will begin with an overview of the community in which the field research was done. This will be followed by a brief history of the association between Norwegians and tobacco in southwestern Wisconsin. The body of the paper will be devoted to a description of the Norwegian-American dairy-tobacco strategy in that region.

BACKGROUND

The ethnographic field work upon which this study is based was done by the authors between 1974 and 1976 in Vernon county, Wisconsin.[3] Vernon county, which lies south of the city of La Crosse, extends eastward for some fifty miles from the Mississippi River. The county is known for its large and active Norwegian-American community and for being one of the two principal tobacco-producing counties in the state.

Vernon county encompasses a landscape of rolling ridges, undulating narrow prairies, and steep-sided, deep stream- and river-cut valleys. The soils are generally good for the production of corn, grains, and tobacco. The climate is typical of the Upper Midwest with a growing season of 150–160 days.

The region was settled, beginning in the 1840s and continuing in significant numbers until the turn of the century, by a series of agriculturally inclined European immigrant populations. The earliest of these settlers were people of "old American stock" who, in local terminology, are referred to as "Yankees." Following closely behind them came Germans, Irish, Norwegians, Italians, and a small population of escaped slaves and freedmen. Toward the end of the century came Czechs and Sudeten Germans, who were locally identified as "Bohemians." Each of these populations settled in different sections of the county. Though there has been some shifting of the boundaries of these "ethnic regions" since the period of earliest European settlement, for the most part the descendants of these immigrant pioneers continue to represent the local majorities in each of their traditional regions in the county. The largest of these immigrant populations was the Norwegian. Their Norwegian-American descendants continue to constitute the largest single ethnic population in the county.

Farming communities in Vernon county are organized in patterns which geographers refer to as "open country neighborhoods." In this form of community organization farm families reside on their own farms in the countryside. Interpersonal relations are structured by social networks which bind farms through ties of friendship, kinship, and proximity. A number of such networks which cluster together and focus upon a country church or school constitute a neighborhood. Several such neighborhoods focus upon a service village, while larger towns serve as marketing and political centers.

In this part of Wisconsin, as in much of the rest of the state, these neighborhoods brought together co-nationals and co-religionists. Neighborhood, religion, nationality, and later ethnicity were tied together into a single social and geographic fabric. Where two national populations bordered each other they would each support their own churches, often within sight of each other, even if they were of the same denomination. If, however, one of the "nationalities" lacked a sufficiently large population to support their own church they would be welcomed, or at least accepted, in the church of their co-religionists of another nationality, language differences permitting. In a similar manner religious differences within a "national population," as for example between Catholic and Protestant Germans, also shaped rural networks and neighborhoods.

Within the Norwegian settlement, community boundaries were differentiated by the settlers' region of origin within Norway. For example, in Vernon county immigrants from the Sogn region of Norway tended to settle in and around the county seat of Viroqua, while people from the Gudbrandsdalen valley clustered in and around the villages of Westby and Coon Valley. These self-identified, intra-community boundaries are still sufficiently strong that Norwegian regional cultural differences, such as local dialects and food preferences, still exist and differentiate Vernon county Norwegian Americans.

The close association between tobacco and Norwegians cannot be attributed to some long-standing agricultural and cultural pattern in Norway which was carried over to the United States by immigrants. When the earliest Norwegian immigrants arrived in the United States, tobacco had never been grown in Norway.[4] Tobacco was introduced to Norwegian immigrants in the earliest Norwegian settlements in northern Illinois and southern Wisconsin. The crop, and the techniques for growing it, had been brought to this region by Yankee settlers from New England. Norwegians worked as hired laborers in the Yankees' tobacco fields and in the process gained the knowledge necessary to cultivate the crop. Tobacco was a highly profitable crop if the producer had an adequate amount of "free," that is family, labor available. The Norwegians, with relatively large families, ignorant of the language and ways of the country and therefore less able to take advantage of other kinds of opportunities which the Yankees could exploit, came to replace the Yankees as the primary producers of the crop.

Tobacco became known among Norwegians as a "mortgage lifter." A few good crops and a man could purchase his own farm, free and unencumbered. "For the Norwegian immigrants, the landless offspring of a society in which land and status, and even personal identity, were inseparable, a land of fierce and unrelenting primogeniture, this opportunity was not to be missed. Labor and obedience [within the family] were expected, had no financial cost, and reaped a rich reward."[5]

These were the circumstances which provoked the link between Norwegian immigrants and their descendants and the cultivation of tobacco. As people moved north out of the original Norwegian colonies of northern Illinois they took their knowledge of tobacco with them and introduced it throughout southwestern Wisconsin. From that point on, however, the dynamics of the association between Norwegians and tobacco were in a constant state of flux, a state which continues until the present day. This association will be examined in a number of key periods during all of which tobacco remained a supplement to a major agricultural product. In the beginning the major crop was wheat but this was later replaced by dairying.

In the middle years of the nineteenth century the economic advantages of tobacco cultivation were immediately apparent to the non-Norwegian neighbors of the new settlers in Vernon county and the surrounding areas. The techniques of cultivation and processing were rapidly transmitted to the non-Norwegians, often by way of intermarriage, particularly with German men.

Initially, the sale of the tobacco, primarily used for cigar-wrapper and chewing tobacco, was made to traveling buyers representing eastern corporations. These buyers usually had to work through local assistants who served as translators in the dealings between immigrant producers and eastern buyers. By the end of the nineteenth century, however, one of these intermediaries, Martin Bekkedal, ventured into the business of tobacco commodity dealing and became the largest buyer in the region. He was Norwegian born, thoroughly rooted in the Norwegian community of Westby; the workers and managers in his business were themselves largely Norwegians from the Westby area, even when quartered in other communities.

By the 1920s other Norwegians from the same region began to develop a producers' cooperative run by and for tobacco farmers. Decision-making in the cooperative was allocated by county and township and reflected the proportion of total sales to the cooperative from a particular regional unit. By this rule Norwegian counties and townships dominated the legislative organs of the cooperative. Thus both private and cooperative commodity purchasing were owned or controlled by local Norwegians. As long as prices were high, all this mattered little to non-Norwegian tobacco producers.

But prices did not remain high. The coming of the Great Depression destroyed the previous price structure of tobacco with disastrous results. Across the region, with the exception of the Norwegian townships and neighborhoods, there was a mass exodus from tobacco production. Even today one can see abandoned tobacco-curing sheds as modern archaeological relics of the crash in tobacco prices. It appeared to people in the affected localities that only Norwegians remained with tobacco during and after the Depression. However, closer examination reveals that this is not the case. Rather, a higher percentage of Norwegians remained with the crop. It is not necessary to repeat here the lengthy argument developed in the authors' earlier study, but in terms of the current discussion it may be appropriate to summarize its conclusions.[6]

In the high-risk economic environment of the depression years, an environment in which the Federal Government sought to control the precipitous fall in the price of tobacco by attempting to discourage farmers from its production, the tobacco producer was faced with a crucial decision. Was he to remain with tobacco or was he to reallocate his resources in land, time, labor, and capital? Disproportionately, Norwegian-American farmers, and their adjacent non-Norwegian neighbors, stayed with the crop while non-Norwegian farmers in their own townships and ethnic communities for the most part chose to abandon tobacco cultivation. The major factor in this decision appears to have been related to the farmer's involvement in Norwegian communities, networks, and neighborhoods where tobacco was a high-priority crop. Non-Norwegians removed from the core tobacco-producing areas quickly restructured their resources and instead devoted themselves almost entirely to dairy cattle, the milk they produced, and the corn forage which they required.

The mechanism of this locally and ethnically differentiated reaction appears to have been the fact that marketing was, by an accident of history, largely concentrated in the hands of Norwegian-managed and -controlled institutions. The predominantly Norwegian communities knew and could evaluate the men who ran the tobacco cooperatives through their social networks, kin connections, and churches. Non-Norwegians who did not reside in close proximity to the

Norwegian communities lacked these sources of information and therefore had less confidence in the future of the crop.

The resulting over-representation of Norwegian farmers among tobacco growers in the region was frozen and institutionalized in the years immediately after World War II by their acceptance of the tobacco allotment system. This system provided crop insurance and a government-guaranteed minimum price if the farmers in a region voted to honor the program's restrictions on tobacco production. These restrictions limited the amount of land each farmer could devote to tobacco production. This amount of land was called his allotment. The allotment was the property of the farmer and could be used by him, rented or leased by him to another farmer, or sold as part of, or separate from, his farm. Although the allotment program could not prevent any farmer from growing all the tobacco he wished, to do so without the guarantees of parity and insurance provided by the allotment program was uneconomic and highly risky. Few, if any, chose that route.

The factor that froze the Norwegians into the disproportionate predominance in tobacco cultivation that still characterizes them was the fact that in order for the farmers in a locality to participate in the allotment program it was necessary for them to vote for it. More to the point was the fact that the only farmers who could vote in the program, and the only ones to benefit from it, were those who had produced tobacco for five years *before* the election was held. In southwestern Wisconsin this meant the election and the program were to be limited to the Norwegians and their neighbors who had stayed with the crop through the difficult years of the '30s and '40s.

However, tobacco had always been a supplement to a major crop. In the nineteenth century it had supplemented wheat. More recently dairying had been the major economic activity in the region for tobacco growers and non-tobacco growers alike. It is this mix of dairy farming and tobacco cultivation, this complex archetypical strategy of the Norwegian-American farmer of the region, that will now be examined.

THE NORWEGIAN FARMING STRATEGY

The current agricultural strategy began taking shape in Vernon and surrounding counties during the 1880s when local farmers, somewhat later than in other parts of Wisconsin, began shifting away from wheat production as their major economic pillar because of the spreading wheat blight and the growing competiton of High Plains wheat growers.[7] This change in productive orientation was signaled by an increased experimentation in the area with fruit growing, cattle, and small livestock production.[8]

In 1880 there were only a few cheese factories in Vernon county; creameries were scarcer still. Some Norwegian farmers in the northern part of the county maintained small herds of goats for milk and the home processing of Norwegian cheeses.[9] After 1880, however, the number of dairy herds in the county increased, as did the frequency of scientific breeding. This development was initiated by "Yankee" farmers but the Norwegians also came to see the value of these practices.[10] A growth in the number of dairy processing plants reflected the increase in the number of dairy herds.[11] As early as 1895 over one million pounds of creamery butter were produced in Vernon and surrounding counties.[12] Within fifteen years of that date outputs of butter, cheese, and condensed milk had established Vernon and neighboring counties as an important dairy region within Wisconsin.[13] Much of the processing was done by local creameries. The important role of dairying in Vernon county expanded in the years that followed.

Dairy farming remains important in Vernon county. In the mid-1970s the county ranked thirteenth out of seventy-two counties in the number of milk cows and fourth in the state in the number of dairy herds. Eighty-four percent of the 2,451 farms in Vernon county are dairy farms. The value of dairy and dairy-related products, including meat animals, which are for the most part culled, overage, non-producing dairy animals, and most field crops in the county, represented ninety-five percent of the value of all agricultural cash receipts. Tobacco, on the other hand, represented a mere .07 percent of the agricultural cash receipts of the county's farmers.[14] It is, then, within this economic context that the adherence of Norwegian-American farmers and their neighbors to the production of tobacco must be considered.

In an overall economic view tobacco is of small consequence. Yet within the region it has a visibility out of proportion to its economic importance and to the relatively small number of farmers who grow it. In southwestern Wisconsin tobacco has assumed a symbolic significance as a marker of rural Norwegian-American ethnic identification. The strength of this identification with Norwegian-American culture led Karl Raitz, in his comprehensive study "The Location of Tobacco Production in Western Wisconsin" (1970), to the conclusion that "Tobacco farming is not an economically viable endeavor which is locationally influenced by climate, edaphic conditions, topography, or historic continuity." He argued that it is, rather, "a residual of an anachronistic social institution."[15]

In their earlier paper the present authors argued against this position on both theoretical and substantive grounds. Theoretically, the view that economic and cultural "explanations" were mutually exclusive was rejected. Rather, it was concluded that "ethnicity [which is to say 'culture'] and economics are better considered as variables in a single equation, the output of which is, in this case, the decision to grow tobacco."[16] Raitz's interpretation was rejected on substantive grounds because it appeared to be based upon an excessively narrow view of "economic rationality." He argues that tobacco cultivation is profitable only when very low cost or free labor is available and that greater profits per acre could be generated by alternative auxiliary crops or by redirecting land from tobacco to the support of additional dairy cattle.[17]

But "economic rationality" need not be defined solely by dollars of profit per acre. Other factors may intervene, such as labor costs, which were recognized by Raitz, but also by the value added to a farm by the fact that it may be sold with its owner's allotment as part of the sale. In addition there are costs involved if a farmer shifts labor, land, and capital from one production effort to another. Finally, there are other constraints upon economic decisions beyond mere profitability. There are also considerations of risk and safety, and the role a particular undertaking and the income derived from it play in a farmer's total production package. In their earlier paper the present authors could deal with only some of these variables in their argument that tobacco production "represents an extremely subtle relationship within the opportunity structure of the region's agro-economy."[18]

In this study some details of tobacco production which help explain the successful symbiotic relationship, the "fit," between tobacco production and dairy farming activities need to be explored. This relationship, the tobacco-dairy complex, is a finely-tuned alignment of farm schedules, crop patterns, and dairy herd management which constitutes a small-farm production strategy for many Norwegian farmers in the Vernon county area. Ultimately it will be suggested that this "traditional" farming pattern has up to now proved to be an effective safeguard for the small farmer against serious economic fluctuations.

THE PRODUCTION PROCESS

As already noted, the geographer Karl Raitz came to the conclusion that soils, climate, and other aspects of the physical environment did little to dictate the distribution of tobacco in southwestern Wisconsin. This fact reflects the hardiness and adaptability of the plant. In spite of this, however, the plant requires that the farmer go through a protracted, complex, and detailed process of production. The most striking aspect of this process is that the cultivation of tobacco has been little mechanized. The work cycle for it requires intensive, hard manual stoop labor.[19]

The cultivation process begins in April with the preparation of seed beds for the initial germination of the plants. These seed beds must be steamed to reduce weeds and control diseases. After the seeds have been steamed, they are planted and the bed is enclosed with a muslin-covered wooden frame

Early in the spring, ground is prepared for the planting of tobacco seed by plowing and then steaming the ground. The steaming sanitizes the ground and reduces weed growth. In the background is a typical tobacco barn. The vertical boards of which the sides are made can be rotated, thereby opening or closing the sides of the barn in order to control the temperature and airflow during the curing process.

After plowing and steaming, the tobacco seeds are planted and the beds are covered with muslin for protection. Here the plants remain until they are mature enough to be transplanted to the fields.

for protection of the young plants when they sprout. By late June or early July, when the seedlings are about six inches high, they are transplanted into the tobacco fields. These have been prepared beforehand by plowing, fertilization, and harrowing. The seedlings are individually inserted by hand in rows by a two-worker team consisting of a tractor driver pulling a transplanter on which rides another worker who takes seedlings and manually plants them in the earth as the tractor slowly pulls them along. A "mechanized" team of this kind can set a five-acre field in three days. Small allotments or poorer farmers may carry out this phase of cultivation completely by hand. In either case, if plants are later found to be damaged or diseased they are replaced manually.

Field care requires hand hoeing, cultivation, and the eradication of insect pests. Once the plant has formed seeds each bud is "topped" manually by having the upper part of the stem snapped off in order to thicken the leaves, stimulate growth, and increase nicotine content. Topping also stimulates axial shoots or "suckers" which must then be removed manually. A good worker can top an acre in three to five hours and remove suckers in an additional four to six hours per acre.

Harvest demands more labor, almost all of it manual, than any other phase of the tobacco cycle. At this point all physically able members of the family are called upon to help and often even with the availability of family labor it may still be necessary to call upon poorly paid wage labor for assistance. Labor demand in the tobacco region is so great during harvest that it is common practice for high school students to be given leaves of absence in order to work in the fields, whether or not they are from farm families themselves.

THE TOBACCO-DAIRY RELATIONSHIP

Tobacco's voracious need for nutrients places heavy demands on the soils unless nutrients are replaced in large amounts by natural or artificial fertilizers. Adequate nutrients not only protect the productivity of the soil but also maintain a high quality of leaf. When the switch from wheat to dairy farming began it had an immediately beneficial effect upon tobacco growing because dairy cows increased the availability of manure to serve as fertilizer for the tobacco fields.

While livestock provided fertilizer for the tobacco fields the cows, in turn, required year-round attention plus adequate feed, in terms of both amount and quality of forage and fodder, in order to insure high milk production. In the developmental years of the tobacco-dairy complex tobacco farmers relied on pasturage rather than fodder for their cattle. All available manure was placed on the tobacco ground while the remaining fields went unfertilized.[20] With the introduction of hybrid corn, farmers were led to devote some of the manure to their corn fields. Yet even today many farmers informed one of the authors that they put three times more manure on their tobacco grounds than on any other fields.

While there are clear advantages to the union of dairying and tobacco in a single operation, there are also disadvantages. The disadvantages appear to affect primarily the dairy side of the equation. The problem in part is a result of conflicting work cycles and agricultural priorities for dairy-tobacco farmers. For example, for modern dairying to be profitable, according to dairymen, at least three cuttings of alfalfa are re-

The only mechanized part of production, aside from plowing, is the use of a tobacco transplanting machine such as the one pictured here. The machine is pulled by a tractor and carries two workers. They place the plants in the wheel, which then inserts the seedlings from the earlier tobacco beds into the soil which has been prepared by the transplanter.

quired for an average-size herd of thirty-five Holsteins. Alfalfa is a semi-permanent hay crop which is first planted in late April. While oats are brought in around May, the first cutting of alfalfa may not occur until the following year, after which it can be cut repeatedly like grass for a number of years. In the second year after planting, farmers try to get a first cutting off by June before planting tobacco. The second cutting is ideally brought in by the Fourth of July. During the 1940s the dairy-tobacco farmer rarely began haying until after tobacco was planted in late June or early July. The lack of modern machinery in the tobacco side of the operation further slowed or delayed the cultivation cycle.[21]

Between about 1920 and 1940 tobacco-dairy farmers generally began their farm activity cycles in early April with planting of oats followed immediately by the steaming of the tobacco beds. In May, corn for silage was planted and tobacco seedlings were tended. In June the tobacco was transplanted from seed beds to the fields, corn was cultivated, and the first harvest of alfalfa was made. Oats were harvested in July, followed by a midsummer slow period during which a second cutting of hay might occur. In early August and into September tobacco was harvested and corn cut, leaving little time for tobacco farmers to get a third cutting of alfalfa. By October and November fall plowing had to be completed. Most often the fields which received priority in the fall plowing were the tobacco grounds, since early spring was the time farmers spent piling up manure and tobacco stalks to spread on them. Consequently, oats might not get planted on time because of the manure spreading, and the crucial third cutting of alfalfa rarely took place. Tobacco, because of its high priority, would not only compete for manure with other crops but by so doing would reduce the amount and/or the quality of feed available to maintain even average milk production in a herd. In other words these farmers sacrificed potentially greater milk production to the immediate demands of tobacco.

The picture today has altered relatively little. Some changes have been made, largely in the mechanization of the production of corn and alfalfa and the introduction of artificial fertilizers and herbicides. Oats have ceased to be a major crop because of a drop in market prices, which in turn reflected the disappearance of the horse as a source of farm labor and its replacement by the internal combustion engine. A first crop of hay (alfalfa) is now put up before tobacco is planted. Also farmers now use several varieties of hay with different maturation cycles, which permits the stringing out of hay cutting over the summer.

Even with these changes many local experts believe that tobacco farmers are still unable to produce adequate hay for their dairy herds. Most farmers would simply buy feed to make up for this shortage. But, say these local observers, "Norwegians have a frugal, tightwad attitude. They don't buy any extra feed, and without that third crop of hay they are never going to get any milk out of their cows."[22]

The tobacco cycle not only competes with the feed and forage cycle; it also is in competition with the production cycle of the cows themselves.[23] A cow generally gives milk only ten months of the year and needs to be freshened annually for milk production. Most modern dairymen seek uniform milk production; thus individual cows are allowed to dry up and are bred on varying schedules. Before modern methods of uniform production, however, if cows came into milk on different schedules, tobacco work would be seriously affected. Tobacco growers, therefore, resorted to controlling their herds simply by manipulation of breeding dates so that cow cycles did not conflict with the tobacco cycle. Thus, they were "tuning" their herds to fit the tobacco schedule. For example, it was expected that replacement heifers added to the herd would freshen in the early fall. To avoid conflicts with the tobacco harvest, tobacco–dairy farmers bred their heifers much later than did other farmers. As a result, the average freshening in Norwegian areas is closer to Christmas, a pattern which continues to the present.

Silage, or stored feed, is also a variable in the dairy–tobacco equation. Before 1920 and the advent of silos in the community farmers generally had more acres in pasture than in cropland. Since "Norwegian" cows freshened around

Christmas the herds were often pastured in the winter when they began to produce milk well. Milk production would increase when a tobacco farmer had more time to attend to his herd. In the summer when these farmers were busiest with tobacco the cows would tend to dry up. The herd, then, was manipulated to fit in with the tobacco cycle. This tended to cause shorter lactation periods, thus reducing overall milk production.

The use of silage reduces the farmer's dependence upon pasturage for milk production by preserving high energy feeds, primarily corn and alfalfa in this region, produced during the growing season for use throughout the year. The most efficient but also the most expensive means of preserving food crops for the livestock is the Harvestore type of silo. These large blue metal vacuum silos are ubiquitous throughout the region. They produce a higher quality silage than the ordinary form of silo, but they are extremely expensive and in order for them to be cost effective a fairly large herd and source of feed and a closely controlled feeding program are required. Such controls are not likely to be found on smaller farms. This technology is generally not associated with tobacco producers, who continue to use older style, less capital-intensive silo technology.

Still another variable in the interaction between tobacco and dairying is the question of the breeds of livestock which the predominantly Norwegian farmers of the region raise as opposed to those breeds usually associated with more modern, large-scale dairy operations. The difference lies between those farmers who raise what are called, in local parlance, "colored cows" and those who raise the most common American dairy breed, the black and white Holsteins. This choice of colored cows (that is, Jerseys and Guernseys) which are preferred by most of those involved in the traditional tobacco *and* dairy production is seen by extension workers and other experts on the local scene as detrimental to local production and is considered by them as counterproductive to the farmers' interests. The first drawback to the non-Holstein breeds are that they do not produce as much milk as Holsteins.

In 1971 Vernon county's 1,725 herds were only 11.7 percent of Grade A quality; in comparison Dane county's 1,639 herds were 73.5 percent Grade A. According to Professor Clarence Olson of the University of Wisconsin the persistence of what he called "the colored cow syndrome" is due directly to the region's Norwegian farmers. This continuing attachment to the Guernsey and the Jersey has been attributed to the fact that the traditional farmer in Norway was accustomed to working with "red" cattle and not the "black and whites" of Germany and the low countries.

Although there has been a reduction in the number and proportion of colored livestock in Vernon county, the Norwegian areas of that county still show the importance of these breeds. While Holsteins make up ninety-three percent of the total dairy herd in Wisconsin, the situation in the Norwegian communities in Vernon county is quite different.[24] According to estimates of the operators of a local breeding cooperative in the heart of the Norwegian settlement, the colored breeds, Brown Swiss, Guernsey, and Jersey, constitute fifty-five percent of the total herd. This is the highest proportion of these breeds in Wisconsin and very likely in the nation as well.

But there is more than ethnic preference and sentimental memory involved in this choice of Guernsey and Jersey. These breeds produce milk of a higher butterfat content than do the Holsteins. Since the turn of the century this region has been a producer of butter and cheese, which demand a high butterfat content in the milk used in their production. In addition milk destined for the butter and cheese market need not meet Grade A standards, which were set for milk destined for direct consumption by human beings.

After the 1920s the growing demand for whole milk led to the introduction of bulk milk equipment and the growing shift to Holstein cattle which produce a large amount of milk, roughly eighty pounds per day, versus about thirty pounds per day by colored cattle. However, this pattern did not emerge as strongly in the Norwegian community of central Vernon county. Small farms were unable to maintain a sufficiently large Holstein herd. Small pastures which could maintain approximately forty Jerseys could support only twenty-five Holsteins. The problem was compounded when hay crops were too small and feed prices were too high.

Barn size was another problem. Norwegian barns were built to last. Made of wood cut from their own farm land, these structures often held up longer than do modern barns. But these barns were built to accommodate the smaller colored cows, and farmers had problems getting Holsteins into stalls designed for Guernseys or Jerseys. A 1,000 pound cow, either a fairly large Jersey or a very small Holstein, was about the largest animal the old barns could accommodate. Farmers who considered remodeling their barns were aware that the cow size/barn size ratio meant that for every 1,000 pounds of cow they could expect 500 pounds of milk per week. But they also knew that after 1,000 pounds of cow, the ratio of income to feed costs actually declines. That is, while the Holsteins produce more milk than the smaller colored breeds their energy efficiency is lower. They produce less milk for a given amount of feed than do their colored cousins. Most smaller farmers felt that the potential increase did not justify the cost of remodeling their barns and changing the breed of their herds. Some implemented a mini-max strategy by attempting to introduce small Holsteins and keeping mixed herds of small Holsteins and colored stock in an attempt to increase their milk production. Replacement cows, however, were expensive, and because of the cost of remodeling few tobacco farmers wanted to take on the necessary debts and risks inherent in any change in production strategy.

Farmers who did respond to the opportunities offered by the expanding market for Grade A milk and modernized their facilities and herds looked down upon the small, traditional Norwegian farmers as conservative. They were seen as merely holding their own and missing the opportunity significantly to expand their operations.

MODERN AND TRADITIONAL FARMERS

The traditional tobacco-dairy farmer sought an operation that was as self-sufficient as possible. This meant minimal capitalization, dependence upon unpaid labor, basically family labor but also neighbor exchange, and as little debt as possible. Responding to opportunities offered by the expansion in the market for Grade A milk, some farmers reacted directly to economic incentives, and indirectly to programs pushed by agricultural extension service workers. These factors encouraged them to expand their land and herds, and invest in modern, expensive bulk–milk–handling equipment and Harvestore silos. They dropped tobacco altogether or at least reduced it to a minor place in their production strategy. It was these "modern" farmers who tended to deprecate those of their neighbors who still placed considerable importance on growing tobacco at the expense of dairy production.

Local farmers, then, see two general categories of farmer, modern and traditional. The distinction is marked by differences in the level of capitalization. The traditional farmers, with limited capitalization, generally have farms in the range of 40 to 100 acres. Nearly sixty percent of the Norwegian farm population around Westby fall into this category. These small farmers grow five acres of tobacco, have little tillable acreage and feel incapable of expanding their operations. They average forty acres of hay and corn and twenty acres of oats without double cropping. Their dairy herds of fifteen to twenty-five cows are mixed, that is, Holsteins and colored, and usually the milk that moves off the farm is not Grade A and is, therefore, not destined for the whole milk market. For these farmers tobacco has priority over dairy production. They feel that tobacco pays the mortgage and the taxes and sends the kids to college, while their dairy operation covers running expenses. On these farms tobacco goes into the drying shed before hay goes into the barn. They do not double-crop but rather rely on a combination of pasturage and a supplement of purchased feed to get them through the year.

According to large-dairy proponents, the traditional farmer sees only the immediate return from his tobacco (about $1,100 per acre at the time of the authors' field work in the early 1970s) and fails to see the long-term return from better milk production. Some critics of the Norwegian tobacco-dairy complex feel that merely taking two acres out of tobacco and putting two to five Holsteins on the land instead would result in a more profitable dairy operation. What the traditional farmer sees in such a suggestion is reduced tobacco profits, additional feed costs, and an extremely problematic improvement in milk production, since the tobacco fields may not be easily accessible to livestock, as they are often on the bottom and sides of steep valleys.

The locally described "modern" farm, while not large by most North American standards, is larger than the local "traditional" farm. Some thirty to forty percent of Vernon county farms, varying in size between 100 and 200 acres, fall into this category. The farmers in this category, many of them Norwegian, gear their operations almost entirely to high production of Grade A milk. With an average of forty to fifty registered Holsteins, they never consider mixing their herds.[25] These farmers are conscientious about their hay crops and will often put in eighty acres of hay with at least two cuttings a year, depending upon the capacity of their silos. The number and type of silos is a visual measure of a farmer's success and a symbol of his economic standing and prestige. These farmers also rely on good commercial feeding programs in conjunction with silage for their cattle.

Even so, these larger farms often have as little as thirty tillable acres. Their crops are primarily a fifty-fifty combination of corn and alfalfa. They feel justified, because of their larger acreage, in purchasing a good deal of labor-saving, large-farm machinery. They maintain good field rotation and generally put in a lot of hay before their tobacco, if they grow it at all.

When grown on larger farms tobacco is viewed as a sideline and not as a major activity. Depending upon market conditions these farmers may vary their actual tobacco acreage within the limits of their allotment. Tobacco provides a nice bonus, but the farmers do not depend upon it as a significant source of income.

As with the traditional farmers, modern farmers also depend upon family labor for tobacco production. At harvest

The tobacco is harvested, one leaf at time, by workers using a tobacco chopping tool. This is typical of the manual stoop labor characteristic of tobacco cultivation.

time family workers will be supplemented by exchange labor with neighbors and/or low-cost labor by high school students released from school for that purpose. When children grow up and leave the farm and the labor required for tobacco becomes costly, then it is likely that tobacco farmers will either reduce their tobacco acreage, rent their allotment in order to maintain their rights in it, or sell it and drop out of tobacco production altogether.

Large-scale family labor is not a flexible resource in the region. Family labor not used for tobacco is not easily reallocated to other income-producing activities on the farm or elsewhere in the community. Non-tobacco farm activities are increasingly capital—rather than labor—intensive. Milking and preparing milk for shipment is largely automated. If a field is redirected from tobacco to corn or alfalfa, topographical conditions permitting, it will be worked by farm machin-

After the tobacco is harvested it is "speared" onto a wooden lathe one leaf at a time, the work being done by the woman in the photo. It is then brought, usually by tractor, to the tobacco barn where it is stored and cured.

ery, not by the wife and children of the farmer. Nor is there much in the way of non-farm employment in the region which will provide income equivalent to that produced in the tobacco fields. No matter what the farm size, reduction or cessation of tobacco growing, as long as "free" family labor is available, is throwing out an income-producing resource without replacing it.

Not everyone agrees that the modern farmers' strategy is necessarily the superior one, a doubt which in recent years appears to be reinforced by events. Even as early as the mid-1970s some local businessmen were seriously concerned about the financial consequences and risks in the "modern" strategy. One informant said that the big dairy operations "just aren't making it, and a lot are over their heads."[26] Some had gone $100,000 into debt with consequent heavy interest payments. At that time they may have been seeing less than $25,000 a year before taxes. The expansion of the "large" dairy farms was occurring on the foundation of rapidly expanding land values. Farms which were valued at only $20,000 at the end of the 1960s were valued at $50,000 by the mid-'70s.[27]

In the opinion of local bankers and agro-businessmen, the farmers that follow the tobacco-dairy strategy are the only farmers in the area with liquid reserves. "The truth is, the small farmer knows his limitations and doesn't go into expensive equipment. He may work a little harder, but it's a nice feeling to have your place clear with a small herd, basic machinery, and not be in debt. It's a conservative strategy."[28]

"Norwegians," stated a locally-based dairy expert, "want to be independent and debt free. They do anything to accomplish those two things." An example of this attitude is a Norwegian estate probated in the Westby region in the mid-1970s which had liquid assets of $100,000, yet the farmhouse itself lacked plumbing and running water.[29]

Events since the mid-1970s suggest that those farmers who followed the tobacco-dairy strategy may, in the long run, have been better prepared to survive the farm crisis of the first half of the 1980s than those of their peers who chose the more "modern" and capital, debt, and interest intensive alternative of straight dairy production.[30] Although the boundary between these two categories of farm is largely determined by farm size, the different ethnic distribution of the farmers who practice these two production strategies results in a larger impact upon the social and cultural life of the Norwegian-American community by the followers of the "traditional" than the "modern" strategy. It is tobacco as a symbol of Norwegian-American identity which has intruded itself into the rural culture of western Wisconsin, not the Harvestore silo.[31]

The traditional Norwegian-American family farm has proved itself a survivor in a random, almost Darwinian response to environmentally selective pressures generated both by the market place and by government policies.[32] However, this does not mean that because the traditional farm has survived thus far it is forever safe. What the effects of reduced tobacco consumption and/or a change in tobacco price supports and allotment programs by the government would be, one cannot say. Although, on the face of it, such developments would appear to spell the end of the tobacco-dairy complex as a viable production strategy one can only wonder if such a development would be any worse for the region's farmers than the wheat blight of the last decades of the nineteenth century or the Great Depression of the twentieth.

CONCLUSION

Karl Raitz, in 1970, was so taken by the close connection between Norwegian-American farmers and the growing of tobacco and the apparent lack of a direct economic link between profit and tobacco cultivation that he turned to a cultural explanation as the motivation of Norwegian-American farmers in southwestern Wisconsin to produce that crop. What the present authors argued in their earlier study, and in more detail here, is that the economic significance of tobacco must be appreciated not in terms of simple profit and loss statements for the particular crop, but rather as part of a complex production plan in which not only profit, but also marginal costs, risks, and goals must be taken into account. From this point of view, tobacco has played a key role in a production strategy that contrasts strongly with a strict dairy strategy which stresses only the profit and loss statement. In the conservative, traditional system which characterizes the preponderance of Norwegian farmers, the role of family labor and the lack of alternative uses for it, the costs of switching cattle breeds, the lack of clearly advantageous marginal benefits in dairy pasturage and feed production involved in shifting tobacco land to other uses, the effects of the tobacco allotment upon the value of the farm, the goal of security, freedom from debt, and the availability of liquid assets, all appear to be maximized by a plan which balances tobacco off against dairy production.

What has kept tobacco-dairy a viable strategy up until the present seems indeed to be connected to Norwegian-American rural culture. But it is not a Norwegian love of tobacco for its own sake, a tradition which is in itself valued, although that occurs among some individuals. It is rather a stress upon the family farm and the personal and community values which orbit around it. It is here that sustenance rather than profit is significant, and financial profit in the strict sense is not the sole goal and measure of satisfaction.

## Notes

[1]In local usage the term "Norwegian" is used to signify both the people of Norway and "Norwegian Americans." Which of the two is meant is usually perfectly clear from the context. Local practice will be followed in the balance of this article and the term "Norwegian American" will be used only when it is necessary to do so for reasons of clarity or emphasis.

[2]Karl B. Raitz, "The Location of Tobacco Production in Western Wisconsin" (Ph.D. dissertation, University of Minnesota, 1970). Arnold Strickon and Robert A. Ibarra, "The Changing Dynamics of Ethnicity: Norwegians and Tobacco in Wisconsin," in *Ethnic and Racial Studies*, 6:2 (1983), 174–197.

[3]This part of the article is wholly based upon the authors' earlier study, "The Changing Dynamics of Ethnicity." All sources for statements made in this section will be found in that article.

[4]In fact, tobacco cultivation was introduced to Norway by immigrants to western Wisconsin who returned to their places of origin in Sogn in the late nineteenth century. It never really caught on as a significant crop in Norway, largely because of a fiscal policy which depended upon taxes imposed on imported tobacco as an important source of government income. See Jan Henrik Munksgaard, "Tobakksdyrking i Sogn 1882–1920," in *Blader av tobakkens historie* (Oslo,1978), 111–137.

[5]Strickon and Ibarra, "Changing Dynamics," 181.

[6]Strickon and Ibarra, "Changing Dynamics," 182–189.

[7]Unless otherwise documented, data for this section was obtained in the course of the field research described earlier. Further detail and documentation will be found in Robert A. Ibarra, "Ethnicity Genuine and Spurious: A Study of a Norwegian Community in Rural Wisconsin" (Ph.D. dissertation, University of Wisconsin, 1976).

[8]See Benjamin Horace Hibbard, "The History of Agriculture in Dane County, Wisconsin," in *Bulletin of the University of Wisconsin No. 101*, Economics and Political Science Series, 1/2 (1904), 67–214; *Wisconsin Rural Resources — Vernon County* (Madison, 1957); Eric E. Lampard, *The Rise of the Dairy Industry in Wisconsin: A Study in Agricultural Change 1820–1920*, (Madison, 1963).

[9]Hjalmar R. Holand, *Coon Valley* (Minneapolis, 1976), 15.

[10]Leola Nelson Bergmann, *Americans from Norway* (Philadelphia, 1950), 71.

[11]See *Vernon County: Overall Economic Development Plan* (Viroqua, Wisconsin, 1967).

[12]Lampard, *The Rise of the Dairy Industry*, 271.

[13]*Wisconsin Rural Resources*, 55.

[14]*Wisconsin Cash Receipts, County Estimates 1965-1973* (Madison, 1975), 683.

[15]Raitz, "The Location of Tobacco Production," 284, 291.

[16]Strickon and Ibarra, "Changing Dynamics," 185.

[17]Raitz, "The Location of Tobacco Production," 275-277.

[18]Strickon and Ibarra, "Changing Dynamics," 189.

[19]The description of the tobacco production process in this section is based upon observation and upon an excellent description of the cultivation process found in Raitz, "The Location of Tobacco Production," 127-135.

[20]Raitz, "The Location of Tobacco Production," 124.

[21]Ibarra, "Ethnicity Genuine and Spurious," 112.

[22]Ibarra, "Ethnicity Genuine and Spurious," 115.

[23]Ibarra, "Ethnicity Genuine and Spurious," 115-122.

[24]"Dairy Herd Improvement Progress Report" (Madison, 1975), 43.

[25]Some larger farms combine feed-lot operations with their dairy production. Feed-lot herds are usually not Holsteins, they do not breed with the dairy herds and are kept completely separate from them.

[26]Ibarra, "Ethnicity Genuine and Spurious," 128.

[27]Ibarra, "Ethnicity Genuine and Spurious," 129.

[28]Ibarra, "Ethnicity Genuine and Spurious," 129.

[29]Ibarra, "Ethnicity Genuine and Spurious," 129.

[30]The "suggestion," of course, derives from newspaper reports which, on a national basis, indicate that smaller, debt-free farms were proving more flexible even before the current "agricultural crisis" than heavily debt-ridden larger operations. See *Capitol Times* (Madison), May 24, 1982. The authors were recently awarded a small grant by the Coordinating Committee for American Ethnic Studies of the University of Wisconsin System which will enable them to return to Vernon county in order to study this question and its effects upon Norwegian-American ethnicity and the tobacco-dairy strategy in this region.

[31]See Strickon and Ibarra, "Changing Dynamics."

[32]Sidney M. Greenfield and Strickon, "Entrepreneurship and Social Change," in Greenfield and Strickon, eds., *Entrepreneurs in Cultural Context* (Albuquerque, 1979), 329-350.

# 2

# Poverty, Overpopulation, and the Early Emigration from Sogn

*by Aage Engesæter\**
*translated by C.A. Clausen*

The causes for the early emigration from Norway to America are among the classic problems raised in the field of emigration research. Scholars have gradually arrived at dissimilar explanations and emphases. Traditionally they have concluded that the causes of this emigration were to be found in poverty and cramped and restricted living conditions. And poverty has generally been regarded as a result of the considerable population increase which took place in Norway after 1815. Concepts such as "population pressure" and "overpopulation" have often been put forth as basic factors. Sogn was one of the areas of the country which had a vigorous emigration movement during the 1840s and 1850s. This movement has been explained as the result of a strong population growth, a manifestation of the fact that too many people had accumulated in the district. The historian Andreas Holmsen launched such an idea during the 1930s.[1] He has been followed by others, among them Rasmus Sunde, who in an article in *Norwegian-American Studies* declares that in Vik (Sogn) around 1845 "the population had reached a saturation point in relation to the area's economic possibilities."[2] He also says that "by 1845–1855 there is definite evidence that overpopulation had reached inner Sogn."

The present article argues against both of these conten-

| INNER | CENTRAL | OUTER |
|---|---|---|
| 1. Lærdal | 8. Leikanger | 11. Lavik |
| 2. Årdal | 9. Balestrand | 12. Eivindvik |
| 3. Luster | 10. Vik | 13. Hyllestad |
| 4. Jostedal | | |
| 5. Hafslo | | |
| 6. Sogndal | | |
| 7. Aurland | | |

Map of Sogn with municipal boundaries in 1865.

tions. In questioning them an attempt will be made to shed some light on the social and economic developments in Sogn during the first half of the 1800s, and the early emigration will be examined in the light of these findings. How strong was the population pressure in this district? Was Sogn "overpopulated," and to what degree can this explain the vigorous emigration movement of the 1840s and 1850s?

Sogn is the area on both sides of the long Sognefjord, which extends more than 100 miles into the land from the west coast of Norway to the foot of the mighty mountain range in the heart of the country. It was from the inner and the central communities of this district that emigration became extensive during the 1840s and 1850s. It is also these communities which have been classified as "overpopulated." Consequently it is conditions in inner and central Sogn which will primarily be examined here.

GROWTH AND COMPOSITION OF THE POPULATIONS

Inner Sogn was the most populous area in Sogn. 12,769 people lived there in 1801. By 1855 the number had grown to 20,787. Outer Sogn had a population of 5,881 in 1801 and 9,659 in 1855. In central Sogn, which had the smallest population, the corresponding figures were 5,500 and 7,737. The population increased in Sogn during the first half of the 1800s, but the increase was not equally large in all parts of the district.

It is not the absolute numbers but the relative growth within each region which is of greatest interest. This development is made clear by figure 1.

The table reveals interesting differences. Outer Sogn had a fairly even growth throughout the whole period from 1801 to 1865, broken merely by a slight slowing down during the decade between 1845 and 1855. In inner and central Sogn, however, it was only after 1815 that the population began to increase.

During the period between 1815 and 1845 it was inner Sogn which had the greatest population increase, but in 1845 the increase in these communities ceased and from 1855 until 1865 the population actually decreased. Central Sogn clearly had a weaker population growth than the other districts. The population grew relatively fast from 1815 until 1835, but then the growth slackened, and was weak during the next thirty years. These population developments alone, however, can not settle the question of the degree of population pressure. In addition one must look at the class composition of the population. It is of interest to look at the relationship between the number of farmers and cotters in the various parts of Sogn,

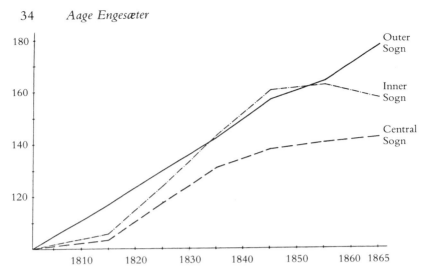

Fig. 1. Population development in Sogn 1801–1865.
Relative figure 1801 = 100.

and how this developed toward the middle of the century. The farmers were those who owned and controlled the resources, while the cotters had no property and sustained life partly by working land which they rented from farmers and partly as hired laborers.

The resources were most unequally divided in inner Sogn. Here there were the fewest farmers in relation to the population. In central Sogn there were more, and outer Sogn had the most farmers in relation to the population. The population grew faster than the number of farmers in all parts of Sogn. The difference was greatest in outer Sogn, while the proportion of farmers in relation to population increase held best in the central communities.

For the cotters the picture was very much the reverse. The number of cotters in relation to population was clearly highest in inner Sogn, equally clearly lowest in outer Sogn, while central Sogn occupied a middle position. The number of cotters grew faster than the population in all parts of Sogn. In inner Sogn there were 2.3 more cotters per 100 inhabitants in 1855 than in 1801, in central Sogn 1.3, and in outer Sogn 1.0 more.

Not even on the basis of these facts can definite conclusions be drawn concerning the population pressure in the various districts of Sogn. It is hardly sufficient to maintain that the population pressure was strongest in the areas where the cotter system was most strongly entrenched. There can be many causes for such a social organization, and it is by no means certain that the overall standard of living needs to be lower in communities with many cotters than in communities where the farms were divided up and the soil resources were more equally distributed. But even if such conclusions were to be drawn, they might indicate that the population pressure was greatest in inner Sogn in the mid-nineteenth century. There the number of cotters increased most rapidly — much more rapidly than the population as a whole, while the number of farmers did not keep up with the population increase.

## AVAILABLE RESOURCES AND POPULATION

The degree of population pressure must be understood as a relationship between the size of the population and the resources within any given area. In order to measure the amount of population pressure it is necessary — as far as possible — to compare the population with the resources available for producing a livelihood. The best method of securing a quantitative measure of the population pressure in an area like this is to examine the relationship between population figures and property taxes (*matrikkelskyld*). These taxes were levied on the gross yield of the farm and therefore are a practical measure of a property's value.

The tax rolls give evidence of the resources at the disposal of every single farm. Fishing, except for salmon, was a resource that was not assessed, which introduces the possibility of error, especially as applied to outer Sogn. In the central and inner communities — which are of greatest interest for this article — the fishing industry was of less importance. One can assume that the assessed property taxes there give a fairly exact measure of the actual resources that were available. Two tax rolls were drawn up for Norway during the nineteenth century. The preparatory work for the first one was done during the 1820s and for the second one during the 1860s.

In 1825 it was inner Sogn which had the greatest number of people in proportion to the property tax. There were then 503 inhabitants per 100 *skylddaler*, the monetary unit used in the tax register. Corresponding figures were lowest in central Sogn with 378; outer Sogn in 1825 showed figures that were about halfway between those for the inner and central communities, 435 inhabitants per 100 *skylddaler*. It was primarily the coastal communities farthest out, where the livelihood to a large extent depended on fishing, which pushed the proportional figures upward in that district.

If one considers the later property register (*matrikkel*), it shows that while inner Sogn in 1855 still had the most people in proportion to assessed property taxes, by 1865 it was outer Sogn that had the largest population per 100 *skylddaler*. This was due to the fact that the population continued to increase in outer Sogn while it decreased in the inner communities. Central Sogn still clearly had the fewest people in proportion to its property taxes.

Everything considered, these figures suggest that central Sogn experienced the least pressure against its available resources. If one takes into account the importance of fishing for the outer coastal communities, it is reasonable to assume that the population pressure was greatest in the inner communities in spite of the high figures recorded for outer Sogn. In this article it is the circumstances in the central and inner communities which are of primary interest. There the situation is not debatable: all evidence indicates that there must have been greater pressure on available resources in inner than in central Sogn.

AGRICULTURAL PRODUCTION AND POPULATION PRESSURE

Thus far, differences between the various parts of Sogn have been examined as regards population growth, class composition, and the relationship between tax rolls and population. Degrees of population pressure have been noted without considering whether this pressure grew as time went on, in other words, whether living conditions became more difficult toward the middle of the century. When Rasmus Sunde and others talk about overpopulation in these communities during the 1840s and 1850s it must mean that living conditions, according to their views, became worse than they had been earlier. It is not easy to measure living conditions. One way to approach the problem is to examine how food production developed in relation to changes in the size of the population. Implicit in the "overpopulation" hypothesis lies the assumption that the food supply did not keep up with the population increase.

Agriculture provided the main source of food production in the district; and this production can be stated in figures, though, to be sure, not without uncertainties in the methodology used.[3] The nutritional value of agricultural production, in the form of energy measured in calories, now appears to be an accepted criterion.[4] The energy production of agriculture, seen in relation to the population figures, should also provide a good indicator as to how well the various districts in Sogn were able to support the growing population during the course of the nineteenth century. The development of the energy production of agriculture relative to the population should be an indicator of whether living conditions became better or worse toward the middle of the century.

The figures cannot be accepted as infallible. They are encumbered with so many uncertainties that they can be used merely as rough indicators. The figures used here are those which appear in the sources, with adjustment of the count prior to 1845 to compensate for the fact that these figures — in the view of all scholars — are too low.[5] The unadjusted figures can mainly be used when looking for differences in the relationship between agricultural production and population in the three divisions of Sogn, while the adjusted figures, in addition, may reveal something about how adequately agriculture in the Sogn communities sustained the population. Experts say that in order to feed a normally distributed population, an

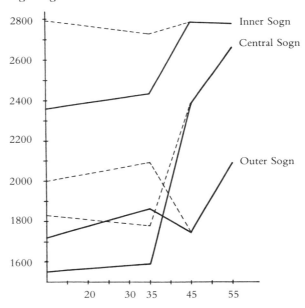

Fig. 2. Energy production from crops and cattle. Sogn 1808–1855.
        Calories per person per day.

average of at least 2,000 calories per person per day is needed.
About 2,600 calories per person is considered a good supply[6]

Figure 2 shows the main results of the calculation. The
solid lines show the agricultural production in calories per
person per day as it was according to the figures in the sources
for inner, central, and outer Sogn. The dotted lines show the
results with adjusted figures.

If the unadjusted figures are examined there are obvious
differences in the registered agricultural production in the various parts of Sogn. Inner Sogn has, throughout the whole
period, the greatest production in relation to the population.
The central communities had very low production at the time
of the first tax roll but came close to the level of inner Sogn
in 1845 and 1855. The registered production in outer Sogn
was somewhat higher than that of the central communities in
1808–1809, but clearly lower in 1845 and 1855.

Though the figures are uncertain, it seems apparent that

real differences exist here. The most striking feature connected with these figures is the low agricultural production per inhabitant in the central Sogn communities during 1808–1809 and 1835. These were the communities which had the fewest inhabitants relative to their resources, as measured by the tax rolls. It would thus be reasonable to expect that production per inhabitant would be great here. It is less surprising that agriculture gave small returns in outer Sogn, since this form of livelihood was relatively less important there than in the communities farther up the fjord.

Even if these figures are not taken at face value it is still difficult to avoid the conclusion that agricultural production per inhabitant was greatest in the inner Sogn communities. That is to say that the areas of Sogn which up to now have been found to be most heavily overpopulated also produced the most food in proportion to the population.

These figures indicate that agricultural production kept in step with population increase during the first half of the nineteenth century. To be sure, there is a great difference between the adjusted and the unadjusted figures. Seen as a whole, though, there is much which indicates that agricultural production in inner Sogn kept up with population growth, at least up to 1845. In the first place, the difference between the adjusted figures for 1808–1809 and 1835 is very small; and second, production increased faster than the population during the decade between 1835 and 1845, no matter which figures are followed. It is reasonable to assume that the same also held true for central Sogn. The numbers for 1835, both the adjusted and the unadjusted, are so small that it is difficult to accept them. It is more likely that the real development would reveal a curve with a more even rise between 1808–1809 and 1845 than that in the chart.

What can perhaps be accepted as the most certain interpretation of this graph is that agricultural production likely slowed in comparison with population during the decade between 1845 and 1855 in inner Sogn. However, it is not necessary to conclude that the district was then overpopulated and the people no longer could derive a living there. It is known, for instance, that various non-agricultural activities were gaining a foothold at the time in several communities.[7] Despite the slowdown, inner Sogn was the part of Sogn where the agricultural yield was greatest in 1858 as well.

The question as to how self-supporting the various districts in Sogn were with respect to agricultural products is more difficult to answer. The problem connected with the understatement of the various numbers then becomes more serious. The most reliable statement concerning agricultural production is likely given by the adjusted figures, but one should be wary about depending too much on them.

If the adjusted figures are to be believed, inner Sogn was self-sufficient in food during this whole period. Central Sogn did not reach the limit of 2,600 calories per person per day until 1855, but it also produced enough food through agriculture in 1845 that the area likely reached the optimum energy supply if fish from the fjord are added. If the figures from the two first periods in the table are accepted, these communities could scarcely have supplied themselves with sufficient food. This is surprising, and one must not depend blindly upon these figures. They are so strikingly low, and the jump from 1835 to 1845 is so great that there are good reasons to doubt their correctness.

Aside from 1845, the figures for outer Sogn are very close to 2,000 calories per person per day. Considering the extensive fishing in these communities, it is likely that agriculture and fishing combined could supply sufficient food.

What the chart shows is how much energy there would have been for every person per day from agricultural production if it had been equally divided among the population. This, of course, it was not and hence little is revealed about the real situation. What it does show is that at least in inner and outer Sogn there was enough food produced during this whole period that, basically, there was enough for everybody, while it is more uncertain whether this was true of central Sogn. If anything certain is to be said about the food situation among different classes of people, then the distribution mechanisms which existed in the communities and how well they functioned would have to be examined. That is something which this study has not attempted. Nevertheless these figures do not indicate that there was a problem of overpopulation in any part of Sogn during the 1840s.

## LABOR MARKET, WAGES, AND PRICES

A number of indicators can, in theory, be used to say something about the degree of population pressure in a community. Land prices can be one such indicator, even though it is not definite how high or low prices are to be interpreted. It is perhaps most reasonable to assume that a strong population pressure will have the effect of forcing land prices upward.

During the 1850s land prices were highest in inner Sogn and lowest in outer Sogn, while the central region found itself, as usual, in between.[8] Land prices were clearly lowest in outer Sogn, probably because the soil had less utility value for people there than for people in the inner communities. Land was not, to the same degree, the only source of livelihood in the coastal areas that it was in the inner fjord communities. Out by the coast there was also another source of income: fishing. But why were land prices in the middle communities also so much lower than in inner Sogn? There were no other sources of income, unconnected with the soil, which would be instrumental in holding land prices down. A reasonable hypothesis can be that the population pressure was stronger in the innermost communities than in central Sogn, and the demand for land was thus greater there.

In a region with strong population pressure it is reasonable to assume that it would be difficult for young people to secure work. Lack of jobs might force them to leave the district. Answers to questions in a circular sent out by the Department of the Interior to local poor commissions can shed some light on the state of the labor market during the 1840s.[9]

It is the labor situation and the income possibilities for young unmarried people that these questions address. They were the ones who had steady employment and for them the answers seem to be quite unambiguous: it was not difficult for young people to secure steady jobs in Sogn in 1840. To the contrary, it seems as if in certain areas (Sogndal, Lavik, and possibly Vik) there was even a shortage of hired help. At least in Sogndal and Vik the reason seemed to be that there were other ways of earning a livelihood which were more attractive than permanent farm labor.

So this was the situation on the labor market a few years before "the dam burst and the emigrant stream went over the ocean," as the local historian Anders Ohnstad puts it.[10] It evidently did not look hopeless. Those who wanted year-round jobs could, without any problem, secure steady employment and those who desired income from day-labor could count on this during certain parts of the year in agriculture. Furthermore, there are many indications that there was work to be had outside the basic industries.

If the information brought to light here is accepted, there are few indications that people had to leave Sogn because of lack of employment. Neither are there any indications that it was more difficult to secure jobs in the inner communities, where it has generally been assumed that the population pressure was most intense at this time.

It is a reasonable hypothesis that there is a connection between the wages earned by servants and day laborers and the degree of population pressure. Population pressure will increase the labor supply and thus, in accordance with usual marketing principles, will play its part in pressing wages downward.

The answers to the questions to the Interior Department in 1840 also contain information about wages. They indicate that the wages were fairly even in the various communities in Sogn. At any rate, they were not lower in the inner communities than in the outer areas. To the contrary, available figures indicate that the wages were somewhat higher in the inner communities than in the outer, especially the wages for men. Overpopulation in the inner communities had, in any case, not caused wages in this district to decline by 1840. This also agrees with the evidence about wages gathered from other sources.[11] The wages in Sogn seem, systematically, to have been higher than in the neighboring districts of Sunnfjord and

Nordfjord, which did not have any early emigration movement. Neither was it possible to find any essential differences between the wages of day laborers in the various regions of Sogn. It is impossible to prove that there was any especially strong population pressure in the inner Sogn communities by using the level of wages as evidence. If there was population pressure in any part of Sogn it did not have any effect on the wages paid laborers.

AN OVERPOPULATED SOCIETY?

In summary, what have the indicators examined so far shown about the relationship between population and resources in Sogn? They have not revealed any unambiguous picture. Neither the labor market, wages, cost of living, nor land prices gave any indications that there was a strong population pressure in any part of the district.

If there was any such pressure, the population increase and the relation between property taxes and the number of people indicate that the pressure was strongest in inner Sogn, while central Sogn seemed to have the most favorable relationship between the size of the population and available resources.

Information about agricultural yield revealed that food production likely kept in step with population growth during the first half of the nineteenth century. In both inner and central Sogn this production, in 1855, was greater than the optimal requirement. In this connection it is worthy of notice that agricultural production, measured in calories per person per day, was clearly highest in inner Sogn throughout this whole period. Thus, it was hardly true that the population increase and a consequent population pressure in this region led to reduced agricultural production per inhabitant and a corresponding shortage of food.

Thus it would seem that the concept "overpopulation" is unsuitable to characterize conditions in Sogn during the middle 1800s. It is therefore difficult to assert that the reason for the great emigration was that the district was "overpopulated."

EMIGRATION

The questions raised can be better addressed by analyzing the early emigration from this district somewhat more closely. The lists of movement in and out of the parishes in the church records of Sogn are the sources for the analysis. All those who emigrated between 1839 and 1855 have been listed and analyzed with the help of a computer.

The number of emigrants was largest from inner Sogn. Here 1,901 emigrants to America are listed during this period. From central Sogn 1,399 people left, while from outer Sogn only 51 emigrants were registered. The absolute figures are, however, not the most interesting. It is more valuable to see how strong the emigration movement was in relation to the population of the three regions. Then the result turns out to be different. This is made clear by figure 3.

The three columns in the diagram show the dimensions of the emigration to America in percentage of the average population. Here it is central Sogn which looms highest. From 1839 until 1855 emigrants numbered an astonishing 18.7 percent of the average population of this region. That is to say that emigration intensity in central Sogn was about twice as high as in inner Sogn, where the corresponding figure was 9.5 percent. From outer Sogn there was scarcely any emigration at this time: only 0.6 percent of the average population left for America.

Figure 4 shows curves for the emigration intensity per 1,000 of the average population in central and inner Sogn.

It is clear that the emigration movement had its origin in central Sogn. Emigrants left from central Sogn in both 1839 and 1843; not until 1844 did registered America migrants leave inner Sogn. Central Sogn also had the highest emigration intensity throughout this period, except for 1855. The differences were greatest during the earliest period and also during the top year, 1854.

This is very interesting and quite surprising. The differences between central and inner Sogn were marked. From the point of view of the traditional explanations, with heavy em-

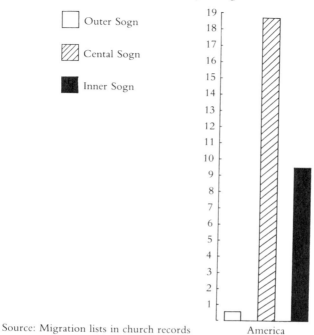

Outer Sogn

Cental Sogn

Inner Sogn

Source: Migration lists in church records

America

Fig. 3. Emigration to America from outer, central and inner Sogn 1839–1855. Percentage of average population.

phasis on "population pressure" and "overpopulation" as causes of the emigration movement, it is strange indeed that the emigration intensity was strongest in the central communities. It has been difficult to prove that there was any strong population pressure in these areas. To the contrary, it is most reasonable to maintain that central Sogn was the region where there was the *least* population pressure. Nevertheless, proportionately far more people emigrated from these communities than from the other districts in Sogn.

In order to come closer to the answer as to why these people left for America, it would be of interest to find out what social status and occupational background or means of subsistence the emigrants had. Unfortunately the information in the church records concerning such matters is meagre and unreliable. Nevertheless, it is possible to estimate the number

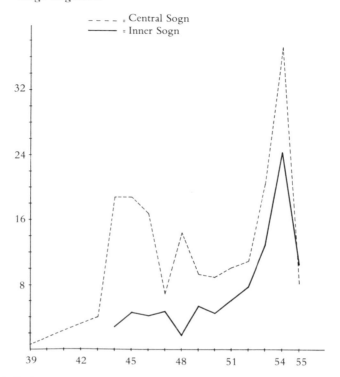

Fig. 4. Emigrants per 1,000 average population per year.
Inner and central Sogn, 1839–1855.

of emigrants in the three following groups: farmers, laborers
or servants, and cotters, and to compare this to the size of
these groups in the population of central and inner Sogn.[12]
The conclusions are as follows: it was the laborers or servants
who had the highest emigration intensity, both in central and
inner Sogn. This could probably have been expected. Servants
were young, unestablished people who were readily mobile;
but at the same time it may seem peculiar that so many of them
could finance the passage to America. It seems as if there was
about the same emigration intensity among farmers as among
cotters, both in central and inner Sogn. In inner Sogn it seems
reasonable to assume that a few more farmers than cotters
emigrated.

Seen in connection with the problem under examination, it is this relationship between the farmer emigration and the cotter emigration which is the most interesting. If the traditional explanations—"population pressure" and "overpopulation"—are accepted as the main causes of the emigration movement, it must seem odd that the emigration intensity among those who controlled the resources (the farmers) was just as great as, or greater than, among the propertyless cotters. Probably a contributory explanation may be that those who left for America were not from the very poorest classes, as the passage itself was so expensive. It is, nevertheless, difficult to place conclusive emphasis on this explanation since so many unestablished servants and laborers managed to finance the trip to America.

In his analysis of the emigrants from Balestrand, Jon Alan Gjerde has found the same social composition of the emigrant mass as that arrived at here: a large number of those who left during this first period of the movement were farmers or children of farmers.[13] He also claims that the farmers who emigrated were above the average in wealth.

Rasmus Sunde has reached about the same conclusion with respect to the emigrants from Vik. Farmers constituted a large proportion of the emigrants; and of 59 farmers who left during the years 1839–1855, 26 came from "large" and 16 from "medium-sized" farms.[14]

WHY DID THE SOGNINGS GO TO AMERICA?

The time is now ripe for a new appraisal of the background and causes of the early emigration from Sogn.

Traditionally too much emphasis has been placed on "population pressure" and "overpopulation" as explanations. It is doubtful that there was any strong population press in Sogn at the time when the emigration started; in any case, the emigration movement was strongest from the central communities, which according to most of the other criteria had the least population pressure. When, in addition, it is revealed that at least as large a proportion of farmers as of cotters emigrated, one is forced to look for other explanations.

No new infallible answer is forthcoming as to why so many emigrated from the Sogn communities during these years. But some factors can be suggested which may offer alternative approaches.

It is reasonable to believe that the great emigration of servants and laborers is an indication that many young and unestablished people looked with misgivings at future prospects in the district. It is also reasonable to assume that population growth was a contributory factor in this case. But the explanations based on population pressure and overpopulation have likely been focused too one-sidedly on purely material, purely economic conditions. There can be reasons for holding fast to the idea that population growth was a decisive factor behind the emigration wave, but the perspective must be widened beyond the usual point of view. The effects of the population increase were not limited to purely economic matters, but had a strong influence on the whole social and cultural life of the rural communities.

Gjerde places great emphasis on just such factors when he tries to explain why so many people left Balestrand. He argues convincingly that they looked with anxiety at the future, and that thoughts about their children's prospects were of decisive importance for very many of those who chose to emigrate.[15] Concern for their children could give relatively wealthy farmers rational grounds for breaking away, because only one of the children could inherit the farm, while the future would be uncertain for all the younger siblings. By going to America a farm family could entertain good hopes of acquiring sufficient land to give all the children a livelihood better than that which anyone in the home community enjoyed. The information about conditions in America which reached the Sogn communities during the 1840s and 1850s gave clear evidence of this. Such information came through letters from earlier emigrants and from newspapers and books which discussed life in the New World. The information obtained about conditions in America was, to be sure, exaggerated at times, but essentially it was correct: possibilities and resources in America were far richer than in the communities at home.

Emigration to America appeared as a new alternative for the Sognings during the 1840s. When they evaluated their prospects for the future, they had one possibility which had not been there earlier. Consequently, it is not necessary to assume that living conditions had worsened in order to explain why so many emigrated.

This is a general explanation of the emigration, which in and of itself does not explain why emigration intensity differed in the different parts of Sogn. When emigration was heaviest from the central communities during the earliest period this apparently grew out of the fact that the first emigrants, more or less by chance, came from Vik. The emigration wave then spread in central and inner Sogn like rings in the water, and was during the earliest period strongest in Vik and the communities nearby. Information about conditions in America came back to Vik in the form of letters from the earliest emigrants. The letters likely made a strong impression and must be reckoned as important liberating causes of the great emigration wave from 1843 onward.

The fact that emigration from Sogn started in Vik and was most intense in the nearest communities up to 1855 can thus be regarded as a chance happening—how *much* of a chance it was can, of course, be argued. If the first emigrants had come from inner Sogn, from Luster or Lærdal, the picture might have been quite different. The contagious effect of the first emigration seems to be the best explanation of the stronger emigration intensity in central Sogn at this time.

It is more difficult to explain the enormous difference in emigration intensity which existed between the communities of central and inner Sogn on the one hand and the communities in outer Sogn and the rest of the county on the other. The traditional explanations of the differences in emigration intensity between inner and outer communities stress that there was less population pressure in the outer regions, and that the fishing industry was of great importance there.

The obvious conclusion is that there is reason to de-emphasize the importance of the dissimilar population pressures. In Sogn the population growth was stronger in the outer regions than in the central communities during the first half of the century, at the same time that the emigration movement was strongest in central Sogn—where the population was lowest in relation to the tax rolls. It is difficult to quantify the importance of fishing to the livelihood of people in the communities closest to the sea and the degree to which it was this industry that kept people in outer Sogn from emigrating. But one should be careful not to place too much emphasis on fishing in this connection. Emigration during this period was also of little importance from the parish of Lavik, which included communities far up the Sognefjord where fishing scarcely had any greater importance than in the communities of central Sogn.

All of this proves that there are many unsolved questions connected with Norwegian emigration research. The great regional differences in emigration intensity are, as yet, not satisfactorily explained.

## Notes

*This article is based on a larger work by the same author, *"Rift om brødet?" Befolkning ressursar og økonomi i Sogn 1801–1855* (Sogndal, 1985).

[1]Andreas Holmsen, "Økonomisk og sosial historie," in *Norske Bygder*, 4 (Bergen, 1937), 80–93.

[2]Rasmus Sunde, "Emigration from the District of Sogn, 1839–1915," trans. by C. A. Clausen, in *Norwegian-American Studies*, 29 (Northfield, Minnesota, 1983), 111–126. The article is based on a thesis titled "Ei undersøking av utvandringa til Amerika frå Vik i Sogn 1839–1915," presented to the History Department of the University of Trondheim, 1974.

[3]Sources used are Regjeringskommisjonen, 1807–1812, and the census for each decade beginning in 1835.

[4]The methodology has been developed by Kåre Lunden. See Lunden, "Poteta og den raskare folketalsvoksteren i Noreg frå 1815," in *Historisk Tidsskrift*, no. 4, 1975, 275–315.

[5]For details of making these adjustments see Engesæter, *Rift om brødet*, 47.

[6]See Lunden, "Poteta og den raskare," 289.

[7]See Engesæter, *Rift om brødet*, 59–62, and also Engesæter, "Sogndalsfjøra 1801–1875. Trekk ved den sosiale og økonomiske historia i ein strandstad," (cand. philol. thesis, University of Bergen, 1976), and Hallvard

Jansen, "Framvoksteren av strandstaden Lærdalsøyri 1801–1865" (cand. philol. thesis, University of Bergen, 1979).

[8]Information about the average value of the tax dollar in the records, "Skylddalerens gjennemsnittspriser," vol. 2 of Department of Agriculture archives in the National Archives, Oslo.

[9]Records of Department of Church and Education, National Archives. Poor Relief (*fattigvesenet*), answers to circular dated April 18, 1848. Packet 105.

[10]Anders Ohnstad, "Dei indre fjordbygdene på veg til pengehushald," academic thesis, published in *Tidsskrift*, no. 13 (Leikanger, 1948), 41.

[11]The published five-year reports of county governors (*amtmenn*) contain information on wages.

[12]Engesæter, *Rift om brødet*, 90–96.

[13]Jon Alan Gjerde, "Peasants into Bourgeoisie: the Migration from Balestrand" (Ph. D. dissertation, University of Minnesota, 1982), 203–204, 214.

[14]Sunde, "Ei undersøking av utvandringa," 133.

[15]Gjerde, "Peasants into Bourgeoisie," 207–210.

# 3

# Sociological Theories and the Great Emigration

*by B. Lindsay Lowell*

The great emigration from Norway took place in a relatively short span of four decades in the latter half of the nineteenth century. From that time to this, historians, sociologists, economists, geographers, and assorted other experts have pointed to certain factors associated with that phenomenon. Sociologists have devised several theories that explain the exodus by placing it against the larger backdrop of social change taking place at that time: the change from traditional to modern society. These theories purport to specify general factors that caused emigration, not just from Norway, but from almost any nineteenth-century society. Sociologists use specific hypotheses as their point of departure and then examine findings from available studies which support or fail to support each hypothesis. The core of this article is a discussion of the logic of three sociological theories and an examination of recent research that illuminates various hypotheses. Further, the accuracy of each theory's hypothesis will be tested with a statistical methodology employed to analyze all of Norway's 535 rural municipalities or communities (*herreder*) between 1870 and 1905. It is the overlap between the case-study findings and the statistical analysis of all Norwegian communities which permits strong conclusions to be reached as to the value of each competing theory.

53

CHANGE AND RESPONSE
(MULTIPHASIC RESPONSE) THEORY

Prevailing population theory in the 1960s interpreted emigration as part of the Malthusian drama of too many people for too little land.[1] The population of Norway grew dramatically during the century preceding the mass departure. In the seventeenth century the population of eastern Norway increased over 150 percent, while western Norway experienced an increase ranging from 40 to 80 percent. By 1865, just prior to the start of mass emigration, Norway's population had experienced a half-century of spectacular and unprecedented growth. High levels of population density became particularly acute in the marginal areas—high mountains, elevated valleys, and the remoter parts of fjord districts. It is no wonder that Norway's foremost emigration historian, Ingrid Semmingsen, has argued that population pressure was a major reason behind the mass movement.[2]

Of course, Thomas Malthus, early in the century, had little notion of the range of transformations which would occur after his time. Urbanization and modern employment can create jobs and markets for goods which eventually absorb rural excess population. The population pressure mechanism implies a pressure on resources, but few contemporary Neo-Malthusians argue that it was overpopulation alone that was responsible for the emigration. Neo-Malthusians argue that there is a connection between rural population density in traditional societies and a general tightening of economic opportunity as farms and jobs become scarce. They focus on the push created by high density agricultural populations, coupled, in the case of Norway, with a lag in urban development and employment in the modern sector of the economy.

If overpopulation purportedly stimulates emigration, then the creation of non-agricultural jobs, assumed to be associated with increases in the urban population, is required to stop it. Figure 1 is a map of Norway that shows the percentage of all workers employed in non-agricultural secondary, or manufacturing, and tertiary, or service, sectors of rural com-

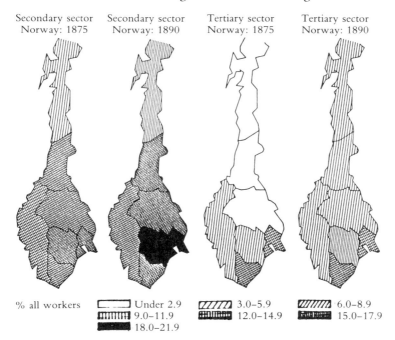

Secondary sector    Secondary sector    Tertiary sector    Tertiary sector
Norway: 1875        Norway: 1890        Norway: 1875       Norway: 1890

% all workers    ▭ Under 2.9    ▨ 3.0–5.9    ▨ 6.0–8.9
                 ▥ 9.0–11.9     ▥ 12.0–14.9  ▥ 15.0–17.9
                 ▆ 18.0–21.9

Fig. 1. Employment in secondary and tertiary sectors, 1875 and 1890.

munities. The statistics for this map are based on official Norwegian census data.[3] The map presents the major subregions
of Norway as they are typically delineated.[4] Here there is evidence that growth in non-agricultural employment was indeed somewhat slow between 1875 and 1890, although there
were especially great concentrations of secondary employment in the south central and Oslo regions. In the Norwegian
South there was a large concentration of tertiary employment
associated with the role of shipping, mainly wooden sailing
craft, in the region.[5]

Oslo, Bergen, Trondheim, and Stavanger were the
largest cities at that time, and nearby rural areas were influenced by urban demand.[6] Urban proximity created specialized agricultural production which demanded close control
over the labor force. These peasants worked on farms where
their labor was purchased to a greater extent than elsewhere

with wages, and their employment was less seasonal. Although urban proximity should be expected to have a restraining effect on emigration, change and response theory clearly argues that only sufficient levels of non-agricultural employment can offset the necessary population response to rural overcrowding.

Still, if change and response theory is correct, population pressure must have been the primary factor causing emigration. However, many inquiries into the classical explanation have found that the assumption of a Malthusian bind does not adequately explain the magnitude of the departure. At the dawn of the mass emigration in 1865 Norwegian farms showed no signs of excessive fragmentation and for the rest of the century agricultural productivity was to increase. Certainly, the change and response thesis requires modification in light of the fact that while coastal areas in both North Norway and Trøndelag just south of it had the greatest population densities, they also had low rates of emigration.

Other indicators of overpopulation likewise tend to disprove the population-density hypothesis. A comparison of wages in various districts demonstrates no consistent relationship with population density. Indeed, wages were the same in mountainous areas with high emigration and in the market-oriented flatlands: emigration may have even created labor shortages, causing wages to rise. Norway's agricultural wage was twenty-five percent greater than Sweden's at the start of mass departure, and Swedish workers found employment in the forests of East Norway. In fact, employment was often high in communities with the greatest emigration, and low farm prices may have reflected a slack demand for land. Ingrid Semmingsen has tempered her original views regarding the importance of overpopulation and has included proletarianization, or loss of status, as an essential element.[7]

THE TRANSFORMATION OF PEASANT SOCIETY

Those who question the population pressure thesis focus instead on the structure of peasant society as it was transformed from a traditional to a market economy. From this perspective

Norwegian emigrants were less likely fleeing destitution and more likely fleeing changes that were occurring in antiquated sectors of the agricultural economy. Rapid population growth in the early half of the nineteenth century was accompanied by traditional technologies and the extension of arable land. Cultivated land doubled in area between 1820 and 1865; thereafter land extension slowed. The Great Transformation (*Det store Hamskiftet*) within the rural areas began in 1857 with a law requiring the consolidation of farms. During the last half of the 1800s farming became increasingly market oriented and agricultural productivity made its greatest gains during the peak years of emigration, 1880 to 1900.[8]

The extension of cultivated land was associated with the swelling numbers of the cotter class (*husmenn*); indeed the proliferation of cotters exceeded that of any group except the freeholding farming class. Family units formed the basis of peasant society and the economic evaluation of goods and labor was for the subsistence of the household together. Cotters contracted with the freehold farmer for a cottage and a small plot of land in return for labor and/or payment, usually in kind. The effect of Norwegian freeholding was such that the farmer was able to determine the structure of the farm. The extension of farm land allowed for more divisions of the household and the creation of more cotter parcels.[9]

Even as late as 1918 just over fifty percent of all Norwegian farms were less than five acres in size. Because farming could not provide a complete subsistence to peasants, members of the family often engaged in activities such as fishing, logging, or animal husbandry. The more traditional the peasant economy and the more reliant on non-wage labor, especially cotters, the greater the resistance to the introduction of agricultural innovations. The established pattern of seeking alternative employment to supplement the family income was pursued by certain family members. Eventually, emigration became an important strategy for peasant families. As a result, workers actually became scarce in some Norwegian districts.

After a period of increase during the first half of the century, the cotters' ranks were rapidly depleted in the last half

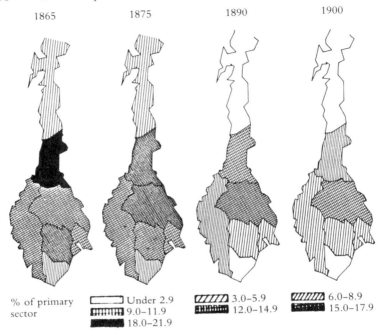

% of primary sector

Under 2.9 · 3.0–5.9 · 6.0–8.9
9.0–11.9 · 12.0–14.9 · 15.0–17.9
18.0–21.9

Fig. 2. The crofter class in Norway: A declining primary sector.

of the nineteenth century. The decline of the cotter class is generally thought to have been a result of heavy emigration. Between 1865 and 1900 the total agricultural labor force declined by some 50,000 persons. In 1865 the cotter class alone numbered 50,000. By the turn of the century its numbers declined to less than 25,000. The cotters who remained were mostly old and infirm.[10]

The distribution of cotters throughout Norway and their pattern of regional decline suggests that they played a large role in emigration. That this is true can be seen in Figure 2, which shows the change in the regional concentration of cotters as a percentage of all workers in rural communities. Those districts with the greatest rates of emigration had the largest relative numbers of cotters and the decline of the cotter class in these districts is notable. In the Trøndelag and north-central districts cotters comprised a share of the primary labor force that was well above the national average throughout the last thirty-five years of the nineteenth century. Decreases in the share of cotters in the Oslofjord and south-central districts took them from just above to well below the national average. The west and north districts had the fewest cotters.

The transformation to a market economy varied, with a dual economy of subsistence and market farming persisting in some districts, while in other districts the transformation was delayed until as late as the Second World War. In part, the availability of alternate income activities and the accessibility of markets played a role in the varied courses of development. Departure from agriculturally dominated Tinn in East Norway started in earnest after 1875 as the market system undermined the old labor-intensive agriculture. Cotters especially fled employment in intensive animal husbandry (*høstingbruk*).[11] A comparative study of three coastal communities in Trøndelag found that when agricultural employment was supplemented with income from fishing, emigration was delayed until the 1880s. Declines in both the harvest and the price of fish worked in tandem with animal husbandry and new roads — market-induced changes in labor demand — to trigger the emigration.[12] Depression in the fisheries also caused people to leave Brønnøy and Vik in North Norway, both communities with traditional and inefficient agricultural alternatives.[13] Paradoxically, the improving agricultural markets and wages of the 1880s may for the first time have allowed the landless cotter class to afford to move on. Witness the great exodus from Torpa in east-central Norway.[14]

## SOCIAL NETWORKS IN TRADITIONAL SOCIETY

Social networks were more important in peasant society than they are today. Indeed, the family, the kinship group, and the community were the individual's intimate social environment. Employment, friends and marriage partners, livelihood and information came from a comparatively tightly interconnected group of persons. Although the potential emigrant had access to newspapers, emigration agents, advertisements, and other commercial sources of information, he was more likely to make his decision to go to America based on information and assurances from the known community.

The greater salience of such social networks in traditional society is closely related to the rise and decline of numerous mass social movements other than emigration. New religious groups began their growth during the period when emigration was beginning. Political movements likewise grew in importance, as did temperance movements, especially after the turn of the century. To some degree the evolution of these phenomena displayed a pattern that is independent of underlying social or economic structures.[15] Social movements often arise through the efforts of charismatic leaders and grow and spread as informal organizations promote the movements' ideals.

Nationwide political parties emerged after 1879 and, with few exceptions, a two-party system predominated after 1882. Liberal political parties had an institutional structure that encouraged individualism. The values associated with the secularization process were generally strongest among dissenting religious groups and the liberal political party. They were characterized by a greater psychological openness to independent decision-making and a readiness to risk leaving a familiar world. However, in South and East Norway, the liberals were associated with the defense of rural language and rural values. Although there was some geographic polarization within parties on issues such as this, the differences between the liberals and the conservatives were greater than intra-party disagreements.[16]

A tradition of emigration from a community also had the well-known effect of increasing the willingness of other individuals to leave. See Figure 3 for the regional distribution of emigration rates over the period of mass exodus. Emigration had an earlier and stronger start from Norway than it did from Sweden. The greatest rates in Norway prior to 1870 came from impulse centers in the West, and in the Telemark and Buskerud provinces in the south-central district. Emigration from Kristians *amt* — the present-day county of Oppland — in the north-central district was especially intense, with six per

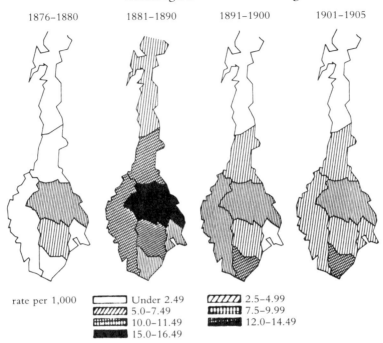

1876–1880          1881–1890          1891–1900          1901–1905

rate per 1,000      Under 2.49      2.5–4.99
                    5.0–7.49        7.5–9.99
                    10.0–11.49      12.0–14.49
                    15.0–16.49

Fig. 3. Emigration from Norway: The decades of mass emigration.

1,000 leaving in this period. The regional distribution of emigration rates before 1870 shows a great deal of stability and reflects the geographic pattern of heavy departure from central Norway throughout the century.[17]

Within a community the tradition of emigration became institutionalized over time. There are several possible elements that combine to make up this effect. Certainly, the changes sweeping over the rural countryside played an important part. Peasant psychology was deeply influenced by the change from a substantive kin-based economy to a formal market economy. Traditional values were resilient and peasants resisted the introduction of new technology, the money economy, and the new cultural elements. Landless cotters, particularly, "voted with their feet" against a mixed system that exposed them to the intensive market economy yet left them mostly under the traditional power of landholding farmers. As alluded to earlier, political and religious changes induced an individualism that further cut against the grain of traditional peasant culture.[18]

The reaffirmation of traditional values was reflected in interpersonal relationships. Social networks influenced the emigration by concentrating the idea of leaving, creating group migrations, and directing the path these migrations would take. Social networks were important in redirecting established movement between Sunnfjord and Bergen to America in the 1880s.[19] When faced with a depression in fishing, the major industry of Brønnøy and Vik, these two communities witnessed the sudden start of mass emigration. Networks of family and friends in America funneled the flow there rather than to more accessible Finnmark.[20] People from Balestrand in West Norway remained closely connected in America, where many fled en masse in a radical attempt to "retain the essential social fabric of their community in a rural environment that was much more conducive to growth."[21]

Social networks facilitated the attempt to recreate traditional values in the relative freedom of America. Such networks often began with a noted leader, such as Cleng Peerson from Stavanger or Per Ivarson Undi from Vik in West Norway. Widely available America letters reported that Ivarson and his family were "doing very well and live like rich people."[22] Such letters exerted a great influence because they were widely read in places where the letter writer was known. Shipping companies knew the power of personal communication and hired returned Norwegian Americans as recruiters. The power of kinship was reflected in emigration from Dovre in east-central Norway where nearly half of all who went to the United States had relatives there. A one to three year lag often existed between the emigration of husbands and other members of a family. Consider that 50 percent of those from Dovre and 47 percent from Balestrand traveled on tickets prepaid by Norwegian Americans, the ultimate in established emigration networks.

THE MULTIPLE FACTORS BEHIND EMIGRATION,
1876-1905

Thus, the fundamentals of three theories of emigration have been reviewed. The theories under consideration are the change and response to overpopulation, the transformation of peasant society, and the social network theory. Each theory hypothesizes factors which may have led to emigration. These factors can be measured for each Norwegian community with available census data. The presence or absence of these factors should, if the theories are sound, dictate the rate of emigration from a community.

All together, twelve factors are considered in the statistical analysis that follows. For the change and response theory the factors considered are the total population divided by land area, the percentage of the labor force employed in non-agricultural secondary and tertiary occupations, and the proximity of one of Norway's four major urban areas. For the peasant society theory the quality of the region's land, the percentage of the rural primary labor force employed as cotters, fishermen, and foresters, and the percentage of all farms larger than fifty acres are considered. The social network factors that are considered include the percentage of all eligible voters who voted and those registered in the liberal party, and the rate of emigration in 1869, just before the start of mass emigration.

For example, change and response theory claims that overpopulation is the most important factor pushing emigration, while non-agricultural employment and urban proximity are the factors that finally slow it. The transformation of peasant society theory posits that landless agricultural labor, primarily the number of cotters, will be the greatest push factor, while high levels of employment in fishing and forestry will serve as restraints. Social network theory apparently specifies only push variables, such as the stimulus from social networks that were most often formed in early periods of intense emigration.

In this research, each of the several factors is measured in such a way that its relative level in each of 535 Norwegian municipalities is known. The strength of such a method is that the association between a community's characteristics and emigration is compared across all 535. About sixty predominantly urban areas, as defined by the Norwegian Central Census Bureau, are excluded because the three theories specifically pertain to the rural experience. The original analysis made four time divisions, but here 1891–1900 and 1901–1905 are combined in the summary table.

In order to test the adequacy of the divergent factors specified by each theory, multivariate regression (OLS) techniques were used. This article will not describe the methodology employed, which is presented elsewhere. Note, however, that the models explain between 40 and 80 percent of the variation in emigration rates. The interested reader is encouraged to consult the more detailed study.[23] Multivariate regression is essentially a data–reduction technique that tells whether "on average" a given factor is empirically associated with more or less emigration from each area, and whether a given factor is more influential than other competing factors.

In Table 1 a schematic presentation of the results is shown for three time periods, as well as for each of Norway's three major geographic regions. The time periods represent the beginning phase of emigration, the peak period, and the declining years. A plus sign (+) signifies that increases in the amount of an indicated factor led to higher rates of departure, or what is known as a push effect. Conversely, a negative sign (−) signifies that increases in the amount of an indicated factor led to lower rates, or had a restraining effect. If a factor is not statistically significant in explaining emigration during a given time period no sign is shown. If one of the listed factors is not significant relative to other factors in any time period it has not been listed. For example, population density, which was entered into the statistical model, is not shown in the table because it was not found to have a significant effect on emigration rates in any period or from any region.

The change and response theory is correct in specifying

Table 1. Simplified Presentation of Multivariate Analysis.

| | 1876–1880 | 1881–1890 | 1891–1905 |
|---|---|---|---|
| **EAST-TRØNDELAG REGION** | | | |
| **Change and Response** | | | |
| Urban Proximity | | | − |
| Secondary Employment | | | − − |
| **Peasant Society** | | | |
| Land Quality | | | + |
| Forestry Employment | − | − | − |
| % of Large Farms | − | − | − − |
| % Primary Cotters | + + + | + + | |
| **Social Networks** | | | |
| Liberal Party Voters | | + | |
| Emigration Tradition | + + | + + + | + + |
| **SOUTH-WEST REGION** | | | |
| **Change and Response** | | | |
| Urban Proximity | | | − |
| Service Employment | | | + + |
| **Peasant Society** | | | |
| Fishing Employment | − | − − | − − |
| Forestry Employment | − | − | |
| % of Large Farms | | + + | |
| % Primary Cotters | + + | | |
| **Social Networks** | | | |
| Liberal Party Voters | | + | |
| Emigration Tradition | + + | + + | |
| **NORTH REGION** | | | |
| **Change and Response** | | | |
| Secondary Employment | + + | + + | |
| **Peasant Society** | | | |
| Land Quality | + + | + | |
| Fishing Employment | | | − |
| % of Large Farms | + | | + |
| % Primary Cotters | | + + | + |
| **Social Networks** | | | |
| Emigration Tradition | | + | + + |

that urban proximity was a significant restraining factor during the declining years of emigration. But non-agricultural or service employment was a strong push behind emigration from the south-west region in the 1890s when the wooden sailing ship industry collapsed in the face of modern steamship competition. And in the North, communities with high levels of secondary employment, primarily manufacturing jobs, actually had the greatest rates of emigration. These results demonstrate that the change and response theory is inaccurate in identifying population density as a push factor. In addition, its theoretical logic is not broad enough to incorporate regional differences in the modernization process.

On the other hand, the peasant society theory correctly specifies the strong push behind emigration rates associated with large cotter populations. This push factor was exhausted by the late 1890s, since most able-bodied cotters had already left and, except for the north region, the basics of market agriculture were already in place. Cotter-dominated labor forces represented traditional, mixed subsistence, and market-oriented farming methods. The early modernization of agriculture in the east-Trøndelag districts can be seen in the restraining influence of market-oriented large farms. Conversely, in the south-west and the north regions the later modernization of agriculture produced a slightly later push for rural emigration. Fishing employment was a restraining influence on emigration rates in the south-west region. The better the quality of land in a district the more likely it was that that district had developed a primarily agricultural society prone to seek agricultural opportunities in America. This latter finding is quite opposite to the change and response hypothesis that better land would support more persons and lead to low rates of emigration.

Finally, the social network theory is correct in expecting emigration to be positively associated with the development of liberal political movements. A relatively large number of liberal voters in a community was associated with high rates of departure from the east-Trøndelag and the south-west regions. Emigration tradition, measured here as the intensity of movement out of each community prior to the period of mass emigration, is the strongest push factor in all regions and throughout most time periods. The tradition apparently began somewhat later in the North, and in the South-west the large exodus from southern coastal shipping communities made this tradition comparatively less important in the 1890s.

CONCLUSIONS

Any perception of the past is always and necessarily partial. The weakness of the theories examined here lies in their single-minded selection of a set of factors out of the many that might have been chosen. Mass emigration was not caused by one factor; indeed it was caused by a number of simultaneous factors. Furthermore, it was caused by different factors at different times. The strength of each theory, however, is the construction of a logical framework which allows one to perceive similar patterns in different settings. The rich analysis by historians has been drawn upon to provide support for, or to cast doubt on, the hypotheses posited by each theory. A brief summary was also given of a regression (OLS) analysis of all Norwegian municipalities to determine statistically which were the significant factors leading to variation in emigration rates. Thus, these findings can now be used to evaluate the success of the theoretical specifications of each perspective.

To be of general use a theory must be successful in capturing an accurate picture of the past. In this study the change and response theory has been found less than adequate in this regard. Historians have pointed to local instances where overpopulation did not differentiate between communities with high and low emigration rates. The findings of the regression analysis substantiate these insights: on the average, population density was not associated with greater rates of departure between 1876 and 1905 for the 535 municipalities analyzed here. The peasant society theory was relatively more successful. Clearly, the major regions incorporated modern farming methods at various times, leading to variations in the start of emigration.

Yet, above and beyond the transformation of the peasant

class, social networks worked to convey an interest in leaving Norway and to concretely organize the emigration. In the regression analysis, emigration tradition was the single most important factor influencing emigration rates.[24] Although regression analysis cannot capture the individual components of such a tradition, several examples have been given of the fashion in which social networks operated within certain Norwegian communities. With its roots in the upheaval of tradition-bound society, mass emigration was driven, paradoxically, by itself.

## Notes

[1]Kingsley Davis, "The Theory of Change and Response in Modern Demographic History," in *Population Index*, 29 (1963), 345–366.

[2]Ingrid Semmingsen, "Norwegian Emigration in the Nineteenth Century," in *Scandinavian Economic History Review*, 2 (1960), 150–160.

[3]Bjarne Kristiansen and Frank H. Aarebrot, "The Norwegian Ecological Data, 1868–1903," in *NSD Report Number 9*, Norwegian Social Science Data Service, Bergen University (1976).

[4]All methods and results reported here are presented in greater detail in Briant Lindsay Lowell, *Scandinavian Exodus: Demography and Social Development in 19th-Century Rural Communities* (Boulder, 1987). The regional clusters chosen are the generally accepted ones.

[5]The maps show non-agricultural employment for rural communities only. Nonetheless, the regional distribution of non-agricultural employment remains relatively unchanged if the urban population is included.

[6]Jan Eivind Myhre, "Urbaniseringen i Norge i industrialiseringens første fase ca. 1850–1914," in Grethe Authen Blom, ed., *Urbaniseringsprosessen i Norden, del 3, Industrialiseringens første fase* (Oslo, 1977), 13–94.

[7]Stein Tveite, " 'Overbefolkning,' 'Befolkningspress,' og Vandring," in Sivert Langholm and Francis Sejersted, eds., *Vandringer. Festskrift til Ingrid Semmingsen på 70-årsdagen* (Oslo, 1980), 43–52.

[8]David Grigg, *Population Growth and Agrarian Change* (Cambridge, Massachusetts, 1980).

[9]Sølvi Sogner, "Freehold and Cottar," in *Scandinavian Journal of History*, 1 (1976), 181–200.

[10]Grigg, *Population Growth and Agrarian Change*.

[11]Andres Svalestuen, "Emigration from the Community of Tinn, 1837–1907," in *Norwegian-American Studies*, 29 (Northfield, Minnesota, 1983), 43–88.

[12]Ragnar Standal, "Emigration from a Fjord District on Norway's West Coast, 1852–1915," in *Norwegian-American Studies*, 29 (1983), 185–209.

[13]Kjell Erik Skaaren, "Emigration from Brønnøy and Vik in Helgeland," in *Norwegian-American Studies*, 29 (1983), 293–312.

[14]Arvid Sandaker, "Utvandring og forandring. Befolkningsforhold i Torpa på 1800-tallet" (cand. phil. thesis, University of Oslo, 1977).

[15]Ron J. Lesthaeghe, "Modes of Production, Secularization, and the Pace of the Fertility Decline in Western Europe, 1870–1930," in Ansley Coale and Susan Cotts Watkins, eds., *The Decline of Fertility in Europe* (Princeton, 1986), 261–292.

[16]Stein Rokkan and Henry Valen, "Regional Contrasts in Norwegian Politics: a Review of Data from Official Statistics and from Sample Surveys," in Erik Allardt and Stein Rokkan, eds., *Mass Politics* (New York, 1970), 190–250.

[17]Svalestuen, "Om den Regionale Spreiinga av Norsk Utvandring før 1865," in Arnfinn Engen, ed., *Utvandringa—det store oppbrotet* (Oslo, 1978), 57–85.

[18]Sogner, "Freehold and Cottar."

[19]Leiv Dvergsdal, "Emigration from Sunnfjord to America prior to 1885," in *Norwegian-American Studies*, 29 (1983), 127–158.

[20]Skaaren, "Emigration from Brønnøy and Vik in Helgeland."

[21]Jon Gjerde, *From Peasants to Farmers, the Migration from Balestrand, Norway, to the Upper Middle West* (Cambridge, Massachusetts, 1985), 239.

[22]Rasmus Sunde, "Emigration from the District of Sogn, 1839–1915," in *Norwegian-American Studies*, 29 (1983), 111–126.

[23]See Lowell, *Scandinavian Exodus.*

[24]It is possible that overpopulation between 1810 and 1840 may have been responsible for early emigration or the establishment of tradition. Another type of analysis is needed to investigate this possibility.

# 4

# "I met him at Normanna Hall": Ethnic Cohesion and Marital Patterns among Scandinavian Immigrant Women*

*by Janet E. Rasmussen*

Marriage patterns among immigrants have interested researchers of ethnic history ever since Julius Drachsler's classic work *Intermarriage in New York City*, published in 1921.[1] A statistical study of the type undertaken by Drachsler generates powerful evidence of the trend toward endogamy, marriage within the ethnic group, among first-generation immigrants. Such an approach fails, however, to convey either the complicated human dynamics that surround choice of a marriage partner or the more subtle signals of cultural adaptation that may exist within endogamous relationships. Oral history interviews offer a vivid and nuanced picture of immigrant courtship and marriage patterns; as a result, a better understanding of the relationship between endogamy and cultural maintenance emerges. It will be seen that Scandinavian women in the Pacific Northwest displayed a high degree of ethnic loyalty in choosing a spouse, yet marriages in the immigrant community bore obvious signs of the new environ-

*A preliminary version of this paper was presented at the Pacific Northwest History Conference, Helena, Montana, May 18, 1985. The author gratefully acknowledges a grant from the L. J. Skaggs and Mary C. Skaggs Foundation of Oakland, California, in support of the oral history collection on which this discussion is based.

ment. Modes of courtship and wedding celebrations changed in response to the rhythms and resources of immigrant life. Single women also boasted a high degree of autonomy, fostered by economic independence, demographic scarcity, and requisite self-reliance; this autonomy added its own flavor to immigrant courtship. For Scandinavians, adaptation coexisted with ethnic loyalty; changes in attitude and behavior took place simultaneously with the forging of endogamous marriages.

Seventy-two women who emigrated as unattached persons and who settled either immediately or eventually in the Pacific Northwest provide the life histories for this discussion of immigrant courtship.[2] An additional fifteen informants who married or became engaged to be married prior to emigration offer valuable perspectives on contemporary courtship and wedding customs in Scandinavia. Viewed together, the women immigrants, eighty-seven in all, display the following profile: they were born in the three decades between 1883 and 1914; they migrated across the Atlantic between 1901 and 1931; and they entered into their first marriages between 1907 and 1943.[3] The majority (fifty-three) of the women came from Norway. Ten Danes, ten Finns, and fourteen Swedes are also included. These twentieth-century immigrants from Nordic countries were found through an informal network of persons and organizations. They represent an important, but hitherto unexamined, regional presence.[4] The interviews with them will become part of the Scandinavian Immigrant Experience Collection at Pacific Lutheran University in Tacoma, Washington.[5]

The technique of oral history was selected for three reasons: first, because interviews capture otherwise unavailable information; second, because oral history allows persons directly, and from their own point of view, to relate their own life stories; and third, because this approach mandates the consideration of human experiences in humanistic rather than primarily statistical terms.[6] These points emerge as especially compelling when the subject under discussion is women's experiences, for women have too often remained silent about their lives. The interviews in our project cover a range of topics and attempt to capture the major features of the individual lives, including social background, reasons for emigration, journey to America, settling in, employment, family life, community involvement, and awareness of heritage. Because of the unique nature of each narrative, topics are discussed more fully in some cases than in others and central points are occasionally overlooked.

Before proceeding with detailed description and analysis of the oral sources, a brief review of the pioneering work on the relationship between marriage and assimilation is in order. To set forth the marital patterns of European immigrants in the country's largest metropolis, Julius Drachsler screened over 100,000 marriage licenses issued in the five-year period between 1908 and 1912 and tabulated the results for 79,704 marriages with identifiable ethnic composition. He urged the use of quantifiable data, such as that presented in his detailed tables, in order that public policies concerning immigrant assimilation might be intelligently formulated. Drachsler stated his understanding of the relationship between intermarriage and assimilation in this way: "Intermarriage, as such, is perhaps the severest test of group cohesion. Individuals who freely pass in marriage from one ethnic circle into another are not under the spell of an intense cultural or racial consciousness. Consequently, the greater the number of mixed marriages the weaker, broadly speaking, the group solidarity" or "to put it differently," as he later suggested, "the higher the proportion of intermarriage, the higher is the degree of assimilation with other groups."[7] A theoretical framework for the relationship between assimilation and intermarriage was provided by Milton M. Gordon who, in 1964, proposed seven stages or types of assimilation. On the assimilation scale, Gordon placed marital assimilation third, after both cultural and structural assimilation, implying that not only familiarity with the host culture's language and customs but also access to its clubs and institutions would normally precede marriage outside the ethnic group. As Drachsler and Gordon both realized, loyalty to one's own group or exclusion from mainstream institutions could not fully explain the immigrant marriage market. Economic considerations and the ratio of men to women would necessarily influence marriage patterns as well.[8] Still, when dealing with a clearly defined ethnic community like the Scandinavians in the Pacific Northwest, the evidence supports Drachsler's view of endogamy as a sign of ethnic cohesion; it also confirms these researchers' understanding of marriage outside the group as an obvious but hardly definitive sign of assimilation. Not only did Gordon place cultural and structural assimilation prior in time to intermarriage, but Drachsler acknowledged that his use of intermarriage data would result in an underestimation of immigrant assimilation.

The perspectives of Gordon and Drachsler provide a helpful point of departure for a consideration of the first-generation Scandinavian experience, although the focus here will be on adaptation to the new urban environment of the Pacific Northwest rather than on assimilation in a purer sense. More importantly, Drachsler's statistical analysis of Scandinavian immigrant women who married in New York City between 1908 and 1912 serves as the best yardstick for judging the representative quality of the oral history data from the Pacific Northwest, since the time period, the immigrant population, and a largely urban environment are points in common. In Drachsler's study, between 63 and 76 percent of the first-generation Scandinavian women married someone of their own nationality. When his data are recalculated to include inter-Nordic marriages, the percentages range from a low of 79 percent to a high of 89 percent.[9] These figures correspond very well with the high rate of endogamy demonstrated by the oral history interviewees. Only seven of the seventy-two unattached women married non-Scandinavians when they entered the marriage market; fully 89 percent chose partners from the broadly defined ethnic group of Scandinavians. Some mixing occurred within the Scandinavian community, but this, too, was very modest. Five marriages joined different Nordic nationalities; in four of these cases, however, familial and linguistic ties supported the choice of mate.[10]

Seven marriages took place with second- or third-generation Scandinavians, though these matches also demonstrated clear loyalty to specific national identity. Leaving aside the non-Scandinavian and the mixed Nordic matches, 72 percent (fifty-two of seventy-two) of the single women married first-generation members of their own nationality.[11] The correlation with Drachsler's figures is striking. Further corroboration comes from Patsy Adams Hegstad's careful study of the 1900 census for Seattle and Ballard; she determined an endogamous/inter-Nordic marriage rate for Nordic-born *men* ranging from a low of 73 percent for the Danes to a high of 85 percent for the Finns.[12] Thus, the general marriage pattern of the immigrants under study here conforms to previously documented trends. What previous investigations have not fully captured is the range of factors behind the matches. Part of the explanation obviously derives from contemporaneous sex ratios.

The unmarried women found the Scandinavian bachelors in the Pacific Northwest most eager to make their acquaintance and it is perhaps not overstating the case to suggest that their relative scarcity supplied them with a certain leverage. Upon learning of a newcomer from the homeland, Norwegian males might waste little time before paying a social call, as this 1923 story from Tacoma indicates: "He was from Sykkylven, Norway. He came to my uncle's house before I even knew he existed, 'cause he'd heard that there was a *nykommerjente* [a girl newcomer] there. He came with my second cousin Oscar Olsen that he'd met here. But I wasn't home that evening when he came over. We met at Normanna Hall, later, through somebody."[13] On occasion, the men formed a reception committee for the arriving immigrant women. Hanna S. recalls her welcome in Astoria, Oregon, in 1919: "When I come here at first, they heard Finnish girls come to here. And they come to see us — boys come to see us. My husband was there. He was Finnish. It happened that he came from almost the same place. We were married in 1921."[14] Before they even had a chance to freshen up after the long cross-country train ride, Greta P. and her companions encountered a group of keenly interested Danish men: "We came into Seattle on the 26th of August [1922]. When we came into the railroad station, they came some of the young fellows from the Danish Hall where they were staying as boarders; they came down to get us. There was a party at the Hall that night. They had to see these here Danish girls, you know. All these young Danes that were staying in this boarding house, they were anxious to see these Danish girls, naturally. But we weren't looking our best. My hair was just like wire, from five days on the train."[15]

The ardent attention paid to the newcomers points to the fact that Scandinavian women were in short supply in the Pacific Northwest. The State of Washington exhibited a high ratio of immigrant men to women, as signaled by the 1910 census (212.1/100); and while Italian and Austrian residents confronted an even greater sex imbalance, Swedish and Norwegian males outnumbered their respective female counterparts by an imposing 187.9/100 and 177.7/100.[16] The percentage of women in the Scandinavian population increased steadily between 1900 and 1940, but females remained in the minority. Figures from the city of Seattle illustrate the trend. In 1900, women made up 29.5 percent of Seattle's Danish population; by 1940 this had risen to 37.5 percent. A similar pattern can be ascertained for the other Scandinavian nationalities in the city, with women constituting around 40 percent of the ethnic population in 1940 (see Table 1).

Table 1
Percentage of Women in Immigrant Population in Seattle

|      | Danes | Finns | Norwegians | Swedes |
|------|-------|-------|------------|--------|
| 1900 | 29.5  | 16.1  | 34.8       | 32.2   |
| 1940 | 37.5  | 43.2  | 39.9       | 41.1   |

Sources: Figures for 1940 are drawn from Calvin Schmid, *Social Trends in Seattle* (Seattle, 1944); figures for 1900 from Hegstad, "Citizenship, Voting, and Immigrants."

Nationwide, too, Scandinavian men outnumbered Scandinavian women; however, the discrepancy was greatest in the western states. This may explain in part why Mina B. had a west-coast suitor while she was working in Chicago in 1917: "I knew him from Norway. He was out here in Seattle. He called me and wrote to me and wanted me to come to Seattle. He was working out here—fishing."[17] A Norwegian bachelor living in rural Montana (later Washington), likewise seized the opportunity to court an eligible woman across the miles. His wife, a nurse, explains: "So one day I had night duty and here come a fellow from America, he was a friend of my sister's husband. I had already asked for my passport and I told him I was coming to America. After he find that out, he just write and write every week and I don't know how often. So I met him in Glasgow, Montana [where the married sister lived] and I don't think he asked me to marry him then. But he came clear to Chicago and asked me if I would marry him and I said yes. So he went back to his job and I was working in Cook County Hospital for two years and then we get married in Chicago in a big church." When the newlyweds traveled to eastern Washington in 1929, Gertie H. discovered to her dismay that the new house was located in a "little God-forsaken country" with "no running water, no electricity."[18] Like electrical power, single Scandinavian women, especially women with Gertie's training, were a scarce resource in rural communities in the Pacific Northwest.

This narrative mentions a referral from Scandinavians in America to a woman in the old country. Other interviews relate similar situations. Jenny P., a twenty-two-year-old seamstress in Esbjerg, Denmark, fancied a Danish American named Chris: "I kind of liked him. He was dressed a little different; he had more American-style clothes on. He wasn't the same type as what we met at home, you know." And how did Jenny and Chris come to know each other? "He visited my sister that lived over on Bainbridge Island [Washington]; they got together all these Danes once a year for a reunion. . . . And so my sister said to him, one day, why don't you go over to Denmark and visit over there and see your mother . . . and I have a sister at home not married, why don't you go home and marry her?"[19] Chris brought greetings from Jenny's sister in

1921 and they were married the following year. Five other women in the group of fifteen married or engaged emigrants had also been courted by visiting Scandinavian Americans. For males, the marriage market was better in Scandinavia than in the Pacific Northwest, since the sex ratio there tipped toward the female side and a Scandinavian American might appear exotic and impressive.[20] The chain of personal ties across the Atlantic grew stronger as direct migration to the Pacific Northwest escalated. Women immigrants, like Jenny's sister, could have had their own motives for long-distance matchmaking, including a desire for female companionship. After Anne H. left Denmark in 1908 to homestead in central Washington — an experience she describes as like "climbing a mountain, starting on the steep side" — her sister followed to marry Anne's brother-in-law and become Anne's homestead neighbor.[21] Thus female kinship networks might play a direct role in the recruitment of brides.

During the early twentieth century, Scandinavian immigrants exhibited considerable transatlantic and transcontinental mobility. As a result, some men compensated for the unfavorable sex ratio in the Pacific Northwest by extending the marriage market to both midwestern settlements and the homeland.[22] But not all immigrant bachelors could afford to travel or were so inclined. Unlike the Italian men discussed by Robert F. Harney in his well-known article "Men Without Women," Scandinavians did not automatically look to the home community for a marriage partner.[23] Instead, the local ethnic scene fostered the principal courtship and mating activity. During this period, Scandinavians in the Pacific Northwest maintained a rich network of secular and religious organizations, a network which provided a forum for socializing between the sexes.

The importance of the ethnic network is shown by a review of the avenues through which the seventy-two unattached women became acquainted with the men they eventually married (Table 2). Most women met their husbands either through friends and relatives or through an organization. Fifty-four of the matches described in the interviews (75 per-

Table 2

Ways Scandinavian Immigrant Women Met Spouses

|  | Scandinavian Husband | Non-Scandinavian Husband | Ethnicity of Husband Unknown | Total |
|---|---|---|---|---|
| Through Relatives, Friends, Neighbors | 31 | 2 |  | 33 |
| Through Churches, Clubs, Lodges | 19 | 1 | 1 | 21 |
| Through Workplace | 5 | 2 |  | 7 |
| Acquainted from Scandinavia | 6 |  |  | 6 |
| Not specified | 3 | 2 |  | 5 |
| Total | 64 | 7 | 1 | 72 |

cent) developed within such a framework; all but four of these were endogamous relationships. The oral testimony reveals that fellowship with other Scandinavians provided a welcome antidote to the initial loneliness and awkwardness of immigrant life. Henny H. felt that her first domestic job was too isolated, so after nine months she quit and took a position close to the Scandinavian neighborhood in Tacoma: "And then I was all set. Then I started going to Normanna Hall where all the Norwegians gathered, you know, and I met friends and then I was on easy street."[24] The single women were employed primarily as domestic servants. Such jobs were in plentiful supply and the compensation was generally favorable. Because they lived in American households, the Scandinavian domestics acquired familiarity with local customs and English vocabulary. This combination of financial security and language facility heightened their sense of personal autonomy and pride. Still, the women gravitated toward the ethnic community during scheduled hours off on Thursdays and Sundays in order to hear their own language, to relax, and to socialize.

The individual church congregations had strong ethnic identities and served social as well as spiritual needs. Laura F. participated in the Danish church in Seattle in the 1920s: "All of us girls, all these young girls, we were all working in homes as domestics and we had Thursdays off. So Thursday afternoon we would meet at the church. We had joined the Danish Young People's Society, and, of course, that got the ball rolling. Then we got acquainted with girls and young people our own age. And it was all clean fun like picnics and basket socials and little plays and entertainment evenings and what have you. And that's where all the young people met. The fellows after work would come in the evening and play croquet out on the lawn."[25] Hilma N. left Norway with several members of her family in 1903; she worked as a domestic in Tacoma and was active in her church and the Good Templar lodge: "Sometimes when we went to church on Sunday evening, I think we went there just for to meet our dates. My husband, he was singing in the choir." Like Laura, Hilma noted the "nice clean fun" that they had while dating and in groups. Her friends belonged to the temperance society; thus a certain screening occurred within the specific ethnic group — "the boys we went out with, they were temperates, they didn't drink."[26]

The secular lodges with their various spin-off activities — singing and dramatic societies, dances and socials — also proved a welcome source of new friends, and eventually of a husband. Arriving in Seattle in 1916, Ida A. found it easy to become acquainted with other Norwegians. She especially enjoyed the chance to interact with a larger circle of people than her home community in Norway could boast: "I joined a mixed group — men and women — that met in Norway Hall, which was of course our meeting place. And that was really nice. Then I met more people from other places in Norway. We'd sing. We had a little choir. I met my husband at Norway Hall, of course, at Boren and Virginia. He was in the Navy at Bremerton. He was a Tacoma boy — of course he was born in Norway. He joined the Navy because he did not want to go in the Army. One of my neighbor boys from home was in the

Navy and that's how I met Andrew." In this case an extra stamp of approval was placed on the already positive fact of Andrew's Norwegian birth by introduction from a trusted neighbor. Ida knew her situation was not unique: "I think lots of young people met husbands through the Norwegian organizations. Sometimes they met someone from their own home place."[27]

Introductions by family and friends were frequent and typically casual. One woman reported, "He came up to the house, because my brother knew his brother and he went together with them."[28] Another said, "My husband was a friend of my uncle. They knew one another, see. So that's how I met him . . . He came over from Norway in 1911, so he was about twelve years older than I was."[29] Anna J., a Swedish-speaking Finn, became acquainted with her husband through a midwest network transplanted to the west coast: "My husband came from Alaska. He had been in the service in World War I and couldn't get a job back east and then he went up to Seattle and hired out on a boat to go fishing in Alaska. And then he came from there. I had known him—he sang in the choir in Bemidji, Minnesota, in a church there. I was slightly acquainted with him there. In Everett [Washington], he had his good suit stored over at Selma Johnson's place and he came over to get his suit. And I met him then."[30]

An example from Astoria, Oregon, reveals the possible interrelationship between the workplace and the ethnic community: "When I got through the eighth grade, I got a job. It was at a department store, it had everything—clothing, shoes, just about everything. I got to work there and he [my husband] and the lady that raised him lived nearby and he came and shopped there . . . I didn't take lunch and I didn't want to walk home for dinner so I used to eat my lunch at the Finnish Boarding House and he was eating there, too, sometimes when he was working. He lived near the boarding house and he came to shop there and I got to know him. We were married for sixty-three years. This was 1917."[31] For Freda R., on the other hand, work in a service job brought contact with a non-Scandinavian spouse. "Then I worked in a restaurant. It was City Restaurant in downtown Tacoma . . . I had to be at work at six o'clock in the morning and make sandwiches and lunches for people who came to buy their lunch. That's what I did. I did that until I met my husband . . . My husband worked at the restaurant; he was a waiter. His name was Dan Ranney. He was from Iowa. His mother was Irish and his father Scotch; but they come over on the *Mayflower*, so they was oldtimers."[32] Interestingly, Freda's first-generation immigrant perspective has exaggerated the husband's American identity.

No special conclusions can be reached about the ways in which the women met their non-Scandinavian husbands. What does distinguish this small group, however, is age at emigration. Five of the seven women who married outside the ethnic network were under the age of confirmation (less than fourteen years old) when they came to this country. Thus, while only a small percentage of the unattached informants married non-Scandinavians (7 out of 72 or 10 percent), a much higher percentage of the subgroup who made the transition from childhood to adulthood after arrival in America did so (5 out of 13 or 39 percent). Three of the younger emigrants entered into unions with second-generation Scandinavians and one, a Dane, crossed national boundaries to marry a Swede. So only 30 percent of the pre-confirmation emigrants married first-generation countrymen, a pattern to which 78 percent of the total group subscribed. Statistical information drawn from the interview sample must not be given undue weight; the important point is not the percentages but the general pattern they suggest, with the evidence here supporting the view that the younger one is upon emigration, the weaker the ethnic loyalty one exhibits.

It has already been noted that eager courting of the scarcer immigrant women by Scandinavian men and the welcoming bosom of the ethnic community helped account for the high incidence of female endogamy. Domestic workers, even though exposed to American household environments throughout the week, used their hours off to socialize with fellow Scandinavians. Certain features of courtship and marriage will now be examined where the matter of adaptation to the American environment may be tested, namely age of marriage, courtship dynamics, wedding customs, and female autonomy.

The first factor, age of marriage, shows obvious continuity from the homeland, with the average age of marriage for the women immigrants close to the Scandinavian norm. During this period, women in Sweden, Norway, and Denmark were, on the average, 26 years of age when they married; the women immigrants were, on the average, just under 25 years old. Once again, the pre-confirmation emigrants display a somewhat different profile, with an average age at marriage of 22 years. Interestingly, this corresponds to the median age at marriage of 22.4 years for women born in the United States between 1905 and 1914.[33]

Though the adult emigrants married according to the Scandinavian timetable, they encountered and adapted to a different set of courtship expectations. In rural Scandinavia, marriages were typically motivated by property and class considerations; appropriate marriage partners could be encouraged by the family and a very low-key courtship carried on until the conditions for marriage (land, inheritance, sufficient capital, pregnancy) were right. Whereas the community was intensely concerned with the propriety of a match and needed to sanction it, courting itself was not conducted in the public eye. Until the late nineteenth century, the established avenue for young people to become better acquainted with each other was night courtship or bundling. Although this custom had largely died out by the turn of the century, the public display of emotions or obvious favoring of an individual prior to an official engagement was still considered improper.[34] The urban environment of the Scandinavian community in the Pacific Northwest fostered a different courtship pattern. The immigrants were by and large wage earners for whom class distinctions based on property ownership were irrelevant. Here courtship consisted primarily of attending social events together: "We used to go to dances and had a wonderful time. We went together about four years before we got married."[35] This represented a reversal of expectations: whereas the choice of a marriage partner was now largely an individual matter, courting itself became a public phenomenon.

According to Ellen Luoma, dances became the principal courtship vehicle among Finnish immigrants, because the "rituals were easy to learn and enforce" and "were not tied to the rural status system." Romance rather than property propelled a couple together: "partners were chosen on the basis of personal characteristics — charm, appearance, the ability to dance."[36] Personal attraction obviously sparked many of the relationships described in the oral history interviews and women were not simply passive recipients of male attention. Sara V. recalls meeting her husband at Normanna Hall in Tacoma: "I remember standing by the steps. I always did like him. He had curly hair and I wanted children with curly hair. He came and asked me, 'Do you want to dance?' So we danced then and we started to go steady for three years and then we got married."[37] Sigrid K., a Finnish immigrant, tells this story: "I met him in the church in San Francisco. He was outside standing with his brother. So we came out; we were quite a few girls. So he told his brother, 'That's the girl I'm going to marry.' His brother said, 'How do you know if she will want you?' 'I don't know, but I'm going to find out!' We were married sixty years."[38] But for persons who had been taught to hide their feelings, there was an awkward and uncertain side to courtship in public. Anna E. had been in Tacoma two years when her future husband attended a Norwegian Christmas party. The meal had been served and the young men were sitting in a row, waiting to start the traditional dances around the Christmas tree. "And so we girls went to sit down on the other side. And I come walking by there and only one guy got up and said hello to me and shook hands with me and that was my husband — isn't that funny? Oh, I felt so cheap. And the rest of the boys, I knew them, and they laughed, and I thought it was so silly . . . So then we started to go around the Christmas tree and he came and got me. He was kinda bashful like, I think. Ole went with me home on the bus, just to the building where I was, so he knew where I lived. He was from Ålesund in Norway. He was down from Alaska for the winter."[39] Anna conveys both her awkwardness at being publicly singled out and the bashfulness she feels her suitor had to overcome ("His brother said to me later, 'I thought he turned crazy that night.' ")

Sometimes the courtship lasted less than a year, but a waiting period of two or more years was fairly common. For one thing, the men held jobs as loggers and fishermen and typically worked away from the cities (Tacoma, Seattle, Everett) for long stretches of time; for another, the women were for the most part settled in good-paying jobs and had no economic incentive to marry. Gunhild S.'s remarks reflect the new context of urban courtship and the individual responsibility she felt for her decision: "I came in '21 and I met him in '22 in the latter part of the year. '23 we got engaged. So I guess I knew what I was doing." She was married in November, 1924. In a bow to old-country tradition, Gunhild's boyfriend wrote to her father in Norway. This was just a courtesy, though, for Gunhild's high opinion of the boyfriend was the only thing the father could judge: "He was kinda nice because he wrote back to my dad and asked him for my hand. There's very few that do that. But he did and told him he would take care of me, you know. Dad didn't quite believe that before I wrote and said how nice he was. Then he wrote, if you say so, it must be."[40]

As celebrated by the immigrants, weddings were a second point of contrast to old-world traditions. Wedding customs were undergoing a gradual change in Scandinavia as migrants to the cities began to opt for civil nuptials and scaled-down festivities, but the rural ideal of a church wedding followed by an elaborate celebration for neighbors and kin retained its force in the early years of the century. Local traditions lent many special touches to these important occasions, but in general the event lasted two or three days, included several full-course meals (some of the food for which was supplied by the guests), a procession of the bridal party and guests through the countryside or village streets, dancing, and ritualized speeches and toasts.[41] Hilda M. married in 1913, a week before emigrating to America with her husband: "We got married in Finland. We got a big wedding party — three days . . . They built a big platform outside where people could dance. There were flowers on it and it was beautifully decorated."[42] In 1922, Elsie M.'s fiancé came home to Sweden from America. One should not be misled by her use of the adjective "little": "They had a little party for us at my grandmother's. There was a *smörgåsbord* . . . So all the farmers that lived there in Mossebo, they came over and then we had a party — a dance, and an accordion player, and lots of food."[43] Olga Ha. remembered her 1926 wedding to a returned emigrant, an event which caused quite a sensation in the northern Norway community and filled the church: "The party after the wedding lasted until the next day. We had that at my mother and dad's house. There was a whole lamb that was butchered for that and we had two cooks there. We had Alexandra pudding [rum pudding] for dessert . . . First we had dinner and then you walk around and some of them, if they want to dance, they had the floor in the barn. Your barn is all washed in the summertime so they were dancing over there; they had an accordion."[44]

The immigrants replaced the stylized ritual with a simple ceremony, often in a parsonage parlor rather than a church, followed by a modest meal. Without the support of a large family, it was difficult to afford or stage an elaborate celebration. Freda R. was married in Tacoma: "I had a very simple wedding. I was married at my sister's house. I had a Lutheran minister come there and marry us. I was married in a nice suit. I didn't have any money. I bought the suit on time. It took me I don't know how many months to pay for it. It was just my sisters at the wedding. Then we went to Seattle for a trip."[45] Olga He. met and married her husband in Bellingham, Washington: "We were married in 1920. We just went to the minister. We invited some people in for the reception, for supper or whatever you call it. You didn't see much of big weddings in those days."[46] Perhaps the most matter-of-fact situation is described by Mira B., who was married the same day she arrived in Seattle from Chicago: "I came from the train, went up to the minister and got married, went back to the apartment and cooked the dinner."[47] A modest celebration was typical. The difference in style between their weddings and those of both traditional Scandinavia and present-day America accounts for the frequent use by the interviewees of terms like "simple," "just" and "no (real wedding, wedding trip, white dress)."

Both courtship and wedding customs became modified in the new country. Women were active participants in the less formal social patterns. The experiences of Anna H. provide a nice example of this point, as well as being representative of the process as a whole. Anna met a fellow Norwegian through an ethnic activity—a snowball fight after an event at Normanna Hall. During their three-year courtship, employment demands kept them seasonally separated. He fished in Alaska during the summer; she was successfully employed as a domestic worker in Tacoma. Anna felt no economic incentive to marry: "There I got $50 a month. That was really good wages for that time, because lots of the men were working and they didn't have more than a dollar a day for working." The sense of autonomy she brought to this courtship is suggested by the active, first-person form of her statement, "I decided to go up to Alaska and we got married up there, in Cordova, Alaska." In other words, she presents this as an independent, personal choice. The marriage ceremony was performed at the courthouse with two of his friends as witnesses. Anna remained in Alaska all summer: "That was a lovely summer up in that fishing camp."[48] Anna's economic independence and self-reliant spirit empowered her to make decisions and take responsibility for herself.

Although one of the interviewees rebuffed a boyfriend by telling him, "I haven't come to this country to get married; I have plenty of chances to get married in Finland," it would be an exaggeration to characterize Scandinavian immigrant women as reluctant brides.[49] They did, however, possess considerable freedom of choice as to whom and when they would marry. They typically spent a number of years in the labor market prior to marriage and in most cases their employment in the homes of American families supplied them with a far more intimate knowledge of American customs and values than that obtained by the bachelor loggers and fishermen. At the same time, they retained a sturdy ethnic pride and looked favorably upon Scandinavian suitors, as evidenced by the striking number who married endogamously.

An endogamous marriage offered clear benefits. For one thing, it seemed natural to associate with persons of a like background. A comfortable relationship is remembered by one who married a fellow Swede: "He had gone through the same thing I had and he had come from the old country, just about eighty miles from where I was. And his mother was dead and my mother was dead and there were so many things. We just clicked together."[50] Social standing, reputation in the home community, and familial approval could no longer function as gauges for a potential spouse. Under these fluid circumstances, it was no doubt reassuring to embark upon a relationship that was at least based in a common ethnic background. And prospective husbands were plentiful; the women encountered a large contingent of single men within the Scandinavian community in the Pacific Northwest, men who were anxious for female companionship. As a result of such factors, Scandinavian immigrant women married predominantly first-generation men of the same national origin. The high incidence of female endogamy, while significant in itself as a feature of the Scandinavian community in the Pacific Northwest, does not, however, convey the changing dynamics and expectations of courtship and marriage. From oral history interviews, one gleans relevant features of the female role, of courtship patterns, and of the transition to married life. While marriage outside the group may well be synonymous with assimilation, it can also be seen that endogamy need not be synonymous with a lack of assimilation. As Thomas Archdeacon points out in his recent book *Becoming American*: "The Scandinavians, in conforming to the American value system, did not have to dissolve their ethnic group connections, and the evidence suggests that the ties remained firm."[51] Through their work lives and through the changing fabric of the ethnic community, immigrant women began to adapt to American ways before they married. Their choice of spouse served as a statement of ethnic loyalty but not to the exclusion of American values. These insights prepare us better to interpret women's roles within the Scandinavian-American family.

## Notes

[1] Julius Drachsler, *Intermarriage in New York City* (New York, 1921).

[2] With the exception of one widow and one woman abandoned by her husband, none of these emigrants had ever been married. The rise in individual, as opposed to family, migration was a marked trend in twentieth-century emigration from Scandinavia; also rising was the percentage of female emigrants. Andres A. Svalestuen provides a useful overview of these trends in "Nordisk emigrasjon: en komparativ oversikt," in *Emigrationen fra Norden indtil 1. verdenskrig. Rapporter til det nordiske historikermøde i København 1971, 9–12 august* (Copenhagen, 1971), 9–60. He reports that during the decade 1901–1910, unmarried adult (15 or older) women comprised 29.9 percent of the total emigrants from Sweden, 24 percent of those from Norway, and 20.4 percent of those from Finland.

[3] One informant who emigrated in 1938 is included here since she was born in 1902.

[4] The major regional studies to date focus primarily on the formative years; these include Kenneth O. Bjork, *West of the Great Divide: Norwegian Migration to the Pacific Coast* (Northfield, Minnesota, 1958); Jørgen Dahlie, *A Social History of Scandinavian Immigration, Washington State, 1895–1910* (New York, 1980); Patsy Adams Hegstad, "Citizenship, Voting, and Immigrants: A Comparative Study of the Naturalization Propensity and Voter Registration of Nordics in Seattle and Ballard, Washington, 1892–1900" (Ph.D. dissertation, University of Washington, 1982); and volume 30 of *Norwegian-American Studies* (Northfield, Minnesota, 1985).

[5] The Scandinavian Immigrant Experience Collection is a special collection of the Robert A. L. Mortvedt Library at Pacific Lutheran University. Oral history interviewing began in 1979 as a class project with undergraduate students and continued as a grant project with staff interviewers. Most of the interviews were recorded between 1981 and 1983.

[6] Two special issues of *Frontiers: A Journal of Women's Studies* focus on the value and techniques of women's oral history: 2/2 (1977) and 7/1 (1983). James Bennett argues for a "humanistic oral history" in his article "Human Values in Oral History," in *Oral History Review*, 11 (1983), 1–15.

[7] Drachsler, *Intermarriage*, 18–19.

[8]Milton M. Gordon, *Assimilation in American Life* (New York, 1964), 71, 80–81; Drachsler, *Intermarriage*, 42.

[9]Drachsler, *Intermarriage*, 97, 159–179.

[10]The inter-Nordic marriages represent the following pairings: Dane-Swede; Swedish-speaking Finn-Swede; Finn-Norwegian (with family ties to Finland); Finn-Norwegian (of Finnish background); Norwegian-Swede (mother a Norwegian).

[11]The marriage partners of the 72 unattached emigrants may be described as follows: first-generation, same nationality: 52; second- and third-generation, same nationality: 7 (this includes one match between a Swedish-Finnish woman and a Swede); first-generation, other Scandinavian nationality: 5 (see note 10 above); non-Scandinavian: 7; nationality unknown: 1.

[12]Hegstad, "Citizenship, Voting, and Immigrants," 146, table 12. Her figures for endogamous and inter-Nordic marriages have been combined. As it will be seen below, women were in the minority in the immigrant population; thus a higher rate of endogamy would be projected for them. Janice Reiff Webster found surprisingly low rates of endogamy for women in her household sample (57% of Swedish women and 62% of Norwegian women), but this may relate to difficulties in interpretation of data; see her "Domestication and Americanization: Scandinavian Women in Seattle, 1888 to 1900," in *Journal of Urban History*, 4 (May, 1978), 282, 289, note 32.

[13]Each interview tape (SPEC T) is identified by number and all quotations from the oral history material will here be referred to by tape number. In an effort to preserve some measure of anonymity, narrators are referred to by first name and last initial only. The quotation is from SPEC T146.

[14]SPEC T87.

[15]SPEC T198.

[16]David L. Nicandri, *Italians in Washington State: Emigration 1853–1924* (n.p., 1978), 31–32.

[17]SPEC T220.

[18]SPEC T274.

[19]SPEC T147.

[20]In his *Flight to America: The Social Background of 300,000 Danish Emigrants* (New York, 1975), Kristian Hvidt analyzes the sex ratio among the emigrants and in Denmark. See especially chapter 8.

[21]SPEC T251.

[22]Webster also reports a pattern of Scandinavian women coming from the Midwest to marry in Seattle in "Domestication and Americanization," 281–282.

[23]Robert F. Harney, "Men Without Women: Italian Migrants in Canada, 1885–1930," in *The Italian Immigrant Woman in North America*, ed. Betty Boyd Caroli *et al.* (Toronto, 1978), 79–101.

[24]SPEC T146.

[25]SPEC T193.

[26]SPEC T233.

[27]SPEC T182.

[28]SPEC T79.

[29]SPEC T149.

[30]SPEC T104.

[31]SPEC T70.

[32]SPEC T203.

[33]Sources for Scandinavia include: *Historisk statistik för Sverige. 1. Befolkning* (Stockholm, 1955), table B7; Erik Høgh, *Familien i samfundet* (n.p., 1969), table 1.4.1; and Sidsel Vogt Moum, *Kvinnfolkarbeid. Kvinners kår og status i Norge 1875–1910* (Oslo, 1981), 36, 63. For the United States, see table 1 in John Modell, Frank F. Furstenberg, Jr., and Douglas Strong, "The Timing of Marriage in the Transition to Adulthood: Continuity and Change, 1860–1985," in *American Journal of Sociology*, 84, supplement (1978), S123.

[34]For more information concerning the custom of night courtship, see Michael Drake, *Population and Society in Norway 1735–1865* (Cambridge, England, 1969), and Ellen Luoma, "Courtship in Finland and America: *Yö juoksu* Versus *the Dance Hall*," in *Finnish Americana*, 22 (1979), 66–76. No mention of bundling is made in the interviews, although familial approval is discussed and the unequal economic status of a Finnish husband and wife was a strong impetus for their emigration to America.

[35]SPEC T225. A. William Hoglund offers a good discussion of these aspects of the immigrant experience in a chapter entitled "Love" in his *Finnish Immigrants in America 1880–1920* (Madison, 1960).

[36]Luoma, "Courtship in Finland and America," 71.

[37]SPEC T115.

[38]SPEC T224.

[39]SPEC T140–141.

[40]SPEC T190.

[41]For a photographic essay on a traditional Norwegian country wedding, see Dale Brown, *The Cooking of Scandinavia* (Alexandria, Virginia, 1968), 62–71. Further information is available in Robert T. Anderson and Barbara Gallatin Anderson, *The Vanishing Village: A Danish Maritime Community* (Seattle, 1964), and Aagot Noss, "Høgtider i livet," in *Gilde og gjestebod*, ed. Halvor Landsverk (Oslo, 1976), 51–71.

[42]SPEC T80.

[43]SPEC T229. They also had cornflakes, which she explains as follows: "There was one from America and she came home and she had it with her. That was something we never had seen before and heard about, so we had that on the table, too! We ate it; I didn't care for it."

[44]SPEC T200.

[45]SPEC T203.

[46]SPEC T256.

[47]SPEC T220.

[48]SPEC T113.

[49]SPEC T83. Luoma quotes a related sentiment in "Courtship in Finland and America," 71–72. Recent research on Irish women in America suggests that they married rather late and with some reluctance. See Hasia R. Diner, *Erin's Daughters in America* (Baltimore, 1983), especially chapter 3.

[50]SPEC T24. A woman who married outside the group commented on the loss of customs and language: "See, I married an American. And he was one of them who didn't want me to even teach the boys any Norwegian. He didn't like any of that Norwegian food; he wanted American food. So I cooked American food." (SPEC T210).

[51]Thomas J. Archdeacon, *Becoming American: An Ethnic History* (New York, 1983), 110.

# 5

# Immigrant Dynamics —
# The Jacobson Farmstead

*by Steven L. Johnson and Marion J. Nelson*

In May, 1977, the Jacobson farmstead seven miles southeast of Decorah, Iowa, was donated by Charlotte, Constance, and Eugene Jacobson of Northfield, Minnesota, and Henning Jacobson of Bayonet Point, Florida, to Vesterheim, the Norwegian-American Museum, as a coherent material record of a Norwegian immigrant family from shortly after its arrival in the mid-nineteenth century to the present. The physical evidence of the farmstead itself as well as the written and pictorial documents remaining on it or with the family reveals an interplay of conflicting forces — the traditional versus the new, the agrarian versus the urban, the mundane versus the spiritual and intellectual — typical of much in Norwegian immigrant culture. Though no conclusions will be drawn regarding the entire immigrant group, the farmstead and its family are presented here as a case study in the dynamics of Norwegian immigrant life.

The farmstead is completely the work of the Jacobson family. It was chosen as the dwelling site on a plot of land claimed by Jacob and Gro (Eggerud) Abrahamson and their three children, who came as one of the first sixteen Norwegian immigrant families to the Decorah area in 1850.[1] It remained in the possession of Jacob's descendants, who followed Norwegian custom by taking his first name to become Jacobson,

Jacob and Gro Abrahamson shortly after their arrival in
America in 1848.

Presumably "Stenbøle" as it appeared in 1898, fifty years after Jacob and Gro left. The log house with a partition near one end facing a barn with a large central doorway corresponds to the early arrangement at the farmstead in Iowa.

until transferred to Vesterheim 129 years later. It had then already been twenty-five years since intellectual and urban pursuits had claimed all the living descendants in the line through which the farm had passed, but familial piety and an awareness of the farm's historic significance had prevented the family from selling it. Having the farmstead go to the Museum as an academically maintained example of agrarian immigrant life was a fitting solution to a conflict that had marked the farm's entire history.

The specific circumstances which led Jacob and Gro to leave their cotter's farm in Vestfjorddalen, Tinn, Telemark, in 1848 are not known, but the name of their farm, Stenbøle (stony place), gives a clue, as does a photograph of the farm from 1898.[2] There was need for more and better land. A letter written home by Jacob while settled temporarily in Muskego, Wisconsin, just after arriving in America indicates that greater opportunities in general also contributed to the lure of the New World. After dwelling at length on the availability of work, the high wages, and the low cost of living in America,

Jacob writes, "I am sure I will live better in America without a farm than I would in Norway with one of the largest farms."[3] The possibility of making a living in America without working the land returns like a leitmotiv in the Jacobson story.

In spite of his praise of opportunity in America, Jacob's own aims remained ultimately agrarian, and his conception of farming remained fundamentally Norwegian. Moving with the vanguard of Norwegian families who left southeast Wisconsin to cross the Mississippi and claim land in the newly opened territory in northeast Iowa, Jacob spent the rest of his life on the farm he obtained there.

The basic elements of the Jacobson farmstead as it stands today were established by Jacob before his death in 1879. The farm was then 173 acres, the size it would remain. The log house, which is the core of the existing dwelling, follows essentially the traditional Norwegian three-room house plan. A close look at illustration no. 2 indicates that this is what the family was used to in Norway. Having doors in both the front and the back is unusual, but the placement of both has prototypes in the rural dwellings of Telemark. One door goes directly into the large room, as in the so-called Akershus plan, and the other (here on the back) goes into one of the two small gable-end rooms, as was typical in older three-room houses.[4] The half story above the ground level does not have a long tradition in rural Norway, but it was far from unknown there when Jacob Abrahamson and his family left in the middle of the nineteenth century.[5] The fact that the wall dividing the gable-end rooms from the main room is only in the upper story and not in the lower is also an unusual feature that may have some incidental rather than traditional explanation.[6] The logs are not tightly fitted as in Norway, but this feature was, for reasons not completely understood, also abandoned immediately by most other immigrant builders.[7]

The placement of the house higher than the barn on a slope leading down to a stream is also in line with Norwegian tradition, although it has a logic so obvious that tradition need not have entered in. Loosely enclosing the space between the

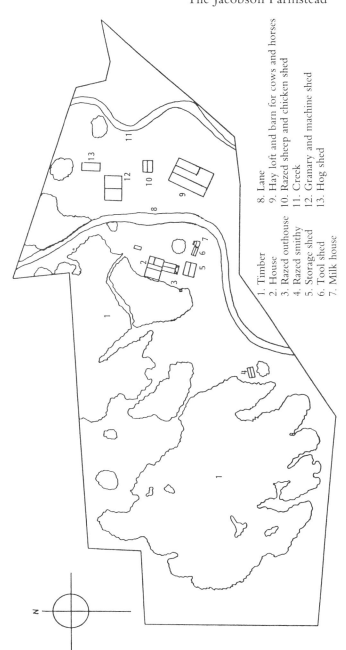

1. Timber
2. House
3. Razed outhouse
4. Razed smithy
5. Storage shed
6. Tool shed
7. Milk house

8. Lane
9. Hay loft and barn for cows and horses
10. Razed sheep and chicken shed
11. Creek
12. Granary and machine shed
13. Hog shed

The Jacobson farmstead and woodlot showing extant and razed buildings.

The Jacobson farmstead as viewed from the northeast in 1913. It had arrived at this state in 1908 and no new construction occurred afterward.

house and the barn by placing storage buildings at both ends is more specifically traditional, as is the placement of the blacksmith shop (now gone but clearly documented) well outside this enclosure.[8] Some of the actual buildings in this secondary group may date from slightly after Jacob's death, but the placement of the earlier ones serving their function would most likely have been the same.

The portion of the barn remaining from Jacob's period deviates from Norwegian tradition in being of stone, but its placement along a steep embankment with the wagon entrance to the hayloft in the middle of the long wall on the upper side has numerous prototypes in rural Norway. Placing the cow barn below the hay loft, on the other hand, is a more American feature. The shift from log to stone was common in large buildings around Decorah because long straight timber was scarce and sandstone with cleavages appropriate for cutting building blocks was readily available. Expertise for its use must also have existed in the community because stone barns from the 1850s and 1860s are found on many surrounding farms.

Assessor records reveal that the livestock on the farm

during Jacob's period also corresponded approximately to that on a small Norwegian farm: about seven head of cattle and two or three horses, sheep, and pigs. These would have provided little more than the needs of the household. Most cash had to be obtained by work in the lumbering industry or other day labor, as was also true in the inner valleys of Norway at the time.[9] Because of the greater tillable acreage, there could have been a greater surplus of grain and potatoes for sale than in Norway.

Jacob and Gro had little assistance on the farm. Their one daughter, Helga, if her obituary is correct, married in 1858 and apparently left the farm, moving eventually to Rock county, in extreme southwestern Minnesota.[10] Niels (1844–1925), the younger of the two sons, left home two years later at age sixteen to become one of the first pupils at Augustana College in Chicago. From there he enlisted in the 6th Iowa Cavalry for service against the Indians. Niels, too, eventually settled on a farm in Rock county, Minnesota, but devoted much of his time to community endeavors. In 1903–1904 he served as a member of the Minnesota State Legislature. His early intellectual pursuits apparently freed him from the most mundane aspects of agrarian life. At sixty-one he retired to the town of Hills, Minnesota, in Rock county, as his sister and her husband had done ten years earlier.[11] There they lived comfortable small-town existences until their deaths in 1925.

Abraham (1836–1910), the older son of Jacob and Gro, the one most expected to assist his parents, was the first to leave the farm. Only two years after the family settled in the Decorah area, when the boy was a mere sixteen years old, he headed for Springfield, Illinois, where he entered the so-called Illinois State University, a school founded and maintained by Lutherans. He remained there for eight years, supporting his studies by working as a custodian and librarian in the courthouse where Abraham Lincoln was making his reputation as a defense attorney.[12] Jacobson's personal connections with the future president were few, but he was a schoolmate and friend of Lincoln's son, Robert.[13] The Springfield period in the lives

Abraham Jacobson, probably around 1900.

of both Abrahams ended in 1860, when Lincoln became president and Jacobson left for Chicago to teach and preach in the Augustana Synod. He was functioning in this capacity at Augustana College when his brother Niels arrived there in 1860.[14]

Although Jacob Abrahamson, the father, chose to remain in a vocation appropriate to someone of his status in Norway, he allowed and possibly even encouraged his children to make use of the opportunities in America of which he had written so glowingly upon arrival. Their early departure from their aging parents—the mother was crippled with arthritis from the late 1850s until her death in 1884—appears to have led to no breach in family relations even though it was not in keeping with rural Norwegian custom.[15]

A pull between the agrarian and the urban, the mundane and the intellectual, existed in the Jacobson family well before its arrival in America. Several generations back, the Jacobsons were connected with the prominent Quisling family of pastors that entered Norway from Denmark in the 1600s. The quality of Jacob's letter from 1848 and the fact that the home at Stenbøle had apparently been a favorite one of the local schoolteacher indicates that a certain regard for culture had been part of the Jacobson family tradition.[16] This does not mean that the family was exceptional among rural immigrants from Norway. One finds the meeting of peasant and official strains in many immigrant family histories.

Abraham is the figure in whom the cultural dynamics were most apparent. He began to show inclinations toward the American, the urban, and the intellectual soon after his arrival from Norway at age twelve. During his first two years in America, while the family was temporarily settled in Wisconsin, he hired out to an American hotel- and store-keeper at Little Muskego Lake. He was so well received that his employer, a Mr. Taylor, gave him lessons in English, got him started in an American school, and even wanted to adopt him.[17] The adoption was resisted by both him and the family, but Abraham's experience with the Taylors undoubtedly prepared the way for his remarkable move two years later when he entered Illinois State University as the first Norwegian at that institution and one of the first children of Norwegian immigrants to enter any American institution of higher learning.[18]

Another indication of Abraham's rapid Americanization was his marriage in 1860 to Mary Hannah O'Connor. Little is known about her because of her death the following year in Decorah, but the name indicates that she was of Irish-American origin, and a photograph suggests that she was a woman of culture and sophistication.

Although Abraham had been in a primarily non-Norwegian environment during his eight years in Springfield, he was ready to reestablish connections with the Norwegian-American community and his own background after the death of Mary. In 1861–1862, he traveled as a missionary to the Norwegians in the newly organized Dakota Territory and to the Scandinavians in the ill-fated colony at Gaspé near Quebec, Canada. In 1863 he remarried, this time to a nineteen-year-old Norwegian-American girl, Nikoline Hegg, from Lier, near Drammen, who lived with her parents on a farm adjacent to that of his family. He actually remained at home as a farmer for three years before heading out again, this time for post-graduate study at Concordia Theological Seminary in St. Louis, Missouri, where pastors for the Norwegian Lutheran church in America were then being trained. After another missionary journey, which took him to west-central Minnesota, he accepted a call to the Norwegian parish at Perry, Wisconsin, in 1869.[19]

While firmly rooted in a rural Norwegian immigrant community, Abraham and his family developed at Perry a gracious style of living, more in line with that of the old official class in Norway than with that of the American farmer. This was very evident to his daughter Clara, who begins her "minder fra Perry prestegaard" with reference to Gustava Kielland's and Elise Aubert's stories of life in the old Norwegian parsonages.[20] It was at Perry that the family's interest in music revealed itself in a material way when the pastor bought a small cabinet organ for the parsonage even before

Abraham Jacobson with his family and hired help as photographed in
the yard of Perry parish parsonage by Andrew Dahl about 1877.

there was an organ at the church. Victorian furniture was purchased from a Norwegian merchant, Gabrielsen, in Milwaukee, and other fine pieces of furniture were made by a local
carpenter from Valdres, Aslak Lie.[21] Modern technology was
also introduced. The Jacobsons were among the first in the
community to have a sewing machine, and the pastor is
credited with being the first person to use one. In line with the
ministers of the enlightenment period in Norway, Jacobson
assisted the parishioners in practical as well as spiritual matters. He instructed others in the use of sewing machines and
helped keep their machines in repair.

Another indication of Jacobson's ongoing fascination
with the new and the cosmopolitan while devoting most of
his attention to the rural Norwegian community at Perry was
his trip with his wife to the Centennial Exposition in Philadelphia in 1876. At that time he also visited New York and
Washington, calling on President Grant at the White House.
His interest in expositions was ongoing. Even after returning
to farming he attended the world expositions in Chicago, St.

*A. Dahl, Landscape Photography*

The parlor in Perry parsonage as photographed about 1877 by Andrew Dahl. All the newly obtained furniture and many of the accessories seen here were taken back to Iowa in 1878 and are still on the farm or with the family.

Louis, and Portland, possibly a record in world's fair attendance for a Norwegian American.[22]

But the pendulum swung back to the farm. In the mid-1870s, Abraham Jacobson bought the home farm in Iowa, perhaps to assist his parents financially and probably with the intent of returning there. Exhausted from the ministry, he and his wife and seven children left Perry in 1879 and settled again in Iowa as the owners and operators of the farm he had left as a sixteen-year-old boy twenty-seven years earlier. The years of exposure to American ways had apparently not allowed Abraham to forget the Norwegian tradition that gave the oldest son responsibility for the family farm. Nature recognized the fate that was directing Abraham as he turned from regular involvement in the ministry to the agrarian life of his immediate ancestors. While the wagons were loading to leave Perry parish, a sudden cyclone swept over the area, removing the roof and upper walls of the parsonage and demolishing the

Abraham Jacobson with his wife, children, mother (directly in front of him), and possibly his mother-in-law photographed about 1883 at the old homestead in Iowa. The pastor is here in the farmer's traditional log chair rather than in the more urban captain's chair of the Perry parish photo.

church. The life of a visitor from the poor farm at Verona, Wisconsin, stopping to say farewell to the Jacobsons was claimed by the storm. "Åsgårdsreien," the turbulent celestial ride of exiled spirits from the pagan world, still hovered over the Jacobsons even after leaving the deep valleys of Telemark.

It is during the thirty-year regime of Abraham from 1879 to his death in 1910 that the Jacobson farmstead acquired those characteristics that most clearly reflect the dynamics at play in Norwegian immigrant life. He is to the second phase of the farmstead's history what his father had been to the first. The original log house, in which the functions of kitchen, dining room, and living room were all combined in the one large space, was expanded immediately to include a frame-construction parlor for the fine furniture brought from Wisconsin and, several years later, a frame-construction summer kitchen. The family was used to both at the parsonage in

When this photograph of three generations was taken in 1912, the house had reached the full extent of its development and convenient interior connections had been established between all units of the house except the second stories of the oldest unit far back on the right and the latest unit to the left. Charlotte, one of the donors of the farmstead to Vesterheim, stands between her grandmother Nikoline and her mother Minnie, who holds a new Abraham, born shortly after his namesake's death. The rider is Olaf J., son of Isaac.

Perry.[23] All additions to the basic log house — the back lean-to, the parlor, and the summer kitchen — could originally be entered only by going out of doors, a continuation of the early Norwegian tradition of having various functional units of the farmstead in separate buildings. These were soon linked by simple frame structures which allowed internal communication between all units, making it, in other words, an American house. By 1908, the summer kitchen had been expanded to include a year-round kitchen, a dining room, and two second-floor bedrooms. The farmstead had reached the full extent of its physical development two years before Abraham's death in 1910.[24]

Unlike his father, Abraham was a gentleman farmer. His grandchildren say that he did not do farm work, and photographs showing him in his top hat by the buggy or writing

The pastor-farmer is here saying farewell to his guests at the old farmstead around 1890. He walked with a cane after a fall on board ship while on his only trip to Norway, in 1888.

at his desk help to confirm this.[25] During his later life he served for over fifteen years as president of the Norwegian Mutual Life Insurance Company of Winneshiek county.[26] From 1903 to 1905 he was a member of the 31st General Assembly of Iowa.[27] For a period he traveled as an overseer for the Mandt wagon factory in Stoughton, Wisconsin.[28] He often served as a substitute pastor in local congregations and even returned to Perry parish in Wisconsin in 1890 to serve in this capacity.[29] At this same time he was also involved in the church controversy that led to the founding of the North Washington Prairie Norwegian Evangelical Lutheran Church, a congregation of the United Church to which he remained faithful until his death.[30]

In many ways, however, the move to Iowa did represent a serious return to agrarian interests and Norwegian cultural roots. One should not belittle Abraham's ability as a farmer. Assessor records show that the amount of livestock on the

During the decade before his death in 1910, Abraham Jacobson spent much of his time writing historical articles and columns for his agricultural series in *Decorah Posten*. He had previously cut a large opening in the wall of the old log part of the house and installed the bay window by which he is sitting.

farm almost tripled after his arrival in 1879, while the acreage remained the same. He devoted much attention to rationalizing farm methods and experimenting with new crops and technology. He is credited with having introduced clover to Winneshiek county, a possible reason for his naming the farm Cloverdale. For fifteen years toward the end of his life he edited a column in the Norwegian-language newspaper *Decorah Posten* entitled "Farmen og haven" (Farm and Garden).[31] The probate record at the time of Abraham's death in 1910 includes a gas engine.[32] Although his wife and children did most of the work, an aspect of Norwegian tradition which Abraham never abandoned, he must have been a good farm manager.

That the return also did mark a renewed interest in his past is evidenced by Abraham's trip to Norway in 1888, a trip on which a fall led to permanent lameness.[33] He was among the founders of the Norwegian Pioneer Association of Winneshiek county, led the erecting of a monument to pioneer Norwegians at the Washington Prairie Pioneer Cemetery in 1887, and did considerable writing about his past and about local history in general.[34] Visitors from Norway were welcome at the Jacobson farm, one being the distinguished Hardanger violinist, Knut Dahle, who appears with his violin in snapshots from Cloverdale.[35]

It was possible for Abraham to keep the complex cultural strains which were part of his background and nature in balance. This was more difficult for the generations that followed and the imbalance generally favored the urban and the intellectual. A grandson of Abraham says that the children were oriented toward college from the time they were young.[36] He was probably speaking of his own generation, but it was undoubtedly true of the one preceding it as well. When Abraham approached his last days in 1910, the options for retaining the farm in the family of eleven children were few. His oldest child, Clara (1863–1949), was a schoolteacher, a distinguished writer of local history, and the family photographer. She never married.[37] The next child, Mary (1865–1954), had become a college music teacher and in 1895 had married Professor I. F. Grose of St. Olaf College. The oldest son, Jacob (1868–1942), did indeed live on a farm, but it was in the second center of concentration for the family, Rock county, Minnesota.[38] Signe (1870–1961) was married to Rev. Knute E. Bakken. Isaac (1872–1925) was originally oriented toward a career in music but was making his living as a sign painter in Minneapolis. David (1875–1955) was a graduate of the University of Minnesota College of Pharmacy who was practicing his profession in Minneapolis. Helga (1877–1948) was a college teacher of English who in 1909 had married Lars W. Boe, later president of St. Olaf College. Otto (1879–1959) was farming in North Dakota but was more inclined toward public service. He had attended St. Olaf College and held the

Clara Jacobson, perhaps on a visit home from teaching around 1890, is dressed in urban high fashion. Since she had already begun photography at this time, the camera being used is probably hers.

position of Registrar of Deeds in Adams county, North Dakota, where he lived. He was soon to enter Luther Seminary and be ordained as a pastor. Christianna (1884–1948), a graduate of St. Olaf College, was teaching English in high school and was still single. Ragnvald (1888–1949) was attending Waldorf College and could not originally have been interested in farming because he joined the United States Navy and served through World War I. He eventually did settle on

Abraham Jacobson and his wife Nikoline are surrounded in this
photograph from about 1890 by all eleven children. Carl, the little boy
in the lower right, was destined to assume responsibility for the farm
through another generation. It may be Clara's camera that is again at
work for this photograph. The intention has been to create the ambience
of a studio picture, but the piece of furniture to the right and the uneven
light indicate that the photograph must have been made at home. The
exaggerated twists and angles of bodies and heads are probably an
attempt to create a professional look that becomes almost a caricature. A
meeting of the traditional and the modern is revealed by the fact that the
four oldest girls are wearing brooches of the rural Norwegian folk type
on dresses in the latest American fashion.

a farm in Glenwood township near Decorah. The lot fell to
Carl (1881–1949), who had attended Valders College in
Decorah and was, according to his family, as interested in intellectual and cultural pursuits as in agriculture. The old sense
of obligation to the family and its property, a lingering heritage from Norway, was probably what determined his fate as
it had previously determined his father's.

With his mother remaining for fourteen years as owner
of the farm and the guardian of her husband's tradition and
with his own skepticism about agricultural innovation, Carl
retained the status quo on Cloverdale to a remarkable degree.

It is popularly said that nothing stands still, everything goes backward or ahead. This was not true at the Jacobson farm. Nothing went into decay, nor was anything substantial added. The practices of Abraham were adequately sound and up-to-date to carry the farm for three decades, but the prospects for its future became increasingly uncertain.

The interest in the intellectual, the urban, and the cosmopolitan must have been as strong in Carl as it was in his father. While a tractor was not used on the farm until the 1940s, the house had a radio in 1927. Both Carl and his wife, Minnie Moen Jacobson, were fond of classical music, and the family would gather around the radio on Saturday afternoons to listen to the Metropolitan Opera.[39] Minnie's brother, Carl Moen, who was to live on the farm after no direct descendants were available to operate it, recalls that there were radios on both the first floor and the second. Reading was also a favorite pastime of the family, certainly of the father.[40]

All of Carl's six children attended college. Three held teaching or service positions in educational institutions. One became a scientist at the Dupont Laboratories in Wilmington, Delaware. Vincent, who had attended St. Olaf College and spent some time in the Navy, was the member left with the responsibility for the farm after Carl's death. Because of personal conflicts, which may or may not have been related to those discussed above, Vincent made his exit from this life on September 30, 1954,[41] as had his brother Abraham fifteen years before him.

The agrarian strain in the Jacobson line was coming to an end. Paternal devotion and lingering regard for the farm led the now urban owners to retain the homestead while the land was rented out. The one direct descendant in whom the duality of his father and grandfather remained most marked was Eugene, who assisted with the operation of the farm while holding a position at St. Olaf College. When illness interfered with Eugene's involvement in the late 1970s the time had come for the Jacobsons' ancient connection with the land to be severed. They had experienced what Jacob had foreseen in 1848 when he told his father in a letter that one could live bet-

By 1940 the bay window, which half a century earlier was cut through the log wall of the original house, formed the backdrop for the latest and finest radio-phonograph. Constance, another of the donors of the farmstead, is looking at an album of Richard Strauss's "Till Eulenspiegel's Merry Pranks." The old and the new, the rural and the urban, are here still in harmony, but the scale is weighted in favor of the new and urban.

ter in America without a farm than in Norway with one of the biggest.

The fact that an intellectual strain in the Jacobson family ran parallel with an agrarian strain had at times created a precarious situation for the farm. Ultimately it was this intellectual strain that led to its preservation. Without it, the family would scarcely have donated the farmstead to be maintained as an example of the agrarian base on which it and much in Norwegian-American culture rest. This strain also contributed to the importance of the farmstead as a visual record of immigrant life. In addition, there is an extensive collection of letters from many members of the family, historical writings from Abraham and Clara, and photographs from Clara and Eugene.[42] The family not only had the ability and made the effort to produce these things, but it had the foresight to preserve them.

The farmstead stands as an accumulative material record of a family caught in the dynamic interplay between inherited conceptions and the budding aspirations nourished by the possibilities in the New World. On the framework of a traditional Norwegian farmstead transplanted to America and still actually including objects brought from Norway or made here according to Norwegian tradition, one finds the addition to the house of a parlor and a bay window, both apparently from the 1880s; a nook for a grand piano (now lost) from only a short time later; a painting by Herbjørn Gausta obtained in 1883;[43] fine American Victorian furniture of urban production purchased around 1870; a bookcase with classic literature and major reference works; and a knicknack shelf with mementos of travels to most parts of the United States, to Canada, and to northern Europe. The dynamics ended when the new elements which put strain on the old structure drew the actors off this stage to a more completely American existence in urban scenes. But the stage remains as a set against which the drama of immigrant life can be better understood than without its visual props.

## Notes

[1] Abraham Jacobson, "Springfield Township, Reminiscences of Pioneer Norwegians," in *Standard Historic Atlas of Winneshiek County, Iowa* (Davenport, Iowa, 1905), Sec. 2,11.

[2] Illustration is assumed to be a photograph ordered by Abraham Jacobson, Decorah, from Knut Dahle, Vestfjorddalen, Norway, and referred to by him in a return letter dated October 8, 1898, in Vesterheim Archives.

[3] Jacob Abrahamson, Muskego, Wisconsin, to his father, Vestfjorddalen, Norway, September 27, 1848, translated by Charlotte Jacobson, in Norwegian-American Historical Association Archives.

[4] Johan Meyer, *Fortids kunst i Norges bygder, Telemark I* (1913, reprinted Oslo, 1977), 5, fig. 1, and 6, fig. 4.

[5] The fig. 4 referred to in note 4 shows a building of this type which appears to be of some age.

[6] According to family tradition as presented in an interview conducted

by Steven Johnson with Henning Jacobson, in Vesterheim Archives, the house was originally one story and was later raised to its present height. If this was the case, the old one-story house with its roof may have become the upper story. Not including the dividing wall in the new lower story would have simplified the raising process and given more flexibility to the utilization of space. The problem with this theory is that no evidence of two stages in production can be found on the building itself.

[7]The lack of close fitting between logs in immigrant building has been explained in several ways. One is that the early houses were looked on as temporary and therefore constructed with a minimum of work. The other is that the irregular shapes of the logs made close fitting difficult. The immigrant type is standard for most American log building. See Reidar Bakken, "En solungs amerikanske hus, tilpasninger til kultur- og naturmiljø," in *Nytt om gammalt*, Yearbook of the Glomdal Museum (Elverum, 1986), 75, 78.

[8]Arne Berg, *Norske gardstun* (Oslo, 1968), 69–72.

[9]*Standard Historical Atlas*, Sec. 2, 12.

[10]*Crescent-Garretson* (South Dakota) *News*, July 26, 1925.

[11]*Decorah Posten*, August 21, 1925.

[12]Typed obituary of Abraham Jacobson, possibly from the *Annals of Iowa*, in the file of his brother Niels Jacobson, in NAHA Archives. Also Abraham Jacobson, "Personal Reminiscences of Abraham Lincoln," an unidentified clipping in NAHA Archives.

[13]Robert Lincoln, Washington, D.C., to Abraham Jacobson, Decorah, November 5, 1883, in NAHA Archives. Also Henry O. Evjen, "Scandinavian Students at Illinois State University," in *Norwegian-American Studies and Records*, 11 (Northfield, Minnesota, 1940), 23.

[14]*Decorah Posten*, August 21, 1925.

[15]*Decorah Republican*, March 10, 1884, and interviews by the authors with Gro's great-grandchildren.

[16]O. Knudsen, Tinn, Norway, to Abraham Jacobson, Decorah, Iowa, October 11, 1909, in Vesterheim Archives.

[17]Abraham Jacobson obituary.

[18]O. M. Norlie, *History of the Norwegian People in America* (Minneapolis, 1925), 217.

[19]Abraham Jacobson obituary. Most of the above biographical information is from this source.

[20]*Symra* (Decorah, 1912), 12. These memoirs were published in English translation in *Norwegian-American Studies and Records*, 14 (1944), 139–158. The information about life at Perry which follows is from this article and the far more detailed account titled "Childhood Memories" still in manuscript at NAHA.

[21]Clara Jacobson does not mention Aslak Lie's name, but the identification has been well established by the research of John O. Holzhueter of the

State Historical Society of Wisconsin. Without referring to the Jacobson furniture, Holzhueter writes about Lie in "Aslak Lie and the Challenge of the Artifact," in *Wisconsin Magazine of History*, 70 (Autumn, 1986), 3–20.

[22]Abraham Jacobson obituary. This is the only source for the visit to Portland. Jacobson's descendants were not aware of the trip.

[23]The most complete description of the parlor is in Clara Jacobson's manuscript "Childhood Memories," 66b.

[24]The chronology of physical changes on the farmstead has been arrived at by checking information from early letters and interviews with family members against evidence on the site itself.

[25]Interview by Steven Johnson with Charlotte, Constance, and Eugene Jacobson, Northfield, Minnesota, March 28, 1981.

[26]"Abraham Jacobson," in *Past and Present of Winneshiek County, Iowa*, 2 (Chicago, 1913), 85.

[27]*Decorah Public Opinion*, May 18, 1910.

[28]"Malla" Jacobson, Decorah, to Clara Jacobson, Beaver Creek, Minnesota, April 30, 1884, in Vesterheim Archives.

[29]Abraham Jacobson, Perry, Wisconsin, to Osten Olsen (Rollag), Christiania, Norway, May 10, 1890, in Vesterheim Archives.

[30]The original Articles of Incorporation of the church dated December 8, 1890, with Abraham Jacobson's signature as secretary, were found in papers on the farmstead and are now at Vesterheim. A letter from Elizabeth Koren, daughter of Reverend U. V. Koren, to Mary Jacobson, daughter of Abraham, August 3, 1889, in Vesterheim Archives, deals touchingly with the personal consequences of the controversy.

[31]O. M. Norlie, *Norsk lutherske prester i Amerika, 1843–1913* (Minneapolis, 1915), 106. In English the column is referred to as "Practical Farming."

[32]The records were with material preserved on the farm and are now at Vesterheim.

[33]Abraham Jacobson obituary; Abraham Jacobson, Rotterdam, Holland, to Osten Olsen Rollag, Christiania, Norway, June 9, 1888, in Vesterheim Archives.

[34]Abraham Jacobson obituary; *Decorah Posten*, August 30, 1887. Among historical writings by Abraham Jacobson is the essay on the Norwegian settlement of Winneshiek county, Iowa, which appeared in slightly different versions in *Standard Historical Atlas*, in *Decorah Public Opinion*, August 25, 1909, and in Norwegian in Hjalmar Holand, *De norske settlementers historie* (Ephraim, Wisconsin, 1909). Others are "Personal Reminiscences of Abraham Lincoln," known only through an unidentified newspaper clipping at NAHA, and "A Pioneer Pastor's Journey to Dakota in 1861," in *Norwegian-American Studies and Records*, 6 (1931), 53–65.

[35]In the collection of Charlotte and Constance Jacobson. Dahle appears to have lived at Stenbøle, since Abraham wrote to him for photographs of

it in 1898. Those that arrived have Knut and other members of his family in them.

[36] Undated interview by Steven Johnson with Henning Jacobson, in Vesterheim Archives.

[37] The information on the children of Abraham Jacobson was supplied by his grandaughter Charlotte Jacobson. Where this has been supplemented, separate documentation has been given.

[38] Martin Ulvestad, *Nordmændene i Amerika*, 2 (Minneapolis, 1913), 509.

[39] Interviews by Steven Johnson with Henning Jacobson and with Charlotte, Constance, and Eugene Jacobson.

[40] Interview by Steven Johnson with Carl Moen, fall, 1979.

[41] *The Decorah Journal*, September 30, 1954, and *Decorah Public Opinion*, October 4, 1954.

[42] Important historical works by Clara not referred to earlier are "A Journey to America in the Fifties," in *Norwegian-American Studies and Records*, 12 (1941), 60–78, and "Memories from Mother's Childhood in Norway and from the Pioneer Days in America," published in Norwegian in *Reform* (Eau Claire, Wisconsin), but known to the authors through a typewritten translation in the archives of NAHA.

[43] This Norwegian-American artist also came from Vestfjorddalen, but there is no indication of early contact between the families. This seems to have come through the Korens, but it continued to the artist's death. "Malla" Jacobson, Decorah, to Clara Jacobson, Beaver Creek, Minnesota, March 8, 1883, and Isaac Jacobson, Minneapolis, to Clara Jacobson, Decorah, January 12, 1920, and December 31, 1921, in Vesterheim Archives.

# 6

# Two Museum Houses: A Microanalysis of Cultural Adaptation in the Upper Midwest in the Late Nineteenth Century

*by Reidar Bakken*
*translated by C. A. Clausen*

The Norwegian Emigrant Museum was established in Oslo in 1952 on the initiative of the Norsemen's Federation (Nordmanns-Forbundet). In 1973 the museum was moved to Hamar, which is centrally located for the two great emigration counties (*fylker*) of Oppland and Hedmark. The greater part of the museum consists of archives and microfilm copies of important source material, especially from the United States, but it also has a collection of objects and several buildings from the upper Midwest. The museum is being expanded as regards both collection and staff and in 1988 was given the official name of The Norwegian Emigrant Museum (Norsk Utvandrermuseum).

In this article attention will be focused on the two dwelling houses which are located in the open-air division of the museum. The first house acquired by the Emigrant Museum was built in the year 1871 at Norman, North Dakota, by Per Bårderud from Grue, Solør. This dwelling has become accepted by people in Norway as the standard Norwegian-American house. (Figures 1a and b). At Grue the house is still standing which the Bårderud family left in 1870. It is being maintained by the Gruetun Museum at Kirkenær. By a trip of an hour and a half between Kirkenær and Hamar one can thus

119

Fig. 1a. Borderud house at the Norwegian Emigrant Museum. The house was built in Norman, North Dakota, in 1871, by Peder Borderud from Grue in Solør. Courtesy Hedmark Museum.

follow an emigrant family from the home milieu in the old country to their new life in America (Figure 2).

The other building is usually called the Gunderson house in honor of the man who built it, the cotter Knut Gunderson from Krødsherad in Buskerud (Figure 3). The house was erected near Vining, Otter Tail county, Minnesota, and the documents which came with the house to Norway state that it was built in 1883.[1] This date has been repeated in later historical literature.[2] The facts of Knut Gunderson's career, however, suggest that this dating must be revised. In Krødsherad the cotter's dwelling which the Gunderson family left is also preserved (Figure 4). It is in a very bad state of repair; but, with the aid of the Emigrant Museum, work is in progress to assure its future. Thus, here also is an opportunity to compare an emigrant's way of life in Norway and in America.

For the Emigrant Museum the most important question is: what happened to Norwegian emigrants, culturally speaking, in their new homeland? The emigrants carried Nor-

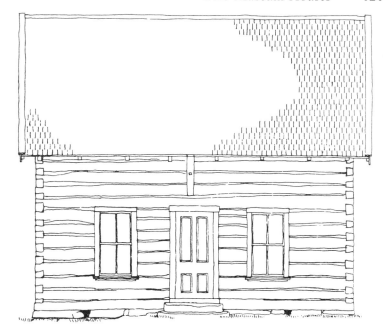

Fig. 1b. Scale drawing of Borderud house by Are Vesterlid.

wegian folk culture to a foreign land; and the development of
a Norwegian-American folk culture forms a part of Norwegian cultural history which the Museum desires to docu-
ment, investigate, and make known. What can these two
houses tell about this subject?

It is the dissimilarities between the Norwegian and the
American houses which immediately attract attention. Were
so few Norwegian traditions carried along to America? Or are
the American houses possibly more Norwegian than at first
glance they appear to be? Here is a debate which has long occupied American architecture students.

## TWO THEORIES IN AMERICA

In considering American log houses (*laftehus*) and their relationship to building customs in Europe, one has to deal with
two contradictory theories. C. A. Weslager, who has under-

Fig. 2. The main building on the Bårderud farm in Grue. The house was probably built toward the end of the eighteenth century. Photograph by Birger Nesholen.

taken detailed studies of American log houses during the pioneer era, maintains that during the post-pioneer period it is absolutely impossible to designate a log house in national terms. He argues that the log houses underwent a development in America which turned them into distinctive American cultural products, even though they had European roots.[3] He further maintains that it is not possible to select specific elements and say, for example, that this is Swedish, or this is Finnish.[4] Weslager thus represents what may be termed the Americanization theory. The heart of this theory is the concept that the log houses through the centuries in America became Americanized and that it is impossible to speak about specific ethnic elements in connection with them. This means that the immigrants who built their pioneer homes chose an American form without paying any attention to old-country traditions. Thus, judged by their early houses in America, the immigrants were quickly Americanized.

Marion Nelson, director of Vesterheim, the Norwegian-American Museum, in Decorah, Iowa, represents the other

Fig. 3. The Gunderson house at the Norwegian Emigrant Museum. The house was built near Vining, Minnesota, by Knut Gunderson from Krødsherad, probably in 1888. Courtesy Hedmark Museum.

theory. Nelson examines the most common type of house among Norwegian Americans during the period 1836–1876, a period when nearly 200,000 Norwegians emigrated to America. An example of this type of house is the Egge house from Decorah, now at Vesterheim. This house was built in 1852 by Erik Egge from Hadeland (Figure 5). It measures a story and a half and the logs are dovetailed. The roof is covered with shingles and is somewhat steeper than, for example, the Norwegian sod roofs. The entry door is placed on the longitudinal wall and has an adjoining window. Houses of this type are whitewashed or sided. Nelson points out that it was earlier believed, because of its deviation from Norwegian styles, that this type of house was developed under American

Fig. 4. Cotter's hut on Andresonbakken, on the Bjøre farm in
Krødsherad. Photograph by Reidar Bakken.

influence. A study of nineteenth-century cotters' and laborers'
houses in Norway indicates, nevertheless, that the type could
have been brought to America by Norwegian immigrants.[5] It
is only the use of whitewashing to draw humidity out of the
timbers that has, as far as is known, no parallel in Norway.[6]
With these ideas Nelson represents what may be called the tradition theory.

With these two theories as background the two houses at
the Emigrant Museum can be examined more closely. It is obvious that neither Per Bårderud nor Knut Gunderson tried to
recreate their houses from the old country; the differences are
too great. The question then arises: do the houses fit into the
general American log-house tradition which extends back to
the seventeenth century, or do they represent a unique
Norwegian-American tradition? Or did the builders have in
mind houses occupied by the lower classes in their home communities when they built their own homes in the New World?
The question may also arise whether they depended on their

Fig. 5. The Egge house, near Decorah, Iowa, now at
Vesterheim, the Norwegian-American Museum. The
house was built in 1852 by Erik Egge from Hadeland.
Drawing by Dana Jackson.

own ingenuity, in which case these houses become, in reality,
a sort of curiosity.

### THE BÅRDERUD FAMILY, FREEHOLD FARMERS

Per Bårderud was a farmer on Bårderud, a middle-sized farm
in Grue, Solør. He was born in 1818, and as the eldest son
took over the farm in 1846. The farm had thirty-eight acres
under cultivation and a smaller area of forest land. Per
Bårderud was married to Johanne Gundersdatter Aarnes from
Brandval and they had six children: Mathilde, Arne, Ole,
Torbjørn, Tea, and Gustava. Family tradition in America has
it that the oldest son wanted to emigrate and all of them left
together in 1870 so as not to break up the family.[7] In Grue it
is rather held that economic causes motivated the emigration.
The fact that the new owner of Bårderud immediately had to
make a lot of improvements in the buildings may also indicate
that Per Bårderud's economic condition was not of the best.[8]
The sale of the farm, however, provided a fine surplus which
the family took along to America.

Per had been a farmer for twenty-four years and was
fifty-two years old when he sold the farm and emigrated. Jo-

hanne was forty-eight and the six children ranged in age from seven to twenty-two. The family spent the first year in St. Ansgar, Iowa, while Per searched for land where they might settle down. This he found in the Red River valley in Dakota Territory. The place was called Norman and was located about twenty-five miles south of the present city of Fargo, North Dakota. Here Per Bårderud became a farmer and took the name Peder Borderud. The Borderud farm was about four times as large as Bårderud in Grue.[9] The Borderud dwelling was completed by the fall of 1871, and Peder and Johanne are said to have lived there the rest of their lives. Peder died in 1890, Johanne in 1894. The son Torbjørn took over the farm and built a new house in 1899.[10]

The older house was not used just as a dwelling place. The first religious service in the settlement was held there on May 8, 1872, and two days later a preliminary congregational meeting organized the Norwegian Evangelical Lutheran Church at the Sheyenne River, Dakota Territory. In 1912 the name was changed to Norman Congregation. Pastor J. A. Hellestvedt came to it as the first minister in 1873, and he lived with the Borderud family for many years. For a long time most church affairs were carried on in this dwelling—a church was not built until 1889.[11] Besides serving as the site for religious functions, the house was also the local post office. The son Arne was postmaster, a position he held until 1880. Furthermore, the building was also a clearing house where Peder Borderud gave counsel and advice to new immigrants. The county board held its meetings in the Borderud home, and reportedly it even doubled as a schoolhouse.

Thus the Borderud house served a number of public functions. That a building of such modest dimensions was utilized for so many different purposes tells a great deal about the pioneer settlement on the shores of the Sheyenne River. It gives a picture of a community which was being established. No institutions or offices were there ready-made—everything had to be built from the ground up. The form of life which people were acquainted with from the old country could not automatically be maintained under the new circumstances.

That the Borderud house was put to such varied uses may have been due to several circumstances. It can be assumed that Peder Borderud held a special status, economic and social, in the pioneer community because he had been a farm owner in Norway. The social position of the family would certainly have contributed toward making the Borderud home a gathering place. Besides, Peder Borderud was one of the first settlers in Norman. But equally important, the house was one of the most spacious in the community.

When Torbjørn Borderud built a new house at the turn of the century, the old house was moved to the Perhus farm near Kindred. Here it also served as a dwelling house for many years. Later, the Sons of Norway lodge in Kindred assumed possession of the house, which was moved still another time and now served as their clubhouse and also as a small pioneer museum. It attracted many visitors until the lodge was dissolved and the museum objects were moved to a building in Kindred. The building stood abandoned when the Norsemen's Federation took the initiative in 1955 to move it to the Norwegian Folk Museum in Oslo, where it remained until 1973, when it was removed to Hamar.[12]

Besides its manifold functions, the house has thus experienced a vagrant existence. It was reconstructed twice in America and twice in Norway. These are facts which must be taken into consideration when studying the house, as the two dissimilar restorations are inadequately documented. A photograph from the 1880s purports to show the Borderud house with an addition and a veranda in front. But in order to make the window opening fit, the picture must be seen as a mirror image (Figure 6). Furthermore, it is unlikely that the addition would have been placed in front of one of the windows. The picture must therefore be of another house. A later picture shows the house the way it appeared while on the Perhus farm. At that time it had no addition (Figure 7). At the Emigrant Museum the house has been given the appearance it must have had at the very earliest period. And it is this period which is of interest here.

Fig. 6. The photograph supposedly shows the Borderud house in the 1880s. If this is the case, it must be a mirror image. Courtesy Hedmark Museum.

### THE COTTER'S BOY KNUT

Knut Gunderson, who built the second house, was born in Krødsherad, March 26, 1863. His parents were Gunder and Berit Torgerson, and the family was referred to in the community as *folket på bakken*, that is, the people on the hill. The whole family emigrated to America, though at different times. Knut left in 1882 on a prepaid ticket sent by a farmer in Beloit, Wisconsin, who was engaged in milk production. Knut had to work a year for the ticket, which is said to have cost $40.[13] The parents emigrated in 1885 and went directly to Folden township near Vining, where they settled on eighty acres of uncultivated ground.[14] Knut is not listed in the Folden township census of 1885, though in the census of 1895 he states that he has been in Minnesota for ten years and eight months. Seven of these years he had spent in Folden. This agrees with information in the family history, which states that he first stayed in Wisconsin for two years.[15] These facts are likely

Fig. 7. Borderud house on the Perhus farm, with Olaf Stengrim Perhus.
Courtesy Hedmark Museum.

based on information from Mason's history of Otter Tail
county.[16] The family further believes that Knut, after the stay
in Wisconsin, worked for his half-brother, whose family
name was Lillemoen, in Austin, Minnesota.[17]

According to this, Knut Gunderson should first have
come to Minnesota in 1884, after his two years in Wisconsin.
The following year his parents settled in Folden. But Knut did
not live there, as some people have maintained.[18] He did not
come to Folden until 1888 — the same year he married Maria
Rakstad. Maria was then sixteen years old and lived with her
parents in Folden. She was born in Filmore county, Minnesota, of Norwegian parents.[19] Considering these facts it
seems quite unlikely that the house was built in 1883. Rather
it must have been built in 1888 when Knut Gunderson married and settled on 160 acres of railroad land in Folden. Many
years passed, however, before he secured a deed to the land.
This did not happen until 1902.[20]

Knut and Maria had eleven children, of whom nine lived

to maturity.[21] Information about the construction of buildings on the farm comes mainly from personal reports. The family states that a new dwelling house was built in 1894. At first there was only a log cowbarn besides the house. A granary was built in 1909.[22] During the period prior to 1909 the old house — the Emigrant Museum house — was used as a granary. It was then moved to a new plot. After 1909 the house was again dismantled and moved — now to serve as a summer kitchen for Maria and Knut. It is said that they were very happy to use it in that way — reportedly, it was very comfortable there. The house served that function through the year 1937. Knut Gunderson died on April 2, 1938. In rough outline the chronology of the house thus becomes as follows:

1888, presumably built

1888–1894, dwelling place for Knut and Maria and their children, up to then four, the youngest born in 1894

1894–1909, used as granary

1909–1937, used as summer kitchen

1962, given to the museum by Wayne Gunderson

1975, rebuilt at Domkirkeodden, the location of the Hamar Museum.

The historical facts can only partially be confirmed through written sources such as real-estate tax lists. The tax for buildings on the farm increased from $12 in 1894 to $20 in 1896. This increase was probably due to the new dwelling house in 1894. In 1900 the tax dropped to $12, while by 1902 it had risen to $15. But between 1902 and 1906 it jumped to $120. It is clear from these figures that Knut Gunderson avoided major improvements until he received the deed in 1902.[23]

### THE AMERICAN LOG CABIN

When the Borderud family moved to Norman in the spring of 1871, they came to the frontier, the boundary line for permanent settlement, which was progressing steadily westward across the continent. But the family had earlier stayed almost a year in more established surroundings, in Iowa. Together with other Norwegians Peder Borderud had roamed widely in Iowa and neighboring states looking for land.[24] When the question is raised as to which building tradition the Borderud house is to be placed in, the question also arises which traditions Borderud was acquainted with. During the course of his first year in America he must have become acquainted with the various solutions found in this country, both during the pioneer stage and in later periods. He would therefore have been in a position to make an informed choice.

The Vining area was certainly somewhat more established when Knut Gunderson built his house there in 1888, even though he also had to start as a new settler. He had been in America longer than Peder Borderud. He must therefore have been well acquainted with the various methods of building a pioneer home. The area around Vining was well supplied with woods, so the material was easily available for the construction of log houses.

Where woods were found in the new settlements it was usual, during the pioneering period, to build a log house with one room, a so-called "log cabin." This is found in many variations, from the most primitive huts to more carefully constructed houses. For a long time Americans were of the opinion that these cabins originated with pioneer settlers in the forests along the East Coast. In 1931, however, Harold R. Shurtlieff disposed of this idea in his book, *The Log Cabin Myth*. But Shurtlieff replaced the earlier myth with a new one. He held that the log-house technique in America spread as a direct result of Swedish immigration to Delaware—Nya Sverige, "New Sweden"—in the seventeenth century. More recent research proves that this hypothesis as well must be modified considerably. It is, to be sure, correct that the Swedes, when they settled in Delaware after 1638, were the first to use the log-house technique in America. But, as Weslager points out, almost fifty percent of the "Swedes" in New Sweden were Finns, who also knew how to build log houses.[25] There were, furthermore, German population groups nearby, especially in Pennsylvania, who also had log-house traditions from their homeland, and they were far more numerous than the Swedes and the Finns. It is assumed today that it was mainly the Germans who further developed the log-house technique on the American continent. The status of research in this field is best summarized by Fred Kniffen and Henry Glassie, who draw the conclusion that the log-house technique, which came to characterize the American frontier, was not an American adaptation to the surroundings; neither was it introduced by Scandinavians, but by Germans in Pennsylvania. It was spread by them, and by a Scotch-Irish group, in all directions from southeastern Pennsylvania.[26] The Scotch-Irish had no log-house tradition from the homeland, but must have learned from the Germans. Kniffen and Glassie have identified a direct transfer of certain traits of Finno-Scandinavian origin to parts of the Midwest, but this took place during the nineteenth century and had no importance in the development and distribution of the American "log cabin" (Figure 8).

The fact that the log-house technique thus has a Central European origin explains some of the characteristics connected with the construction of the log cabin. A main line of separation in the European log-house technique is drawn between the Nordic and the east-central areas of Europe. In Nordic log houses the logs are fitted longitudinally by a so-called *meddrag*, a groove cut into the timbers to hold the logs tightly together. In the rest of the European log-house regions this *meddrag* is lacking and the spaces between the logs are caulked with various types of material. Warren Robert points out that practically all American log houses have a space between the logs, often several inches wide.[27] This characteristic element is construed by many as a proof of the Central European origin of the American log-house technique. But a few also argue that these spaces may have been simply an adaptation to the local situation in regions where there were no supplies of the straight-growing spruce and pine so common in the Scandinavian countries. Claire Selkurt, for example, accounts for the poor workmanship found in a certain Norwegian-American region, Luther Valley in Wisconsin, on this basis.[28] For Marion Nelson this is the main explanation of the absence of *meddrag* in Norwegian-American log houses.[29]

Fig. 8. Overview of the spread of various methods of log construction and their frequency in the United States. The Finno-Scandinavian eastern influence is found around Lake Superior. The overview is based on about 1,000 examples. Map from Kniffen and Glassie, "Building in Wood," 60.

Crooked timber made the use of *meddrag* difficult. When examples of this technique are found, they are an exception to the rule, even in areas where straight-growing timber was available.

Another characteristic element connected with the American log houses is noteworthy, namely the extensive use of different types of dovetailing. There has been some uncertainty among scholars concerning the age of this technique in Scandinavia, but it can be said with full assurance that dovetailing was not usually known or used there until long after the American log cabin was fully developed. Hence dovetailing is presumably also an element borrowed from the Central European log house.

When the Borderud house is considered in relation to these characteristic elements, it is clear, first of all, that the *meddrag* is missing. As already pointed out, this is no doubt due to the lack of suitable material. Peder Borderud's building material consisted of hard and somewhat crooked oak trees. But the logs are hewn flat inside the house and partly also outside. Borderud evidently chose the toilsome flat-hewing of the timber in preference to the traditional Nordic *meddrag*. The Borderud house has dovetailing of a type called "half dovetail." Borderud was a carpenter and it is reasonable to assume that he performed the work himself. He was undoubtedly acquainted with dovetailing from his carpentry work and this style of log construction was also known in Solør when he emigrated. The fact that he used it may therefore have its origin in Norway. But at the same time it falls within the framework of the general log-house tradition, where dovetailing had a higher status than joints with projecting ends (*laft med hoder*).

The materials in the Gunderson house are also oak logs, though smaller and straighter; but there are no traces of *meddrag* here either. The Gunderson house is built with extended log-ends. This is a feature which can be conceived as a traditional Norwegian element. This way of building had a high status in Norway and was not unusual in dwelling houses even as late as the 1880s. But the log-ends in the Gunderson

Fig. 9. Projecting log-ends at the Gunderson house. The tear-shaped
ends are an American element. Courtesy Hedmark Museum.

house are of a shape rarely found in Norway. They have clear
traces of a special type of V–notch which is tear-shaped. Here
the American influence is clear (Figure 9).

The same is true of the windows. Both houses have
double-hung sash windows of American type, with small
panes in the Gunderson house and large panes in the Borderud
house. But both windows and doors were bought ready-
made and hinged windows were not often available. The same
goes for the use of American shingles. Other roofing methods
were certainly tried by Norwegian pioneers, but they worked
poorly (Figure 10). Cedar shingles were practical and easily

Fig. 10. Parsonage in the Red River Valley. The climate was not suitable for a sod roof. Here it is gradually being replaced by boards. Courtesy Vesterheim.

obtainable. That the houses are whitewashed both inside and out is in accordance with American tradition, while this method is unknown in Scandinavia on unplastered timber walls.

In summary it can be said that both houses fit into a general American log-house tradition. The question then arises: how do the houses stand in relationship to a Norwegian-American tradition?

NORWEGIAN–AMERICAN LOG HOUSES

Thus far very little research has been done on the distinctiveness of Norwegian-American houses. Norwegian-American houses with *meddrag* are found only rarely. Whitewashing was general. These are both breaks with Norwegian tradition. What other elements characterize the early Norwegian-American houses?

Curator Darrell D. Henning at Vesterheim has identified two main types of log houses on the basis of studies in northeastern Iowa, a region which was settled by various ethnic groups during the 1840–1860 period.[28] The most common type of log house there was one room with a loft above. On the basis of this type he set up the following survey of features with varying degrees of standardization.

Very standardized:
— one-room ground plan
— facade — entry door slightly off center on the long wall, with a window beside the door
— the stovepipe placed indoors on a shelf, at or near the center of the gable wall
— a finished ceiling and a combined attic and second story

Less standardized:
— placing of the other windows
— placing of the stairs

Little standardized:
— method of joining logs
— other construction details

The survey builds on the degree of variation in the different elements mentioned; a great variation in a certain element shows a small degree of standardization. Henning's other type of Norwegian-American house has a two-room ground plan, and consequently is not relevant here.

How the logs are put together and other construction details are, according to Henning, little standardized. Hence there are grounds for saying that in this field there are no firm Norwegian-American traditions. Most common in Henning's findings is "full dovetail," but no statistical information is presented on which to build. This type and "half dovetail" are also common among other ethnic groups. Dovetailing on the Borderud house may just as well be an American as a Norwegian-American element. But it may also, as already mentioned, be of Norwegian origin. The saddle-notching on Gunderson's house may be both Norwegian and American, but the shape of the ends of the logs has, undoubtedly, an American source.

Nor can the less standardized features give any certain basis for placing the houses in a particular building tradition. But
here the possible variations are more limited. Even though the
placing of the windows varies, it is normal to have two windows in addition to the window by the door. One window is
then frequently placed directly across from the door, on the
opposite wall, and another on the gable wall. In the Borderud
house, the first of these extra windows is not found, but there
is a window on the gable wall. Hence the house is atypical as
regards the placing of windows. The Gunderson house has the
window directly across from the door, but lacks a window on
the gable wall. Thus this house is also atypical. The stairs can
be placed in the corner, either to the right or the left of the entry door — most often to the left. The Borderud house has the
stairs in the right corner on the inner wall, and thus deviates
also in this respect from the customary. The Gunderson
house, however, follows the norm here. The stairway — or the
ladder in this case — is placed to the left of the door.

It is, nevertheless, by considering the most strongly standardized elements that one can best decide whether a house
falls within one definite tradition. These elements grant the
least leeway for variation. As regards the Norwegian-
American one-room house, the facade, the placing of the
chimney, and the utilization of the loft are very standardized.
The fact that the loft is utilized gives this type of house its
characteristic proportions, with great height in relation to the
width. The loft is used in the Borderud house, and the house
is so large that the second story has been divided into two
rooms. The roofs are steep on both of the houses; in the little
Gunderson house there is only room to sit in the upper story,
but even so it was used as sleeping space.

The chimney is usually placed in or near the apex of the
roof on the gable wall, in compliance with Norwegian-
American custom. This is true in the Borderud house, but
there are traces in the ceiling that suggest the chimney has
been moved several times. In the Gunderson house the chimney was placed in the apex of the roof, in accord with the
Norwegian-American standard. The facade would normally

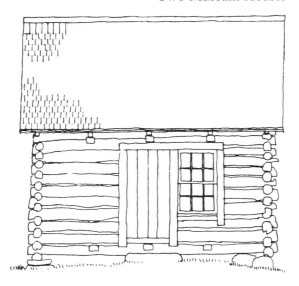

Fig. 11. The Gunderson house at the Norwegian Emigrant
Museum. Scale drawing by Are Vesterlid.

have the entry door a little off-center of the longitudinal wall
with a window near the center of the wall beside the door. The
facade was thus given an asymmetrical shape. The Gunderson
house has this characteristic facade arrangement (Figure 11),
like the earlier-mentioned Egge house in Decorah (Figure 5).
The Borderud house, however, has a symmetrical facade with
one window on each side of the door. This arrangement is said
to have been more commonly used among the German
Americans.[29]

After this what can be said about the relationship of the
two houses to the Norwegian-American tradition? One can,
in the first place, disregard the elements which are very little
standardized and affirm that the placing of the windows,
which was a firmer tradition, deviates in both houses. The
stairs are placed "wrong" in the Borderud house, but are found
in the most common location in the Gunderson house. Most
decisive are deviations in details of the facade, which are most
strongly standardized. The symmetrical facade makes the
Borderud house atypical among Norwegian-American pi-

oneer houses. The moving of the chimney in this house also deviates from the norm. The facade of the Gunderson house, however, is entirely in accord with custom.

The question then arises: where did Borderud find his model when he built his house in Kindred? It appears quite unlikely that it was among the Norwegian Americans. Hence one must look back to Grue in Solør.

### AN ELEMENT FROM SOLØR

The Borderud house in Grue was likely built in the last part of the 1700s. It is a comparatively large two-story log building (Figure 2). Externally the house is still as it was when the family emigrated in 1870, but internally some alterations have been made. The dissimilarities between it and the American house are so obvious that a comparison here would serve little or no purpose.

As Marion Nelson points out, it is in houses from other social groups that parallels with the Norwegian-American houses may eventually be found. They might be sought in a certain type of cotters' house in the home district of the Borderud family. The reason for looking in this direction is the size and also certain similarities in design between this type and the Borderud house. In these houses the logs are joined only at the four corners, but the placing of the chimney reveals an interior division into two-room or three-room floor plans. In Grue today at least three or four such houses can still be found. Several others have been torn down in recent years. In the archives of the Gruetunet Museum are still more of the same type. The log construction of these houses varies. Some have dovetailing — others have extended log-ends. As a rule the gable is sided and the houses have raftered ceilings. Both these features are found in the Borderud house. Some houses are fitted with an entryway in front of the door, while others have a small Swiss-style veranda. In many cases the entryway leads directly into the main room (Figure 12).

One single element, the arrangement of the facade, is the essential feature which sets the Borderud house apart from the usual Norwegian-American houses. Peder Borderud may

Fig. 12. House at Grinder in Solør. Photograph by Birger Nesholen.

have gathered impulses from German–American houses, which are said to have had similar facades. But the facades of the small cotter houses in Solør have the same symmetrical or- ganization as the Borderud house. Hence it is possible that this one element from the old country is present in the Borderud house. It is, however, not derived from traditions of his own class, but from a certain type of cotters' house.

A TYPICAL HOUSE

Knut Gunderson, however, belonged to the social stratum from which Peder Borderud possibly gathered impulses for his pioneer house. He should, therefore, still be close to the originals. But his house is not like the one he left behind. The cotter's house on Andresonbakken in Krødsherad has three rooms, with a somewhat old-fashioned floor-plan (Figure 13), a type of house which has been in use ever since the Mid- dle Ages. The dissimilarities are obvious in a number of respects, including size, ground plan, *meddrag*, fireplace, and roof construction. It is clear that Knut Gunderson did not try to recreate this house in Minnesota. But when it is seen how closely his pioneer house resembles the usual Norwegian-

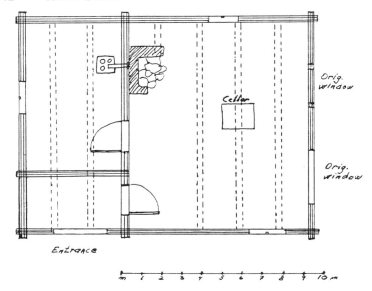

Fig. 13. Floor plan of house on Andresonbakken in
    Krødsherad. Scale drawing by Reidar Bakken.

American immigrant's house in the upper Midwest, especially
with respect to the standardized elements, it is reasonable to
regard this house as a typical first house for Norwegian immigrants in this region.

Knut Gunderson not only came from a different social
group than Peder Borderud, he was also considerably
younger and hence took a longer time to establish himself in
America. For six years he roamed about through Norwegian
settlements before he built a house for himself and Maria. His
relationship with Norwegian America must therefore have
been closer than Peder Borderud's when the latter — after only
a year in America — built his house. Furthermore, it is quite
unlikely that a cotter's son had any strong desire to transfer his
home surroundings to America. He had become Norwegian
American, just as his house was to be.

It is a paradox that the Borderud parents, who were relatively well-off when they came to America, occupied their log
cabin as long as they lived. They had built a roomy house and

Fig. 14. The new house built in 1894 at the Gunderson farm near Vining, Minnesota.

found it quite adequate. Knut Gunderson and his wife Maria, on the other hand, built a large new log house after living only six years in their first little house (Figure 14). Thus the cotter's son had a much better house to live in than the oldest generation of the landowning Borderud family.

ADAPTATION TO THE ENVIRONMENT

To return to the two theories, the tradition theory and the Americanization theory, support can be found for both. There are parallels to the Borderud house in the general American log-house tradition; it can be seen as an American cultural product, as the Americanization theory supposes. But the Borderud house diverges in essential points from the Norwegian-American tradition. Of special importance is the divergence in a strongly standardized area, namely the facade. For the facade, parallels can be found in a group of cotters' houses in the home community of the Borderud family. The model is thus found in Norway, as the tradition theory states, though not where it might be expected. The divergences from Norwegian building styles are, nevertheless, so great that in summary it seems most reasonable to talk about a break with the traditions of the homeland. The question will then again arise how this fact can be explained: how could it develop that Peder Borderud built such an un-Norwegian house after having been in America only a year?

When, in this case, support is present for both the main theories about the origin of the Norwegian-American log house, indications are that neither theory, standing independently, is adequate. Consequently, new factors must be considered. It will thus seem reasonable to look more closely at conditions in the new physical and cultural environment in which the Borderud family found themselves.

The region where the house was built was a typical prairie landscape—flat and treeless as far as the eye could reach. Only along the nearby Sheyenne River were there any woods. But these were woods of a different type than the Norwegian spruce and pine forests. As building material Borderud used hard and rather crooked oak trees. There were no sawmills. The logs had to be hewn into proper shape as well as possible with an axe. Here Nelson's and Selkurt's explanation of the absence of the *meddrag* can be understood. It was impractical to notch such hard and crooked pieces of timber. A break with tradition thus resulted from adaptation to the local supply of timber. The crooked timber, furthermore, made it simpler to utilize the height of a house than to build it out in the longitudinal direction. A one-room house thus got a second story and its unusual proportions by Norwegian standards.

In a pioneer culture such houses were one of the methods of solving the housing problem. Hence the formal elements of the house were also an adaptation to a new culture. Peder Borderud did not build simply in accordance with his own ideas or the traditions of his homeland. He adapted himself to a new environment. The lack of buildings for public functions was a characteristic feature of these new settlements. People had to make use of the possibilities which presented themselves. The spacious Borderud house consequently became church, schoolhouse, and public meeting place.

Most of the one-room houses were considered as temporary dwellings until a larger house could be built. Some American scholars speak of a division between what they call a "pioneer form" and a "folk form."[30] The distinguishing feature of the first category is that the houses are primitive in construction and merely intended to satisfy the basic demands for living space. When conditions in time permitted, houses were built which also satisfied other cultural demands. These became houses of "folk form" — in general, second houses for the pioneers. It is here that one can best detect cultural impulses and choices because they did not come into being as a result of an immediate need.

The Borderud house has several characteristics of houses of the "folk form," even though it was the first house Peder Borderud built. It is relatively large. The carpentry work, the hewing of the logs, and the joining show good workmanship and there are no indications that the men were in a hurry. The long time during which the house was in use also proves that there can be no talk here about makeshift architecture or "pioneer form." In this sense also the house is somewhat atypical, which can be explained by the fact that Borderud was himself a skilled craftsman. He could also afford to hire help.

The Americanization which marks the Borderud house does not necessarily say anything about the assimilation of the family itself. It does tell about the new situation of a farm-owning family in a strange world. This becomes especially clear when the Borderud building in Grue is compared with the Borderud house at the Emigrant Museum.

The Gunderson house also supports both the Americanization and the tradition theories. The extended log-ends are an example of possible transfer of tradition from Norway, while the absence of *meddrag* is an example of Americanization. But in this house the oak logs were straighter and therefore better suited for *meddrag* than in the Borderud house. Hence the adaptation must be due more to the cultural than to the physical milieu. The tear-drop-shaped log-ends are also American in form. But the Gunderson house also has prominent Norwegian-American features. The strongly standardized element, the facade, is an important example of this.

It may be possible to explain this phenomenon through the time factor. It took time to enter fully into the Norwegian-American world. Knut Gunderson had likely stayed here long enough to achieve this identification. The typical Norwegian-American one-room house would then be a natural first home for this newly-married couple.

In regarding the house as a temporary dwelling place he also followed the practice of many other Norwegian Americans. Thus, the house has features which can be characterized as "pioneer form." For instance, the logs are not flat-hewn but used in their round shape. And the many and varied uses to which the house was put can also be regarded as an element in a flexible and adaptable Norwegian-American folk culture.

Thus, for the Gunderson house, neither the tradition theory nor the Americanization theory can offer an adequate explanation. Considering the few studies which have been made of Norwegian-American houses, it is important not to cling to definite, inflexible theories which aim at explaining every phenomenon. Research is still in its preliminary phase and the limited material available is characterized by many subtle variations. In the meantime it is important that items of cultural value be well cared for on both sides of the Atlantic. This will preserve material for the study and dissemination of the exciting cultural development which Norwegian emigrants went through in a new land.

## Notes

[1]*Pioneer Norwegian Log Cabin located on the Farm of Wayne Gunderson near Vining, Minnesota, U.S.A.*, illustrated brochure in the archives of the Norwegian Emigrant Museum.

[2]See, for example, Anne-Lise Svendsen, "Utvandrermuseet," in *Museumsnytt*, 3 (Oslo, 1977).

[3]C. A. Weslager, *The Log Cabin in America* (New Brunswick, New Jersey, 1969), 238–239.

[4]Weslager, *The Log Cabin in America*, 84.

[5]Unpublished manuscript by Darrell D. Henning, curator, Vesterheim, the Norwegian-American Museum, Decorah, Iowa, 1973.

[6]Marion Nelson, "The Material Culture and Folk Arts of the Nor-

wegians in America," in Ian M. G. Quimby and Scott T. Swank, eds., *Perspectives on American Folk Art* (New York, 1980), 82–85.

[7]Per Hvamstad, "Pionéren Peder Borderud og hans 'log cabin'," in *Årbok for Glamdalen*, 11 (Solør, 1967).

[8]Insurance assessment for Bårderud, in the archives of the Gruetunet Museum, Kirkenær.

[9]Hvamstad, "Pionéren Peder Borderud," 13.

[10]Hvamstad, "Pionéren Peder Borderud," 21.

[11]Hvamstad, "Pionéren Peder Borderud," 15–16.

[12]Hvamstad, "Pionéren Peder Borderud," 15.

[13]Interview with Orvie Gunderson (born 1905) in Vining, Minnesota, September 23, 1982.

[14]John W. Mason, ed., *History of Otter Tail County* (Indianapolis, 1916), 791.

[15]*Familiehistorie i bilder*, in the archives of the Norwegian Emigrant Museum.

[16]Mason, *History of Otter Tail County*, 791.

[17]Interview with Orvie Gunderson.

[18]Mason, *History of Otter Tail County*, 791.

[19]Mason, *History of Otter Tail County*, 792.

[20]"Knut Gunderson gets a warranty deed from Northern Pacific May 21, 1893." Register of deeds, county court house, Fergus Falls, Minnesota. The deed was actually recorded in Norwegian.

[21]*Familiehistorie i bilder*.

[22]*Familiehistorie i bilder* and interview with Orvie Gunderson.

[23]Real-estate tax records in County Auditor's office, Fergus Falls, Minnesota.

[24]Hvamstad, "Pionéren Peder Borderud," 12.

[25]Weslager, *The Log Cabin in America*, 150.

[26]Fred Kniffen and Henry Glassie, "Building in Wood in the Eastern United States. A Time-Place Perspective," in *Geographical Review*, 56 (January, 1966), 65.

[27]Warren Roberts, "Folk Architecture," in Richard M. Dorson, ed., *Folklore and Folklife* (Chicago, 1972), 290.

[28]Claire Selkurt, "The Domestic Architecture and Cabinetry of Luther Valley," in *Norwegian-American Studies*, 30 (Northfield, Minnesota, 1983), 247–272.

[29]Nelson, "Material Culture and Folk Arts," 83.

[30]Henning, "Log building study," undated paper. Vesterheim.

[31]Henning, interview, October, 1982.

[32]Mark H. Knipping and Richard J. Fapso, "The Anders Ellingsen Kvaale Farm. Early Norwegian Commercial Agriculture ca. 1865," unpublished manuscript, 1978, in Old World Wisconsin, Eagle, Wisconsin, 28–29.

# 7

# A Letter of 1852 from Eldorado

*translated and edited by J. R. Christianson*

Two Norwegians traveling on skis arrived at Fort Atkinson, Winnebago territory, in the dead of winter in 1843. They had come skiing from the Rock Prairie settlement in Wisconsin, had crossed the Mississippi near the old fur-trading center of Prairie du Chien, and had skied along the military road through the wooded hills and across the natural prairies of the Winnebago lands for sixty miles until they came to the fort, a few miles from the Winnebago agency. Northeastern Iowa was still Indian territory, occupied by the Winnebagos; hostile Sac and Fox roamed to the south, and the warlike Dakotas to the north. The area was not officially open to white settlement and would not be until the year 1848, so these first two Norwegians in northeastern Iowa found employment by teaching agriculture to the Winnebagos who farmed near the fort.

Two years later, however, in 1845, one of these two Norwegians claimed land along the military road south of the Indian reservation, in Clayton county, Iowa. The other man went back to the Rock Prairie settlement, west of Beloit, where he told still others about the varied lands in the hills to the west of the Mississippi. In 1848, he returned to settle near his companion.

By that time, Norwegian settlers had begun to trickle into the area formerly reserved for the Winnebagos, which was now officially open to settlement. In 1849, several Norwegian families from Rock Prairie arrived and settled in the Clayton county area, along the military road which ran to the north of the Turkey River. Others settled at Glenwood and Washington Prairie in Winneshiek county, and along Paint Creek in Allamakee county. This was the beginning of the first Norwegian settlements in Iowa.[1]

A Norwegian named Bertel Osuldsen (or Bartel Ossuldson), author of the letter that follows, was among these arrivals of the year 1849. Like many of the Norwegian pioneers of northeastern Iowa, he came from the Rock Prairie settlement. Holand said that he was originally from Åmli, north of Arendal.[2] He may have had ties to a group of emigrants who left that part of Norway in 1846 and settled in widely scattered areas including Texas and Missouri.[3] When Osuldsen wrote to his relatives in Norway in 1852, he addressed the letter to his brother Jacob who lived at Søvik, near Grimstad, not far from Arendal.[4]

Religion was a matter of primary importance to this God-fearing emigrant from the southern coast of Norway, as it was to many of the Norwegian pioneers in Iowa. Establishment of regular patterns of worship was one of their first concerns, and the primary permanent structure of community in their settlements became the Lutheran congregation. In northeastern Iowa, religious life among the Norwegian settlers took shape through a three-stage process. Lay preachers were active from the very beginning: this was the first stage. The second stage came with the visits of itinerant Lutheran clergymen from Wisconsin, who preached, baptized, and helped to organize formal congregations. The third stage was when these newly organized congregations were able to call a resident pastor. Bertel Osuldsen, an active Christian layman, wrote his letter at a time that allowed him to offer a glimpse into all three of these stages.

Pastor C. L. Clausen of Rock Prairie had been the first itinerant Lutheran minister to visit the Iowa settlements. During the summer of 1851, he had ministered at the Paint Creek settlement and at two places along the Turkey River.[5] Bertel

Osuldsen was almost certainly one of his former parishioners from Rock Prairie whom Clausen saw in Iowa.

In that same summer of 1851, Pastor Nils Brandt emigrated to Wisconsin from Norway. One of his sisters had emigrated earlier with her husband and family. By 1851, they had settled near the upper reaches of the Turkey River, northeast of Fort Atkinson, in what became Winneshiek county. Brandt wanted to visit these relatives, and at the same time he planned to minister to the scattered Norwegian settlers in Iowa. He went first to Rock Prairie, in order to visit Pastor Clausen and get the names of some of these people. One of the names was very likely that of Bertel Osuldsen, who would have been an excellent contact for Brandt. Armed with this list of names, Brandt crossed the Mississippi in the autumn of 1851 and visited the chain of new Norwegian settlements. Upon his return to Wisconsin, he received his first regular call in America, to the Rock River pastorate, not far from Beloit.

Brandt made a second mission journey into northeastern Iowa in the summer of 1852. He organized three congregations—Turkey River, Little Iowa, and Paint Creek—and he helped these congregations to draft a joint letter of call for a resident minister from Norway.[6] Family tradition has it that Bertel Osuldsen was the one who wrote that letter of call.

It was about this time that Bertel Osuldsen sat down to write a letter to his brother Jacob and other relatives in Norway. He had come to Iowa three years earlier from Wisconsin. Since then, he had claimed and cleared a piece of land near Gunder in Clayton county, then sold it and moved farther west along the Turkey River. He was now living near Eldorado, some six or eight miles southeast of Fort Atkinson, in a valley as picturesque as its name. The Winnebagos were gone now, and the area was acquiring a scattering of ethnic settlements, including a fair number of Norwegian ones.

Bertel Osuldsen wrote in a regular hand and a polished, precisely grammatical Norwegian which reveal him as a man of good education. Perhaps he had attended school in Grimstad or served an apprenticeship as clerk to a merchant in that little coastal town. In any case, he did later serve as a pastor's assistant and teacher among his countrymen in America. His letter also reveals that he was a man of sincere piety.

The purpose of his letter was to inform the family at home concerning conditions in. America, and to induce some of them to emigrate. It was not really written from one individual to another, as a modern letter would be, but from one community to another: from an immigrant settlement on the frontier of the New World to the home community in Norway. In the Eldorado settlement there were several families who had come from the same part of Norway and were known to the people back home. The letter contains greetings to a number of specific individuals, special greetings from Marte to Aunt Helga, and even a paragraph dictated by one Ole Torjusen, who seems to have been a neighbor in the Old World as in the New.

This letter gives a factual account of pioneer life, with details concerning dwellings, livestock, crop yields, prices, and land values, as well as religious conditions. It tells a good deal about pioneer days in northeastern Iowa, and it must have been well received by its original audience. The recipient, Jacob Osuldsen, later emigrated to America and brought the letter with him. He gave it to his niece, Berthe Ossuldson. Her heirs have owned it until the present, displaying it in a frame with double glass so both sides could be seen.[7]

Eldorado Settlement in Iowa
the 8th August 1852

Dear Relatives and Friends,

Our correspondence goes very slowly and, I fear, also uncertainly. I have sent three letters to you but have received only one reply. This is a bit sad—that we cannot be informed more frequently about each other. I answered the letter of April 14, 1851, which I received from you, father-in-law. I replied some eight weeks after that date, and I asked you to reply but have received no answer. I now intend to tell all of you something about our situation here, and I hope that you will send us a letter as quickly as possible, so that we can hear about you.

Last autumn, I sold my *klem* [claim] or land to an Irishman, and this past spring I claimed land again, ten English miles west of where I lived before. On this land I have now cleared ten acres, six of which are fenced and sown with maize and potatoes, together with some vegetables. About twenty Norwegian families have settled here where I live, and I believe that more will come here in time. Some have come here directly from Norway this summer, and they say that grain prices are high and day wages low in Norway. It is a pity that more of you cannot come over here, where day wages are at least half a dollar and up to $1.25 for common laborers, and the highest price of wheat is fifty cents a bushel.

We live two English miles from the town of Eldorado, where there is a sawmill and a grain mill. The house we now live in was built by me this past spring of basswood, and I bought boards in town for the floor and the roof. I have now hewn new house timbers, mostly of oak, and intend to erect a new dwelling in the autumn and use the old one for a cow stall. It is true that the newcomers, here in America, live in utterly simple dwellings, but when they are finished and well covered with whitewash they are quite warm and could compare favorably with ordinary farmhouses in Norway, at least internally if not externally. As a whole, however, our good Norwegian people cannot compare to Americans with respect to cleanliness.

I do not have any other news to tell you except that we now have our third child, a girl named Berthe. She was born on the 12th of July last, and we are all healthy and living well. We can satisfy our material needs in abundant measure here, and I believe that the religious life is more active than in Norway. We gather regularly each Sunday for meetings in homes, taking turns around the settlement or parish. There are some pious Haugeans, in particular, who preside at these meetings, speak, and recite prayers.

Nor do we lack clergymen, but they are somewhat at variance with our ancient Lutheran teachings, and consequently, we have cooperated with several nearby settlements this summer in seeking a pastor from Norway. Our temporary Lutheran pastor is a Pastor Brandt from Wisconsin, who came over here last summer, a young man, but to the best of my knowledge pious, capable, and good.

The harmful potato rot is found here as in Norway, and I believe I lost 200 bushels last harvest. This spring I bought two bushels for seed for two dollars, and they are still good. We have eleven cattle (six steers and five cows), fifteen pigs, some chickens, and all the necessary equipment. The land I now have is especially suitable, with woods, arable land, pasture, and good spring water right by the house. I have claimed 160 acres but have not paid for it yet. Most of the settlers usually occupy the land for two or three years or more without purchasing it. The American government is presently working on a law which would allow anybody to acquire title to 160 acres of land for nothing — without paying.

Marte sends greetings to her Aunt Helga and would like her to come over here and bring one or two of the Homstøl children if they can get permission to do so.

I, Ole, send greetings to your father and mother, as well as your brothers and sisters. Do what you can in order to get help to come here, and I promise to pay your transportation when you arrive. If you come next summer, you can let me know and I will meet you in Milwaukee in Wisconsin and help you get here. I am now working at a sawmill and have been getting $16 per month, but I think that I shall soon get more. I have now begun to cut with the aforenamed saw. Since last we corresponded, I have been quite well and comfortable.

Live well, all of you,
Ole Torjusen

In conclusion, we send most hearty greetings to all relatives and friends. May the Lord's blessing be upon you in bodily and especially in spiritual matters.

Jacob my brother! I cannot imagine that you will decide not to come over here when you learn that the difference between Norway and America is so great. Come, all who can pay the transportation, and you will not find such distinction between persons as in Norway. I do not want to expand on this matter, but everyone who comes here will discover the difference for himself, although there are without doubt . . . [The script is illegible here where the paper is torn on a fold.] the world over.

Father! I have frequently wished that you were with us, but above all else, I should wish that you were with our common Father, or that you were prepared for Him by faith in the Savior.

Let sinners confess to one another and pray for one another. Pray without ceasing. Yes! Let us all pray! Live well. My address is Mr. B. Osuldsen, Eldorado P.O., Iowa, North America.

Please be satisfied with our incomplete correspondence and greetings, with the most hearty regards from all of us,
   B. Osuldsen.

At Christmas time in the year 1853, the first resident pastor to the Norwegian Lutheran congregations of northeastern Iowa finally arrived from Norway. This was U. V. Koren, and the arrival was well documented in the diary of his wife Elisabeth.[8] Bertel Osuldsen was mentioned on January 12, 1854, in the minutes of the first congregational meeting held after the arrival of Pastor Koren.[9] A committee met on February 22, 1854, to divide the pastorate into districts, and six districts were established. At the second congregational meeting on March 10, 1854, pastors' assistants were elected in each of the six districts. Bertel Osuldsen was chosen in the Sixth District, which lay farthest south, in the area that later became Stavanger congregation. This meant, among other things, that on Sundays when Pastor Koren was not able to hold divine services in that district, Bertel Osuldsen was responsible for holding a devotional meeting with prayer, singing of hymns, and reading of the text for the day and of a sermon from a good Lutheran book of homilies.[10] Presumably he continued to get on well with the "pious Haugeans" who had formerly assumed similar duties. He also served as the congregational schoolmaster for the district, and as host to Pastor Koren when he came there on his pastoral circuit. The letter of 1852 indicates that Bertel Osuldsen was an excellent choice for these responsibilities.

## Notes

[1]Carlton C. Qualey, *Norwegian Settlement in the United States* (Northfield, Minnesota, 1938), 83–86. George T. Flom, *Chapters on Scandinavian Immigration to Iowa* (Iowa City, Iowa, 1906), 65. Robert C. Wideraenders, "Lutheranism in Iowa," in Michael Sherer, ed., *Iowa District ALC 1976 Congregations Directory* (n.p., 1976), 11.

[2]Hjalmar Rued Holand, *De norske settlementers historie* (4th ed., Chicago, 1912), 332.

[3]Frank G. Nelson, trans. and ed., *Pathfinder for Norwegian Emigrants by Johan Reinert Reiersen* (Northfield, Minnesota, 1981). In a private letter of April 23, 1981, Frank G. Nelson informed me that he knew of no connection between Bertel Osuldsen and Osuld Nielsen Enge, a leader of the 1846 emigrants, though the documentation is somewhat incomplete.

[4]O. Rygh, *Nedenes amt*, vol. 8 of *Norske gaardnavne* (Kristiania, 1905), lists no place named Søvigen or Søvik. *Fortegnelse over matrikulerede eiendomme og deres skyld i Nedenes amt, affattet i henhold til kgl. Resolution af 29de mai og 6te december 1886* (n.p., n.d.), lists a place named Søvig, apparently a cottage belonging to the farm of Vestre Augland in Fjære parish, Nedenes *amt*.

[5]Qualey, trans. and ed., "Claus L. Clausen, Pioneer Pastor and Settlement Promoter: Illustrative Documents," in *Norwegian-American Studies and Records*, 6 (Northfield, Minnesota, 1931), 12–29.

[6]Wiederaenders, "Lutheranism in Iowa," 12. Adolf Bredesen, ed., "Pastor Nils Brandts erindringer fra aarene 1851 og 1855," in *Symra* (Decorah, Iowa, 1907), 97–122. Erling Ylvisaker, *Eminent Pioneers* (Minneapolis, 1934), 56–62.

[7]Information kindly supplied in 1975 by his descendant, Mrs. Elton Bradley of Decorah, Iowa. The letter has been donated to Vesterheim, the Norwegian-American Museum.

[8]David T. Nelson, trans. and ed., *The Diary of Elisabeth Koren 1853–1855* (Northfield, Minnesota, 1955; reprinted Decorah, Iowa, 1978). See also U. V. Koren, "Nogle erindringer fra min ungdom og fra min første tid i Amerika," in *Symra*, 1905, 11–37.

[9]Charlotte Jacobson, trans., "Minutes of the Congregational Proceedings in Little Iowa Norwegian-Evangelical Lutheran Congregation Begun January 12, 1854." Typescript in photocopy (Decorah, Iowa, 1981), 1.

[10]Jacobson, "Minutes of the Congregational Proceedings," 5, 10, also 11–12 and 14–15.

# 8

# Letters to Immigrants in the Midwest from the Telemark Region of Norway*

*by Øyvind T. Gulliksen*

Scholars who have studied Scandinavian immigrant letters have focused almost entirely on letters sent by immigrants in the United States back to family and friends in Scandinavia. For historians of Scandinavian immigration to the United States, these letters provide valuable source material. They contain firsthand observations and comments about American life, written by newcomers to inform readers back home about life in the New World. People in Scandinavia then often decided whether or not to emigrate on the basis of these letters.

The label "immigrant letters" could possibly be extended to include that part of the correspondence which went the other way. The study of "Amerika-brev" (letters from America) has not given enough attention to the fact that letters back to Scandinavia were part of a two-way process of communication. Reading Theodore Blegen's extensive collection

*Earlier versions of this essay have been presented as the annual Knut Gjerset Lecture at Luther College, Decorah, Iowa, in 1984 and at the conference of the Society for the Advancement of Scandinavian Study at the University of Illinois, Urbana-Champaign campus, in 1985. The Council for Cultural Affairs, Telemark county, and The Norwegian Research Council supported the research by travel grants.

of America letters published in the volume *Land of Their Choice* (1955) one wonders what happened to the letters from Norway which at least some of these letters writers must have received.

What do letters sent to immigrants in the United States from various parts of Norway during the period of mass immigration tell us? Obviously these letters do not reveal much about immigrant experience, but they may tell us something about the effects of emigration on those who stayed at home. Letters sent from the Old World did not contribute to such important changes as did the letters from America, although they may perhaps have convinced some immigrants to stay in America and others to return home. But on the whole such letters had another function. If letters from immigrants in America informed Norwegian readers of a world they did not know, the purpose of letters from home was primarily to help the immigrants stay in touch with a known world, a familiar world they did not want to forget and could not completely let go. Of course many recipients of these letters, at least before the turn of the century, realized that they would not see their mother country again. Letters from home helped to keep alive that private world which had shaped the immigrants before they decided to leave. The letters, for as long as they kept coming, were reminders of a past which the process of assimilation could not eradicate.

The most serious problem for the scholar who wants to study letters which immigrants received from home is the lack of available source material. Surprisingly little has been done to study or even to collect letters in this category, despite the fact that such letters to Norwegian settlers in the Midwest must have been almost as numerous as letters going from Norwegian-American communities back to Norway. It may already be too late to acquire a significant number of these letters from the time of mass emigration, 1837 to the early 1920s. Most such letters are irretrievably lost. Since they were the only written records left behind by a good many people, the loss is a tragedy. Such letters could have contributed to our understanding of regional history in Norway, particularly of life in rural communities in times of great change.

Because of the scarcity of collected material in public archives, a scholar interested in this particular kind of research must undoubtedly devote much time and effort to hunting for sources himself. Easiest to find are letters from home printed in the Norwegian-American press. Sometimes private letters of more general interest were sent to such newspapers; some letters were even written for newspaper publication, just as were some letters sent the other way. Letters seem to have been a popular genre in newspaper publishing on both sides of the ocean. In *Decorah-Posten*, for instance, letters from various regions of Norway were offered to the readers all over the Midwest. One particularly interesting example in this context is the letters written by Torbjørg Lie. For close to thirty years, from the 1890s to the early 1920s, Torbjørg sent about 145 letters from Upper Telemark to be published in *Decorah-Posten*. The wife of John Lie, a regional writer much read among Norwegian settlers in America, she recorded in her letters what she experienced as a woman on a small farm in Telemark in those days. She wrote about visits to neighbors, and about going with her children to the nearest large town. She told about her own household and those of others, about livestock, weather conditions, food prices, sickness, and people who have died in her community. She used local gossip and humor. Her letters often have a touch of poetry. In 1894 she submitted a series of letters titled "bregneblad" (fern leaves). She was no doubt conscious of her readers' interests. Sometimes she would include her own childhood memories specially for the readers of *Decorah-Posten* who came from her own area of Telemark, sometimes also a poem of hers, intended, she said in a letter of 1891, "to lull the immigrant reader into pleasant dreams about bygone days in the old country." The editors of *Decorah-Posten*, well aware that letters from home would be popular among readers in the United States, also encouraged subscribers to submit letters they received. During World War II, when firsthand information from Norway was sometimes hard to come by, the newspaper ran a special column called "Breve fra Norge" (Letters from Norway).

In all likelihood, however, the most interesting letters written to immigrants never saw the printed page, largely because they were considered to be too private, or of little interest outside the family circle. In cases where letters were kept, they often disappeared when the person who received them died. Letters from home may be difficult to trace today simply because they were sent to people who lived in a much less stable society than those who stayed in the old country. Letters from immigrants to friends and relatives in rural communities in Norway and the other Scandinavian countries have been collected in public archives in fairly large numbers. Letters·from America were kept by those who received them and handed down to the next generation as part of the family treasure. In a society where farms tended to be kept within the same family, such letters were not easily discarded. In the Midwest, however, where farms changed hands more rapidly, letters from home often disappeared in the process. In addition letters written to the first immigrants did not have the same meaning for the next generation of Norwegian Americans, who did not share the memories or interests of their parents, and who in some cases did not even share their language. Much too often one hears the sad story of how letters from home were dumped when "the old folks" retired from farming and went to live in a house in town.

The present study is limited to letters sent from just one region of Norway, Telemark *fylke* (county). Telemark was an area with an exceptionally large number of immigrants. It has been estimated that between 1837, when the first group of families left Telemark for the Midwest, and World War I, approximately 45,000 people left this area to settle in the United States. Letters must have poured from the area to immigrants in the Midwest. On the basis of the letters examined here, it seems that even if they felt they had not much news to tell, they definitely had questions to ask.

In order to gather material for this study, information

about the project was sent in 1984 to local newspapers in areas of the midwestern states where people from Telemark had settled in fairly large numbers. By the end of 1985 roughly 500 letters had been collected, including the above-mentioned letters of Torbjørg Lie to *Decorah-Posten*; copies of all of them are now in the archives of the Telemark College Library in Bø. In this same collection there are about ten letters to an immigrant farmer in Whitewater, Wisconsin, from before the Civil War. There are some twenty letters to an immigrant woman in Elbow Lake, Minnesota, from the 1920s and 1930s. But close to two hundred of these letters come from one family only. This substantial collection of letters reads like a novel. Most of them were written by a father in Telemark to his oldest son, an immigrant in Hawley, Minnesota. They bear witness to an unusually intimate relationship between father and son. There are also letters from the immigrant's stepmother and from his brothers and sisters. Most of these family letters were written during a period of twenty-five years, from the 1880s to the time of Norwegian independence in 1905. This particular collection is of special value because it provides the family background of an immigrant who later became a prominent Farmer-Labor politician in Minnesota. His name was Knud S. Wefald. His work for the Norwegian-American press has been honored by a Wefald room at the Norwegian-American Museum in Decorah.

The arrival of a letter from home was undoubtedly a special event for all immigrants. Before the turn of the century a letter could of course take months to reach its destination. It is known from several America letters that immigrants became impatient when they had not heard from home for a long time. Indeed the main drive behind a letter from the Midwest to Norway would often be the desire to have one in return. "I can hardly describe the excitement when I opened your long letter," explained an immigrant from Telemark in a letter home. In a letter of 1896 to his parents in Telemark another immigrant in Minnesota related how eagerly he and his brothers were looking forward to receiving a letter: "It does not matter much whose name is on the envelope when a letter from Norway arrives. We do not follow the commonly accepted rule as to who gets to open it. The one who first lays his hands on it will open it and read it, because his curiosity must be satisfied."

If there were several immigrants from one family, a letter would often be forwarded from one to the other. Some of the early letters from home were addressed to "our unforgettable and faraway brothers and sisters." No wonder such letters were kept and read over and over again. It is of course impossible to use information gathered in these letters for statistical evidence of any sort. But in these letters to immigrants the family at home would reveal brief glimpses of rural life, not as written about in textbooks, but as actually experienced by members of the household. The letters also clearly show how much the midwestern immigrants were tied to the past, to places and people in their home community. In some of the letters the writer from home would ask if the immigrant remembered such and such an episode or something important which was said, and then would retell the story as if to make sure that he or she did. One would probably expect letters to immigrants to be responses and commentaries to America letters, but entries of that type are scarce.

Letters were sent both ways to settle financial questions. When parents died, questions of inheritance had to be settled through letters to sons and daughters in America. The letters reveal that heirs far from home were not always given their due share. In a letter of 1931 a sister wrote to her brother in Wisconsin to inform him that his father's estate had been settled. This was done in a way that may have been fairly common: "Perhaps you think this strange, but your father told those who helped set up his will that he wanted to divide his belongings as he himself thought best. And he thought that you over there had more than enough already. We would be grateful if you would accept this arrangement." Another father was more concerned about the rights of his son in America. In a letter the son was asked to appoint a reliable person to act for him, so that when the time came for the settlement of the father's estate, it would not have to go through a costly court procedure. When the son suggested that his brother should act as his representative, the father wrote back to advise against that arrangement, since, wrote the father, his brother might not send him a fair share.

Not all families had money to send. Some wrote to their family in the United States to ask for money, and of course wrote notes of thanks in return. If the letter writer did not ask directly for money, he would at least sometimes ask his brothers to guarantee a bank loan for him. To many it must have been a humiliating experience to ask for money. Such requests usually came at the end of a letter, after careful preparation. In 1897 Abraham Jacobson, whose farm outside Decorah is now part of the Norwegian-American Museum, received a letter from a nephew of his in Upper Telemark. The conclusion of the letter reads like this: "I have lots of work to do every day. This winter I have been working as a lumberjack. I had to stay away from home for long periods then, leaving my wife alone with the children. . . . We have two cows and a few sheep. That is, we do not own the cows yet, because we have borrowed them from somebody else. I guess I do not have more to tell you, but I would like to ask if you could please send me one hundred *kroner*, so that we could buy a cow for ourselves. We would of course also be happy with less than a hundred *kroner*." Whether Jacobson sent the money is not known, but the letter writer at home must have been quite convinced that his uncle in Iowa had become a man of means. Begging may not have been common, but sometimes money was lent to help the farm economy at home. In a letter from the 1920s a farmer in Telemark wrote to his brother in Wisconsin that he would soon try to pay off his debt: "Please don't refuse the thousand *kroner* which I will send you in the spring, provided I am in good health."

Since the farm economy was the domain of men, most letters in which money is a concern seem to have been written by them. Women wrote about different things. Apart from the large file of Wefald letters, most of the letters discovered seem to have been written by women in Telemark and kept by women in America. Maybe women at home wrote more often than men, and women were in all probability better keepers of letters. Women who had grown up together in Telemark kept in touch through writing. In one such letter of 1905 addressed to a friend in North Dakota, a young woman wrote that she had received *The Ladies' Home Journal*, and that it had helped her to gain insight into the education of women in the United States.

The conception of the young American woman as illustrated in the popular press at the time may have appealed to young Norwegian readers, but mothers may have been more worried. When Knud Wefald announced his engagement, his stepmother in Norway sent him her sincere congratulations, saying: "From what you write in your letter, I know that she must be beautiful, but is she also kind and good? Is she a good housekeeper? Pay attention to that . . . . If she has few intellectual interests, you should help her to gain some. I know that in America the woman participates in all things on an equal footing with her husband."

Some letters were written by mothers who worried about their children who had emigrated. Many of these made use of religious language. The writer would often conclude her letter by expressing a wish that they would meet in heaven, if not before. It is not surprising that people at home, who had experienced heartbreaking scenes of farewell, thought of heaven as a place "where there is no more parting or breaking up," as one mother wrote. Below is an excerpt from such a letter written by a widowed mother to her son in Minnesota in 1909. Her handwriting is poor, her spelling inaccurate. It must have been one of the few letters she ever wrote. She admitted that she was afraid of becoming a burden to friends in her community:

"My dear son. Thank you so much for remembering me, and for the money you sent. The Lord will pay you back. For according to the Word of God, great gifts will be bestowed on those who help their parents.

"The Devil has tried to convince me that you were dead, and that I had no more support here on earth. But, thank God,

I know now that you are alive. Poor Terje [another son], though, it is as if he is dead to me. If you see him, tell him that his mother loves him with all her heart and that she never tires of praying for him.

"You mention that you would like to send a ticket for me and my daughter this spring. But she says she does not dare to travel with me alone, so that is quite impossible. Perhaps you do not even remember how old I am now. I am 68 years old.

"I will not see your face again in this world, but I hope to see you again in our heavenly dwelling."

A similar letter, written by a mother to her immigrant son in Iowa during the 1920s, reads in part:

"Dear Son. I am not much looking forward to Christmas this year. Too many painful memories. We do not have our own songbird at home any longer. He flew away to a foreign land in the west. I do not know if he will use his good voice out there. Perhaps he still sings the songs of Zion in a foreign land? Does he?

"A neighbor brought us a newspaper in which you had written a column. I enjoyed reading it, but I did not like what you wrote about having picked up American swearwords. That hurt me so much I could not sleep until late that night."

Religious language as used here reveals a sense of loss on the part of the letter writer. If repression of emotions is a common trait among Norwegians, the religious language in these letters provided an important emotional outlet. Through the religious diction in the letters a collective mentality of the period may be traced. In some letters the writer will also give information on religious conditions in the community, such as pietist revival meetings around World War I. One such letter records how the youth of Seljord were divided: at the local 17th of May observance after the church service was over, they split into two groups with widely different ideas of celebrating.

Letters written by women reveal their special interests and duties. They tell about having to take care of an old mother, they mention weaving and crochet work. Sometimes their own needlework, a handkerchief, a garter, an ornamental

towel, would be included in their letters, often with the typically modest note: "it is so ill-made and coarse, I do not know
if you will even care to use it."

People who rarely wrote to family in America at least had
to notify their relatives about the serious illness or death of a
parent at home. There was little the immigrant could do to
help in such cases, except write a comforting letter back. A letter writer from Kragerø had expected more concern:

"That you forgot her at the end was a great disappoint-
ment to her [their mother]. You did not even send her or us
a friendly greeting when she was on her deathbed. You who
have children of your own know how the heart of a mother
suffers from such neglect . . . . [But] perhaps your relatives
here failed to tell you in time."

Like many America letters, mail from home also con-
tained everyday information about the harvest of barley, rye,
and potatoes, about cattle, or a new horse perhaps, about
weather and farm prices. If immigrants boasted about their
new farms in the Midwest, their families at home also felt the
need to send news of prosperity, although on a lesser scale.

Letters from home also brought the latest shocking news
and gossip concerning people in the community. Some letters
would tell about recent accidents, who had been sent to prison
in Skien and for what reason, and who was reported to have
been in bed with whom. For example, Ole Helgesen, a teacher
in Calmar, Iowa, wrote a diary in the 1870s in which he
recorded notes from several such letters sent from his friends
in Upper Telemark.

In wartime people complained about the rationing of
food. "In America, I suppose you have wheat flour in abundance," wrote a farmer in 1917. Often letters would have long
lists of names of people who had died. Letters of 1918 and
1919, sometimes opened by United States censorship,
brought news of the devastating effects of the Spanish flu epi-
demic in parts of Telemark.

Letters written over a period of a hundred years will naturally differ in style and content. The early letters, written

from father or mother to their immigrant son or daughter, or
from siblings at home to brother or sister in the Midwest, bear
witness to a once-shared world. A father wrote from
Kviteseid to a son in America: "When you tell about your children, I visualize them in my mind gathered around the table.
What you write brings to life my memories about the years
when you and your brothers and sisters grew up here." In a
letter of 1873 a father complained to his son that he had become terribly short-winded and was barely able to walk up-
hill. Once an active farmer, he was now able to do puttering
work only (*noget pusleri*). The letter ended in a typical tone for
its kind: "Many have died in the parish this last winter. On
Christmas Eve nine corpses lay unburied here. I will not have
to wait long for that final trumpet either, since at present there
are just five men older than me in the community."

Sometimes a family connection was kept up between
branches in both countries through correspondence into the
next generation. Naturally cousins who had never seen each
other would pass on a different kind of information than the
first generation. To her cousin in the Midwest a young writer
included a flower in her letter: "This is a Norwegian flower.
It is called geranium."

It has been noted that few immigrants wrote home to say
that they regretted having left Norway. Most of them were no
doubt better off in their new country, but some may also have
felt that an expression of regret would disappoint their relatives in Norway, and consequently they refrained from com-
plaining. In a letter in 1874 to his brother in Minnesota, we
find the following statement: "I truly wish I had not helped
you go to America, if it is true that you regret the voyage
now." In cases when there was no one living on the Telemark
farm left by the immigrants, neighbor families reported the
sad sight: "Everything is so quiet and dreamlike up there now.
One cannot help thinking of all the struggle and toil that once
went on there."

Letters would also inform immigrant readers of social
changes that had taken place in the region after they had left.
It has been noted that immigrants or their descendants who

went back to Norway on a visit would often be disappointed because what they found did not correspond to the vision they had. Letters from home, however, gave little support to nostalgia. Readers of such letters could not possibly expect Norway to have remained the way it was when they left it. Here is one such realistic description of social changes in an immigrant's home community, recorded by a brother in Telemark shortly after World War II: "Things have changed since you left. People are much better off than before. When I was young they went to America, now they take to the cities for work, both boys and girls. Lots of young people leave their farms. If this trend continues, we will pretty soon see the mountainous districts of Upper Telemark depopulated. . . . On some farms now they no longer bother to plant wheat. As long as America can sell us wheat, they may be all right, but we have no guarantee that that will also be the case in the future."

Several writers from about this time and earlier mentioned how hard it was to get farmhands and dairymaids. But some things had improved. One farmer boasted that he was able to buy a new suit in a local store now "just like in America." Letters from the turn of the century and the next decades also reflect the growing industrial life in the region. A writer from Vrådal recorded in the early 1920s: "This is May 1st, Labor Day, the day for the Socialists to celebrate. You probably have some of them in America as well. We have quite a few here now. Mostly in the cities. Farmers do not often become Socialists."

During this era American-made automobiles and motorcycles came to Telemark. One writer related how the new vehicles scared the horses: "During church hours now there are motorcycles parked against the entire church wall."

Letters from home also provide an interesting source for the study of written language. The earliest letters are written in the official Dano-Norwegian, a standard which not all letter writers had mastered equally well. Later, dialect words are included in the letters. Some letters, or parts of them, are in New Norse. Apparently writers did not feel the need, or perhaps have the ability, to be consistent. In letters after World War II people would sometimes turn to a very elementary English in their letters to immigrants. One such woman, who for years had written in Norwegian to her relatives in the Midwest, now felt the need to try a letter in her own fumbling English: "We in Skafså have not electric lighting, but now build they a electric power station. We shall *faa* electric lighting in 1952."

In contrast to the more or less scattered nature of the material referred to so far, the large Wefald collection of letters has the advantage of a sharper focus in time and place. The letters provide an excellent source for regional history in Telemark, a source which is largely untapped. Most of these letters also have the distinction of having been written by an excellent letter writer and storyteller. In this particular case the recipient also deserves to be singled out for a few comments. Knud S. Wefald of Hawley, Minnesota, entered state politics in 1912. He won a seat in the United States Congress in 1922, a position he kept until 1926. Until his death he was active in state politics in Minnesota. An essay of his is included in a volume called *Third Party Footsteps*, an anthology of writings of Midwestern political radicals published in 1966. James Youngdale, the editor, introduces Wefald as an outspoken defender of the common man. Wefald's support of the Non-Partisan League and later of the Farmer-Labor Party must to some extent have been influenced by his father's ideas and earlier letters from home. Wefald was also an able poet in the Norwegian language.

In several of his letters Knud's father discussed his political views in detail with his son in Minnesota. The father comes across as a strong supporter of the small farmer and of the emerging laboring class. He related how he got into bitter quarrels with the local establishment: with the big farmers, the influential middlemen, government officials, and also — occasionally — the minister of the state church. Indeed Wefald's father seemed to expect more from the rising working class than from his farmer friends. "Too many small farmers," he complained, "have fallen asleep. They are totally blind. Too often they will kiss the hands of those who beat them most severely." Even if he felt that he stood alone in his community, the father knew that he would have "the miserable, the beaten, the poor people who have fallen into the poisonous swamps of the capitalists" on his side. Not only did he use his letters to teach his son about politics in Norway, he also sometimes offered his opinions about American politics. With Norway still under the reign of the Swedish-Norwegian king, the elder Wefald was strongly in favor of a republican system of government. "As a good republican", he wrote to his oldest son in Minnesota in 1889, "I wish all kings would go to blazes." But he was also skeptical about the future of American politics, as seen from his vantage point in Norway: "A better party must emerge in America, a political party consisting of small farmers and of workers in both country and city, a party powerful enough to beat both the Republicans and the Democrats off the field. If not, American politics will end in disaster."

It was only natural that Wefald of Hawley, Minnesota, would transfer this Norwegian radicalism by way of Jeffersonian ideas of the small, independent farmer onto the then-contemporary progressive platform. In Wefald's case some of his American third-party footsteps can actually be traced back to his father in Telemark in the 1880s. In a study titled *A Voice of Protest: Norwegians in American Politics 1890–1917*, Jon Wefald, a great-grandson of the letter writer, argues that one of the reasons a number of Norwegian-American politicians sided with the left wing in midwestern politics was their past experience of a "cooperative spirit" in the farm communities back in Norway. These politicians, claims Jon Wefald, based their political views on "the spirit of the old country" or "the neighborly relationships" or "the concern for the public good" in the rural Norway they had known. If the author had had access to his great-grandfather's letters, he would probably have drawn a less favorable picture. In almost all the Wefald letters from Telemark—the son's letters back have unfortunately been lost—the father told of neighbors who were fighting each other. There were sometimes fierce battles in the community over patches of forest and land. There is more than one account of farmers who refused to help each other even in times of great need. Knud Wefald sent money home to help his father out of poverty and debt, but apparently also to help him in necessary lawsuits with other farmers in the district. Letters from immigrants in America may have influenced a democratic spirit among Norwegians at home; the Wefald letters suggest that the influence went both ways. As a Minnesota politician Wefald truly learned from his Norwegian background and from his father's correspondence. But in his case the rural life and experience from Telemark must have provided him with a negative political example.

Seen in this context the Wefald letters may contribute to Norwegian-American scholarship in the United States, but most of all they will add to our understanding of regional life in Telemark during the period when they were written and sent to Minnesota. The letters appear to be a gold mine of information about daily life in southern Telemark shortly before the turn of the century. There are descriptions of the routines of daily work, of the quantity and the quality of the annual harvest of potatoes, cabbage, and turnips, as well as poetic impressions of nature. Not only politics, but also family life was important to the elder Wefald. He complained in one of his last letters about getting old: "I wish I had your age and strength, combined with my own life experience and the spirit I once had," he wrote to his son. He sent a moving letter to inform Knud about the sudden death of Knud's ten-year-old brother. He noted children's play around the farm, summer and winter. A lover of nature, he described the spring flowers and many a sunset on the nearby lake, a sight he would not give up, he said, for all the riches in the world. He was constantly fighting poverty. More than once he complained about not having money enough to pay for postage. Yet he informed his son that giving in and moving to America was absolutely out of the question.

The letters also bring vivid reports of local fairs, of parties, weddings, and funerals. The writers are honest enough to reveal some of the less commendable aspects of Telemark life. In 1890 a brother of Knud wrote about what he had witnessed at the county fair in this way: "There were not many cattle, but plenty of beer. Fifteen cases full in all. People [were] drunk to such an extent that they looked more like animals than the cattle in the show. They fought and quarreled. It was wild." At a local wedding that same year, the writer related this extraordinary episode: "For their church wedding the pastor gave a sermon on the value and importance of a good home. He said that Per [the bridegroom] had not grown up in a particularly good home, since his brothers were such heavy drinkers. This was too much for one of the brothers, who at this point was quite drunk, and when time came around for the church offering, he rose and said, loud and clear: 'This sermon was nothing to pay for!' The pastor told him to keep still in the house of God, whereupon the brother took his hat and left."

After Knud's father died, Knud's stepmother had to ask for more money from Minnesota. In 1902 she wrote: "Perhaps I could ask you for twenty *kroner* so that I could buy a sack of flour. All my pension now goes to paying rent and taxes on the farm." At the same time she continued to send her advice to the stepson in Hawley. When he complained in a letter home about losing weight, she wrote back: "Please, boil some seed of hemp in milk, strain it, and drink it as soup every day, and you will put on weight again." She also added her own blessing with the Biblical words: "The promise of the 4th Commandment is given to you, and you will live long in your country."

This essay has attempted to give some brief glimpses into what letters from Norway to immigrants in America might reveal. Such letters will certainly shed light on various effects of immigration on those who did not go, as well as on regional history in Norway. They not only ought to be studied as source material for history; they are also part of a true folk literature. The letters deserve to be studied along with the America letters as an essential part of a two-way communication. This type of research will rest totally on source material in the United States; unfortunately, much of it has already disappeared for good. Collecting what remains demands a joint effort, an effort which is essential if this important material is to be preserved.

Below is a list of the letters referred to in the essay. The Telemark College Library has copies of all of them. All translations from the letters are the present author's. Quotations from America letters are from Telemark Historielag's collection, also at Telemark College Library.

180 letters to Knud S. Wefald in Minnesota and North Dakota from family in Drangedal, 1887–1911.

145 letters to *Decorah-Posten* from Torbjørg Lie in Fyresdal, 1891–1920.

55 letters to Torjus Larsson and family in the Goodbridge area, Minnesota, from family and friends in Mo and the Porsgrunn area, 1928–1971.

30 letters to Mrs. Alfred Carlson (Alice Nerison) and her mother Mrs. Knute Nerison (Ragnhild Strand) in Houston, Minnesota, from family in Vrådal and Vinje, 1912–1980.

25 letters to Mrs. Ole S. (Egelev) Olson in Elbow Lake, Minnesota, from family and friends in Seljord, 1916–1935.

10 letters to Niri Nilsson, Louisburg, Minnesota, from family in Brukaasa, Lunde, 1872–1880.

10 letters to Helene Gjermundsdatter Alseth in the Rochester area, Minnesota, from family and friends in Tinn, 1934–1940.

10 letters to Peder Kjostolfsen Haatvedt (Peter Kestol) in Whitewater, Wisconsin, from family in Holla, 1852–1862.

7 letters to Abraham Jacobson and family, Washington Prairie, Iowa, from family and friends in Tinn, 1898–1909.

7 letters to Gaute Ingebritson Gunleiksrud and his family in Stoughton, Wisconsin, from family in Tinn, 1889–1891.

7 letters to S. Gudmundsen Opsund from family in Kviteseid, 1871–1885.

5 letters to the Vasend family in McIntosh, Minnesota, from family in Høydalsmo, 1954–1961.

4 letters to Sigurd Hansen Sanden in Rio, Columbia county, Wisconsin, from family and friends in Sauherad, 1895–1899.

4 letters to Jacob Torgrimsen Bjørtuft in Decorah, Iowa, from relatives in Tinn, 1851–1857.

3 letters to Sveinung Tovson Rauland in McIntosh, Minnesota, from a brother in Rauland, 1917–1923.

3 letters to Jacob Grimstead, Lake Mills, Iowa, from family in Nissedal, 1932–1952.

2 letters to Ragnhild and Jacob Knudsen Mæland in Racine, Wisconsin, from family and friends in Tinn, 1849.

2 letters to Halvor Pedersen Næsund in Milwaukee from family in Kragerø, 1845–1856.

2 letters to Joraand Opegarden Midtveit in Willmar, Minnesota, from family in Vinje, 1919 and 1922.

2 letters to Tor and Olav Langeli in Canada and Minnesota from their mother in Vrådal, undated.

2 letters to Jørgen (George) and Torjus Felland in Viroqua, Wisconsin, from family in Mo, 1905 and 1931.

2 letters to Bergit Norjoret in Minnesota, from family in Vinje, 1915.

2 letters to Lake Mills, Iowa, from Aslak P. Vehus, Vinje, 1921 and 1940.

2 letters to descendants of Kari Haugen Tveito Olson, Fillmore county, Minnesota, from Tinn, 1955 and 1959.

2 letters to Signe Hustveit Aslaksen, Sheyenne, North Dakota, from a sister and a friend in Vinje, 1894 and 1905.

1 letter to John Aasten, Seattle, Washington, from Hovin, 1945.

1 letter to O. O. Otterholt in Sugar Creek, Wisconsin, from family in Gjerpen, 1881.

1 letter to S. S. Urberg in Blair, Wisconsin, from a brother in Bamble, 1915.

# 9

## Twelve Civil War Letters of Col. Hans C. Heg to his Son*

*edited by E. Biddle Heg*

The Civil War was a major catalyst in the Americanizing of the Norwegian immigrants who arrived here between 1825 and 1860, molding them in some ways very subtly and in other ways more obviously. Few immigrant Norwegian Americans escaped the influence of this upheaval, if not on the battlefield then certainly on the economic and social fronts. Those on the home scene who assumed the duties of business, farm, and family were passively influenced, adjusting to the attendant deprivations and daily changes, not always aware that they were participants in the struggle of their adopted country. Others, more aggressive, were drawn into the vortex of the war on the several battlefields away from home. On whichever front they found themselves, the immigrants came to feel at home in America during these Civil War years. So it was with Hans Heg, who "became the war hero of the Norwegians, the personal symbol of their contribution to the preservation of the Union."[1] His short life is a microcosm of

*The following twelve letters by Hans C. Heg were preserved by the Heg family until they were donated to the Norwegian-American Historical Association. In December, 1939, the Association presented the letters to the State Historical Society of Wisconsin at Madison, there to become part of the larger Fowler/VanDoren collection of Heg manuscripts.

immigrant Americanization; for him as for many others, the Civil War was a decisive stage in this process.

For the Norwegian immigrant in the Middle West, one can identify four general phases leading to the Civil War years: the frontier years, the years of settlement, the years of social and cultural beginnings, and the first steps toward political involvement. From 1825 when the first Norwegian immigrants arrived in America, these phases followed swiftly as the tides of immigration flowed west after 1836, when Wisconsin became a territory. By 1840 the frontier years were at their height there. By 1845 the years of settlement had turned villages into towns and towns into cities;[2] and this same year the Norwegian immigrants in Wisconsin felt secure enough in their new home to issue a "declaration of independence," the Muskego Manifesto, acknowledging allegiance to their new country and emphasizing the basic philosophy of their Americanization — "freedom and equality," the very principles for which Hans Heg was to give his life just eighteen years later.[3]

Hans Heg was well prepared for his role as an American when at the age of eleven he arrived on the Wisconsin frontier. Born in Lier on December 21, 1829, to parents who had made the most of individual enterprise in a land of farmers, this youth spent his most impressionable years in the shifting panorama of coastal life in Norway at an inn operated by his father. To young Hans, this inn was like his father's great barn on the shore of Wind Lake in Wisconsin; his eleven years in Norway imbued him with a sense of wide horizons which he later pursued in leading other immigrant settlers farther west, and in his adventuresome trip to the California gold fields in 1849. His strong sense of identity with America was fostered during the ten years before he was twenty-one by an intimate knowledge of the territory in which he lived, its wilderness, its towns and cities, and its people;[4] by his close association with the Norwegian-American cultural and political activities of his father. Even, who was a vital participant in the affairs of the Muskego settlement until his death in 1850; and by an open and friendly warmth of personality that made him admired by those who knew him.[5]

In 1851, Hans Heg, a wiser, more experienced, and more worldly man, returned to Wisconsin from California to take over his father's farm, and on December 10 of the same year, eleven days before his twenty-second birthday, he married Gunild Einung in "the old log house" on the farm.[6] The next ten years Hans devoted to family and career as he supervised his 320-acre farm with the help of Hans Wood and Ole Luraas.

With a strong sense of dedication to his adopted land, his state, and his Norwegian heritage, he began the final step in the Americanizing of an immigrant—assuming his political identity. He first moved into local and county politics in 1852, when he became a justice of the peace and a town supervisor in the town or Norway, Racine county. In this same year, on September 22, James Edmund, the first of his four children was born. In 1854, Hans Heg was named chairman of the town board of supervisors, a post to which he was reappointed the following year. As chairman he automatically became a member of the county board of supervisors. This affiliation in turn led to his being appointed as one of the commissioners to supervise the Racine County Poor Farm. In 1857, Heg entered state politics by becoming a delegate from Racine county to the Republican State Convention in Madison. Then, in 1859, he won the Republican nomination for the office of state prison commissioner of Wisconsin, to which position he was elected for a two-year term.

The same year, Hans moved his family from Waterford, where he had recently opened a mill and general store, to their newly purchased home near the state prison in Waupun. It was here in Waupun that his three-year-old daughter Annetta died in 1860, and his fourth and last child, Elmer, was born.[7] Although he was renominated for the office of state prison commissioner, Hans Heg left Waupun after receiving his commission as colonel in the Union Army on October 1, 1861. By the time he assumed leadership of the Fifteenth Wisconsin Regiment in the winter of 1861–1862, he had moved his family back to Waterford, where they had their general store, until then tended by his partners. At that time young Edmund was nine years old, a shy and somewhat frail child. In Waterford he continued the education he had begun at the log school near his father's farm and later at Waupun. He was schooled enough to write to his father at Camp Randall in Madison, and old enough so that he and his sister Hilda[8] could travel by train to visit their father at camp on February 19, 1862.[9]

Throughout the time that Colonel Heg was in the army, Edmund was at home under the care and guidance of his mother. His father's letters to him, with notes to Gunild often appended, reflect the love and concerns of an absent parent. Hans's letters to his son also carry indirect admonitions, advice, and suggestions to his wife, as he was always aware of her responsibility in managing a farm and household, and mindful of her role as a mother to three young children. Self-made in the full sense of the word, Hans Heg believed in education and the ethic of hard work. "I want to give the *boys* a good education, but no money—let them work for it as you and I have done."[10]

The colonel saw the value of his son's learning German and Norwegian, and frequently reminded his wife to encourage the complete education of their children. To this end, five years after the death of her husband at Chickamauga in September, 1863, Gunild Heg moved her family to Beloit, Wisconsin, where Edmund entered college in 1868. There he studied law, but during his college years he became quite deaf and decided to take up journalism instead. He was graduated in 1874. That same year he married Ella C. Clark in Beloit, where they lived for the next two years. From 1876 to 1895 Edmund Heg and his wife lived at Lake Geneva, Wisconsin, where all six of his children were born.[11] There too he began his work in journalism by becoming owner and editor of *The Lake Geneva Herald*, a weekly newspaper.[12] He served as president of the Wisconsin Press Association in 1891 and 1892. During these years Edmund also became general superintendant of the Green Bay Reformatory, which he was instrumental in organizing. Finally, in 1895, he sold his interest in *The Lake Geneva Herald* and moved to Rahway, New Jersey, where he helped start a new reformatory. After he had completed this work, he became president of the Automatic Heating Company, with corporate offices in New York City and some twenty branches throughout the country. He moved from Rahway to Elizabeth, New Jersey, where his sister Hilda lived with her husband Charles N. Fowler. After the sudden death in 1909 of his son Walter, who had charge of the Chicago office of the Automatic Heating Company, Edmund moved his family to that city, where he lived until his death on April 6, 1914, at the age of sixty-one.

1.

[N.D.][13]

Dear Edmund—

I must not forget to write to you. I am very glad to get letters from you, and to hear that you take good care of the Ponies. You must tend to my business till I come back home.

If you learn to do that now when you are a boy, you will be a smart man when you get older.

You must sell off some of the sheep this fall—so that you keep about 40 or 50.—The ponies you must do the best you can with, if you can sell them you had better do that perhaps—When I come home I intend to bring you a fine little pony to ride.

You must practice writing, so that you learn to write a good hand—and bye and bye I will take you along with me as *Aid de Camp*—do you know what that means? Every General has several boys and men to ride around and carry messages for them. When you get to be one year older, I will get a commission for you as *Lieutenant* and have you with me as my *Aid de Camp*—dress you up in fine uniform, and get a nice pony for you to ride but you must learn to write a good hand—and you must be a good boy—You must learn to ride too—

I am telling you this, to keep it to yourself—When you

get old enough, and are a smart boy, I can find a good place for you — Write to me as often as you can and see that Elmer is a good boy and do not plague him any —

Your Father — Hans C. Heg

My Dear Hilda,
I have not room to write much to you — but I will write you a long letter pretty soon — I am coming home to hear you play on the Piano before long.

Good Bye<br>Hans C. Heg

2.

Bowling Green Ky                                                    Oct, Nov[14]

My Dear Edmund,
    I wrote to Ma yesterday and I will write to you and Hilda today. I have not had any letters from you for a very long time, but today I got an old letter from you by Willard,[15] he came here to day. I am very glad that you have sold the Ponies and I hope you have got the Pony I sent you. I am expecting [a] letter from you and I want to know how you like the little Pony.[16] I am very glad to see that you attend to my matters at home, you must take care of my things till I come back —
    Write to me as often as you can and let me know how El- mer and Ma is [sic] — I want to see you all very much, and will try to visit you sometime this winter and next spring. The war will probably be over and I will come home and stay with you. You must go to school and learn to write so that you can write me good long letters, and tell me all the news. I am very anxious to hear from home. I have been sick for a few days and I am nearly well again to day.[17] The Regiment came in to this place today, and camped close by here. I can not tell how long we will stay, we will go from here to Nashville. Write to this place, and if I am not here I will have it forwarded to where we are. When I come home for good I will take you and Ma

and Elmer and Hilda all with me up on a visit to Minnesota,[18] and a good many other places — We will have very nice times, if you are good children while I am away. I am getting good wages and will [have] plenty of money to buy many nice things when I get home. Furgeson [sic] is here to see me just now, he has been sick at the hospital in this place for sometime.[19] Bert Willard is very sick but he is getting better now I believe. I must stop this time, write to me immediately and direct it to Bowling Green Ky.

Be a good boy, and I will write to you often

Your own Pa Pa —

Dear little Hilda

I must not forget to write a few lines to you, then you will write to me again, I am so glad to see your nice little letters. If Edmund's Pony has come home I want him to let you ride on him sometimes. I will try and get a saddle for you when I come home.

I have been in the Battle several times and seen a great many men killed, and the Rebels have shot at me too,[20] but if you are a good girl and Edmund is a good boy, they will not hit me, but I will come home again to you soon, and we will have very nice times — does your Piano play good now?[21] Write me a good long letter soon and give Elmer a kiss for me.

Good By My Dear Hilda
Kiss Ma for me too.                                    Your Pa

3.

Camp near Nashville Tenn.
Dec. 9th 1861

My Dear Edmund,

I wrote to Mother last night and I will write to you to day. The Paymaster came here yesterday evening and paid us up for the months, July and August.[22]

My pay is cut down some — I received $410.00 and today

I sent by Express to the Farmers and Millers Bank $400.00 to be deposited for Mother, to pay her for what I borrowed of her while I was with you — she can not say now that I owe her anything.[23] And you can tell her that we are even again now.

I have got a nice warm tent, and I bought me a light stove yesterday for 5. dollars — I board together with the Doctor and am living well — we have plenty to *eat*.[24]

I hope you will try to learn to write well, and write to me often. I am very anxious to hear from home, and want you to keep me posted. I send you an Illinois Bill that I can not use down here. You may give Hilda half of it and keep the balance your self. I am very busy since I came back. My tent has been full every day and it is hard work to get a [chance] to write letters. I make many mistakes in writing because I have to do so while my tent is full.[25]

I have nothing more to write about this time and must close — I expect to hear that you are a good boy and that you help your Mother all you can, that you are good to Hilda and Elmer.

I think we may have a Battle here before long, and if you are good children, God will let me come home again to you safe.[26]

The weather is very warm and fine today, it was cold Sunday and yesterday. Good by — my Dear Boy —

Your Father
Hans C. Heg

Capt. Johnson just came in and gave me his Picture — Take care of it — [27]

Hans

4.

Camp near Nashville, Dec. 18th 1862

Dear Edmund,

I have written to Hilda, and Mother, a letter a piece — and I owe you one this time.

I got Ma's letter day before yesterday, her letter was dated Dec 9th with Clausen letter in with it.[28]

I am very glad to hear you get along well, and I will try and write to you as often as I have chance to send the letters. Yesterday I went out with two Regiments, my own and the 101st Ohio and a Battery of Artillery, and 125 Waggons, to get corn and hay.

We saw the rebels, but they did not try to fire on us. There was [sic] about 500 up on a big hill about two miles from us, and I tried to get my waggons loaded early enough to have got time before dark to go up and see them, and try if they would fight, but I did not get time to do it. General Davis promised that I should get permission to go out to day or to morrow to look after them, but I have had no orders yet.[29] The weather is very pleasant indeed. It was cold last night but the sun shines nearly every day, and then it is warm and pleasant.

We have lots of good things to eat and I am just as well again now as I was before I was taken sick. If you get a chance to send any thing down here by Lt. Thomson, you can send me a box of cigars, of the same kind that I got when I left home. On the 10th of December I sent $400.00 the the Farmers and Millers Bank[30] and asked Holton to send the check to Mrs. H.C. Heg at Waterford, so that you can tell Ma that I do not owe her once cent.[31] And if she wants to borrow any more money from me I will lend her some after New Year. You may tell her that I will lend her enough to buy her a House and Lot if she wants to and I collect it from her when I come back home — Dr. Wooster of Racine is commissioned as Assistant Surgeon for this Regiment, and I suppose he will be here very soon.[32] I am very glad he is coming, for I know he is a very good man. I asked the governor to appoint him.

I shall expect to get a letter from some of you to day — We get the mail at 2. o clock every day — I subscribed for the Sentinal before I left Milwaukee, and get it regular.[33] I got the one giving account of the drawing on the 11th but I did not remember the number of your Ticket so I could not tell whether you drew anything or not. I sent a Magazine to you by mail, and in it is 3 Pictures of our Camp on Island No 10.

One of the Picture belong [sic] to Dr. Himoe—and you must send it to Andrea.[34]

[incomplete]

5.

[N.D.][35]

My Dear Boy,

Your letter that was inclosed with one from Ma came to day—It is so long since you wrote to me that I was really glad to get your nice letter—I hope you are going to school and learning to read and write fast. When school is out you must stay at home as much as possible, and not run around the streets too much nights—it is only bad boys that will do that. Tell me in your next letter how the sheep are doing, and how it is with the Pony and black Horse—If Gipsom will take good care of the Horse, and break him to work for a Buggy good—you may let him have him to use, as long as you please—I want you to learn to write good till I come back, so that when I start a store again you can do the business for me—We will go in partnership then—Tell Hans Wood to write to me—[36] and tell Hilda I will write to her the next time I write home—and tell Nebby I am sorry he has lost his dinner, but if he is big enough to wear bosom Shirt, he ought to lose his dinner—     Good Bye—I expect to hear that you are a good boy—

Your own Pa

Did I ever tell you that Furgeson is dead? He died in Bowling Green.

6.
Camp at Salem March 19th 1863

My Dear Edmund,

To day I recieved [sic] yours and Ma's and Hilda's letter. I was really glad to get so many letters at one time and such nice interesting ones. I wrote to Ma to day with Pencil. I had no pen and ink. I hope you will get your new house soon, and you will be near the store.[37] Mother says you are a strong Republican, I am glad of that, [if not] you would be like the Democrats, and help the *Secesh*. I see that the Black Horse is well again too, — If you can find somebody that will take good care of him, — you may let them have and use him and learn him to work in a harness, so that when I come home I can use him for a Buggy horse. I have sent home plenty of money to pay for your house, and to build a stable. The House, if you get it is to belong to Ma, and I want she shall build a good Barn, and paint it Blue, so that we can have as nice a place for our horses as anybody — I am sorry the Sheep is not doing well.[38] You must buy some grain and give them. I am going to come home next fall — and stay for good, unless I can get command at some place where I can have you all with me, and as soon as I come home I will go in partnership with you in a *Store*. But you must learn to write good if we shall keep store together.

You can tell Ma and Hilda that I will write to them soon, and answer their letters.

Old Rosy wont let your Mother come down and visit me — although he has his own wife down here — He thinks women are not good soldiers.[39]

I have not time to write any more now, it is very late, and I must go to bed — Good Bye — be a good boy —

From your own
PaPa

Dear Nebby,

You little Rat you — you would like to come down to visit with Ma — and see PaPa — I will have to come up and see you soon —

Nebby I know is a good Boy, and he is Pa Pas Boy —

7.

Camp Near Murfreesboro Tenn
April 1st 1863

Dear Edmund,

I got a letter from each of you yesterday but I was out on Picket at the time and did not get time to write to you till to day. I was very glad to get so many letters, and to hear that you are well. Elmer sings a song about the Copperheads. I send you [a] song that the boys down here sing about them — I will Explain to you what some of the names in the song means — a "Pup Tent" is a small Tent that Every soldier has to carry on his back, and is so small that the boys call them Pup Tents or Dog Tents.

"Sow Belly" means "Bacon" — some of the Bacon when it looks poor, the boys call it "Sow belly" because it is a part of the belly of some old Sow.

"Hard Tack" means Crackers — The soldiers sing this song very often. They do not like Copperheads at all — But I hope there will soon be no Copperheads up North. — They ought to be loyal all of them. I was very glad to get so many letters, and I hope you will write to me again soon. I will write to Hilda to night and put a letter in here for Ma. — I would like very much to have you all come down here and see me, but I can not send for you now, I am afraid we would move, before you could come — As soon as I get settled down in a place, then I will have you come down — If not then I expect to come home to you next fall. You must be a good boy take good care of Ma and learn to write a good hand. I shall want you for my Aid De Camp, when I get to be a General — or a clerk if I go back to Wisconsin to Keep Store. I want to have you learn to ride Horseback too — do you ever ride on the Pony?[40]

You must let me know how Turk is getting along[41] and how my Black Horse is doing — I have sent Ma a good deal of money and you must keep my accounts and let me know how much she owes me — I think she must owe me a good deal when I have paid for her house and Lot. — I wish I could see little Nebby — I know he must be a funny fellow now. Does he go down to the Store often? and has Ma made him any Military clothes yet? She must make him a pair of blue Pantaloons and an officers Coat for Summers. — He will make a fine little officer wont he? Tell little General *Ellsworth* that he must write to his papa — soon — [42]

I think I shall go up to Nashville in a day or two, and if I get time I will take my Photograph and send home to you —

Good bye — be a good boy — show this song to the Union *Men* — Those that like the Copperheads wont like it much.

Good Bye
Your own PaPa

8.
Murfreesboro — April 24, 1863

Dear Edmund,

I have not had time to write to you for a good while — I have expected letters from you but I have not got any — You do not write very often — How is Turk now, is he still alive?

I send Hilda some money in her letter the last time and I intended to have sent you some in this, but I am a little afraid it may get lost — I will wait till I hear if Hildas came through safe —       Are you going to the German School yet?[43] I want you to learn the German language — and not to forget the Norwegian — You will see that it is necessary if we shall keep store.

If you and I go in partnership keeping Store we shall have to hire *Nebby* for our clerk.

How does the little Rat like his new house? You must write me some good long letters and tell Hans Wood to do so too —       Next fall I expect to come home to you for good — and I hope to find you a good smart boy — I will not write to you till I get a letter from you now

Good Night
Your PaPa

Good Night to Hilda & Nebby too

9.

3d Brigade May 12th 1863

My Dear Edmund—

I get letters from you very seldom—You dont write as often as I think you ought to. I am sorry to hear that Ma complains of you sometime—You should keep away from all the bad boys around the streets, and try to be a real good boy. If you are a good boy then I will come back to you soon and stay at home all the time with you.—I dont want to come back and find a bad boy.—I suppose Ma had the *Blues* and I suppose when she wrote to me about you being a bad boy sometimes—she said that for an excuse.

Have you been up to see how it looks up on the Farm lately? I want you to tell me all about it—how are the sheep? I heard that you was [sic]going to the German School—have you quit? I want you to keep on steady where you begin—if you go to one school—you must keep on at that one all the time—and not run from one thing to another or you will never amount to anything at all.

Tell how the Store is running—has Ole got much goods[44]—Write often to me and I will answer you—and give the letter that is in with this one to Ma—I shall expect to hear that you are a *real good boy always.*

Your PaPa

10.

3d Brigade June 3d 1863

My Dear Edmund,

I wrote to Hilda yesterday, and promised to write to you this time. I got your letter. I am glad to hear that the Sheep are washed, and to hear that you are going to school and learning fast. You must try to write often, and by and by you will be able to write a good letter.

I have bought a very handsome Horse now, that I will try and take care of so that I can bring him home with me when I come. He is very big and handsome. And I have got a very pretty mare that I shall bring home for Hilda, and if you will learn to ride on the Black Horse, I suppose that will have to be yours now. And Ma & Nebby will have the Pony—you dont tell me any thing about the Pony, have you got him yet? You dont tell me if Turk is alive or not. You ought to write to me often. You may tell Ma that Albert Skofstad[45] got a letter from the 3d Regiment saying that Simon Thorsdal is dead—And tell her that I will write to her next time. I am coming home in the fall, perhaps for good—You must see that your sheep are taken good care of and that Ole Luraas does not keep any Bucks with them during the summer. I can not write any news—I get the Milwaukee and Madison Papers, and the Racine Advocate.[46] I must close—give Nebby a kiss for me and give Ma one too.

Good by. Be a good Boy<br>From your PaPa

11.

July 7 1863

Dear Edmund—

I get very few letters from you. Why dont you write to me oftener? I wish you would tell me what sort of a celebration you had on the 4th and how the wheat up on the farm looks—

Do you want me to build a store on Ma's lot?[47] One that you could keep store in—in company with me? If you will learn to write well, and be a smart man—I shall have to do as Waage has done—take you in Partnership with me and start a good big store. In your next letter you may send me a few Postage Stamps—and I want you to send Mothers Photograph with Even if you can get her to take it.[48] I do not care about a daguerreotype—I want a good Photograph—I want you to see that she puts on her best clothes and dresses up like a *Generals Wife*—I would like to get Nebbys Picture too—and if the little rascal wont send me his picture I shall have to give him a good spanking when I come home.

Nebby must write to me too.

Good Bye my Boy<br>From your PaPa

Dear Hilda, I have [no] time to write a letter to you today —
but I will write to you to morrow or next day. I am glad to
hear you have a music teacher.[49] I know you will be a nice
young lady by the time I get back home — and I shall be very
proud of having a smart little girl like you —      I will take
you along with me to a good many places when I get home
from the war — Your Mare is very fine — I ride her every day —

Good by my little Darling,

Your PaPa

12.
3d Brigade July 28, 1863

My Boy,

In Hilda's letter I promised to write to you next time — I
got four letters all right and I only wish you would write
oftener than you do — You should practice writing so that you
learn to write a good hand.

When I was as old as you are I could write very well and
I had not gone to school but very little. If you was down here
I would let you see what fine Horse I have got — and I have
got me a good Buggy too — just as good as the one we had at
Waupun — I can not tell you when I am coming home — but
when I come I shall let you know it and have you all meet me
in Chicago. — I suppose you get all the wine you want to drink
now that Ma has made so much — you must live well up in
your new house — I think you have the best place in Waterford. I only wish I could come up and help you build a good
Barn and fix up everything for you well —      I send you
$200 and $100 for Nebby. I sent him some in Hildas letter, tell
the little rascal that he must not say that he is not my boy or
I will not send him any candy money —

Good night, be a good Boy

Your PaPa

# Notes

[1] Theodore C. Blegen, *Norwegian Migration to America: The American Transition* (Northfield, Minnesota, 1940), 392.

[2] The population of Milwaukee in 1840 was 1,712 and in 1846, 9,655. Bayrd Still, *Milwaukee, The History of a City* (Madison, Wisconsin, 1965), 570; James S. Ritchie, *Wisconsin and Its Resources; with Lake Superior, Its Commerce and Navigation* (Chicago, 1858), 86.

[3] Clarence A. Clausen and Andreas Elviken, eds. and trans., *A Chronicle of Old Muskego: The Diary of Søren Bache, 1839-1847* (Northfield, Minnesota, 1951), 143.

[4] Joseph Schafer, "Five Wisconsin Pioneers," in *The Wisconsin Blue Book* (Madison, Wisconsin, 1933), 38.

[5] Leola N. Bergmann, *Americans from Norway* (Philadelphia, 1950), 262–263; Blegen, ed., *The Civil War Letters of Colonel H.C. Heg* (Northfield, Minnesota, 1936), 65.

[6] Blegen, *The Civil War Letters*, 154, 249.

[7] Annetta is buried in the Norway churchyard, Muskego.

[8] Hilda Heg married Charles N. Fowler, congressman from New Jersey. She died February 20, 1932.

[9] Blegen, *The Civil War Letters*, 56.

[10] Blegen, *The Civil War Letters*, 226, 225.

[11] The children born to Edmund and Ella were Walter (died 1909), Lois (1877–1961), Katherine (1878–1953), James Elmer (1884–1971), Ernest Clark (1887–1968), and another child who died in infancy.

[12] *The Lake Geneva Herald*, April 13, 1914.

[13] This letter was probably included with another written to Gunild. Reference to "the Piano" places the letter after Heg's return on June 4, 1862, from a leave in Wisconsin. Evidently he had bought the piano for his family when he was on leave. Blegen, *The Civil War Letters*, 91–93. Heg's mention of selling the sheep "this fall" indicates that the letter must have been written in the early summer of 1862.

[14] This letter was probably finished on November 1, 1862, when Heg was recuperating from a cold at the Morgan House Hotel in Bowling Green, Kentucky. The regiment was expected to catch up with him at this place "sometime tomorrow." Blegen, *The Civil War Letters*, 150–151.

[15] DuBartus Willard of Racine. Blegen, *The Civil War Letters*, 105, 151, 235.

[16] Blegen, *The Civil War Letters*, 140–142, 148.

[17] Blegen, *The Civil War Letters*, 150–151.

[18] Heg had bought some land in Minnesota, apparently as an investment. Blegen, *The Civil War Letters*, 191, 205.

[19] Fergus Ferguson was a corporal in Company D and Heg's orderly.

[20] The Fifteenth Wisconsin had participated in the Union City, Tennes-

see, expedition in March of 1862 and in the battle of Perryville, October 8, 1862.

²¹Blegen, *The Civil War Letters*, 87.

²²At one time, the paymaster was as much as four months late. Blegen, *The Civil War Letters*, 87, 101. The remuneration paid to Heg was between $200 and $250 per month, on which he paid a federal tax. Blegen, *The Civil War Letter*, 232.

²³Heg had been home on leave for thirty days. Blegen, *The Civil War Letters*, 153n.

²⁴Dr. Stephen O. Himoe, Heg's brother-in-law, was surgeon of the Fifteenth Wisconsin from November 11, 1861, to November 13, 1863. Blegen, *The Civil War Letters* 49n, 156; E. Biddle Heg, "Stephen O. Himoe, Civil War Physician," in *Norwegian-American Studies and Records*, 11 (Northfield, Minnesota, 1940), 30–56.

²⁵It is interesting to note how very few errors in spelling and rhetoric are made by Heg in the many letters he wrote to his family during the war, especially as his formal education was quite limited. In editing, the spelling has in a few instances been regularized. He "attended the common schools, but there is no evidence that a thought was ever given to the possibility of a higher education for him." Blegen, *The Civil War Letters*, 8. It is quite possible that he was a member of a "school" class organized by Claus L. Clausen or his wife Martha. Nils N. Rønning, *The Saga of Old Muskego* (Waterford, Wisconsin, 1943), 20.

²⁶The Fifteenth Wisconsin was involved in the action at Knob Gap on December 26, 1862, and in the battle of Murfreesboro, between December 30, 1862, and January 2, 1863.

²⁷Captain John M. Johnson of Madison, Wisconsin, second captain of Company A.

²⁸Claus Lauritz Clausen, first chaplain of the Fifteenth Wisconsin. Blegen, *The Civil War Letters*, 69n; Rønning, *The Saga of Old Muskego*, 18, 28–29.

²⁹General Jefferson C. Davis, Division Commander.

³⁰The Farmers and Millers Bank in Milwaukee, incorporated in 1853 under the 1852 free-banking law, later became the First Wisconsin National Bank "and one of the most influential banks in Wisconsin finance." Leonard B. Krueger, "History of Commercial Banking in Wisconsin," in *University of Wisconsin Studies in the Social Sciences*, 18 (Madison, Wisconsin, 1933), 62.

³¹Edward D. Holton (1815–1902), an entrepreneur, was one of several influential civic leaders in early Milwaukee. Still, *Milwaukee*, 53–54. Holton had some connection with *The Milwaukee Daily Sentinel* newspaper and was president of the Farmers and Millers Bank from 1852 to 1862. John C. Gregory, *History of Milwaukee, Wisconsin*, 1 (Chicago, 1931), 399–400; Blegen, *The Civil War Letters*, 107, 174.

³²Blegen, *The Civil War Letters*, 176n.

³³"The *Sentinel*, published daily, tri-weekly, and weekly (Republican),

is the oldest and most widely circulated. As a political and commercial journal it is regarded throughout the north-west with general favor. Jermain and Brightman, the publishers, have materially improved the sheet within the last two years, and widened its circulation accordingly." A. C. Wheeler, *The Chronicles of Milwaukee* (Milwaukee, Wisconsin, 1861), 286.

[34]Andrea Heg, sister to Colonel Heg, was born in 1835 in Norway, and married Dr. Stephen O. Himoe, surgeon of the Fifteenth Wisconsin.

[35]The date of this letter is difficult to establish. It appears that Heg sent the black horse and his Negro servant, Gipsom, home to Wisconsin with Even Skofstad, who left camp January 7, 1863. It is probable that this letter was written between January 8 and February 16, 1863, when Heg wrote again to Edmund. Blegen, *The Civil War Letters*, 169–170, 175.

[36]Hans Wood was a close friend of Heg. He was employed to look after Heg's interests in Waterford and at the farm and to help Gunild Heg with the management of house and store. At one point, Gunild has some question in her mind as to the expense of employing him. Blegen, *The Civil War Letters*, 55, 92–93.

[37]Heg and his family had owned a house in Waupun, where he was State Prison Commissioner from January 2, 1860, to January 6, 1862. He sold this property in late 1862. Blegen, *The Civil War Letters*, 153–154. The Heg family had previously bought a store property in Waterford. However, Heg wanted a separate home there for his family; and after the sale of the Waupun property, he became more interested in such a purchase. Finally, between the middle of February and the end of March, 1863, Gunild purchased the Hovey property in Waterford. She and the children moved into their new home in the first part of April, 1863. Blegen, *The Civil War Letters*, 197–198, 205.

[38]The sheep were kept on the Heg farm about four miles north of the town of Waterford, This farm was purchased by Hans Heg's father from John Nelson Luraas, who came to Wind Lake in 1839. George T. Flom, *A History of Norwegian Immigration to The United States* (Iowa City, Iowa, 1909), 68, 241–242. The purchase was made in the late spring of 1843, at which time (by the end of May) John Luraas had moved west to Dane county. In the spring of 1863, a purchase offer apparently having been made to him, Hans Heg considered the value of his farm to be $25 an acre. Blegen *The Civil War Letters*, 201. The farm was approximately 320 acres and contained the family homestead and the great barn. After Hans and his family moved to Waterford in 1859, he left the farm in the care of Ole Luraas, who is mentioned many times in Heg's letters to his wife. Evidently Luraas managed the farm completely, though not always to Heg's full satisfaction. Blegen, *The Civil War Letters*, 200, 217. On the farm Luraas raised such livestock as horses and sheep as well as grains and other produce. Some time before 1866 the farm was sold to Tollef Jensen and his wife. Then on December 6, 1866, it was sold sold by the Jensens to Halvor Bendickson, who married Anna

Anderson, daughter of Ole Anderson who came to Wisconsin with the Heg family in 1840. Ella S. Colbo,*Historic Heg Memorial Park* (Racine, Wisconsin, 1940), 10, 61.

[39]Major General William S. Rosecrans. Heg's estimate of Rosecrans is given in his letter to Gunild, October 26,1862. General Rosecrans discouraged Heg on several occasions from having Gunild with him while he was on duty in the South. Blegen, *The Civil War Letters*, 193, 204, 211, 213.

[40]Heg writes to Gunild, September 26, 1862, "I have one of the prettiest little Ponies you ever saw, that I bought on Edmunds Birthday." Blegen, *The Civil War Letters*, 140. He sent the pony home to Edmund and inquires in several letters how his son likes the pony. In one letter to Gunild, he is annoyed because Edmund is afraid to ride the pony. Blegen, *The Civil War Letters*, 201.

[41]Turk is the family dog, much beloved by the children. Turk was killed by someone in Waterford at the end of May, 1863, and Heg named his new horse after Turk. Blegen, *Civil War Letters*, 54, 115, 216.

[42]Hans Heg facetiously calls his youngest son, Elmer Ellsworth Heg, the "little General," as he was named after General Elmer Ellsworth, the Zouave commander.

[43]At the time of this letter, Edmund was ten years and five months old, old enough to attend an elementary school.In the town of Waterford, the first school was established in 1840, and the first schoolhouse was built at Rice's Corners some years later. In the early days, before the state organized the school districts in 1858, many of the school activities were held in local churches. Such was the case in Waterford. In the early 1860s school was held in the basement of the old Congregational Church at the west end of Main Street. Colbo, *Historic Heg Memorial Park*, 58. For a discussion of early education in Wisconsin see Consul W. Butterfield, *The History of Racine and Kenosha Counties, Wisconsin* (Chicago, 1878), 140–142, 146–147, 484.

[44]Ole Heg, the Colonel's younger brother, was born in Norway June 2l, 1831, and died at Burlington, Wisconsin, April 18, 1911. He was quartermaster of the Fifteenth Wisconsin Regiment until his resignation on June 6, 1862. His first wife was Smilie Christenson, who died in 1856. On January 27, 1861, Ole married her sister Nanna, whom he took with him in the service until she became ill and returned to Wisconsin in early April, 1862. Hans Heg sold his interest in the Waterford store to Ole for $2,000 in 1862. Later Ole took Christen Hatlestad as a partner in the store business. Blegen, *The Civil War Letters*, 57, 78, 109, 237. In 1874 Ole Heg was a member of the Board of Supervisors of Racine county, a position which his brother Hans had held in 1855 and 1856. Butterfield, *The History of Racine and Kenosha Counties*, 316. Hans was most critical of his brother's lack of enthusiasm for any war service.

[45]"Albert" was Anthon Skofstad, the son of Johannes Evensen Skofstad and Berthe Olsdatter, sister of Sigrid (Siri) Olsdatter, Hans Heg's mother.

Anthon was born in 1839 and with his family came to America in August, 1840, on the *Emilie*, when he was nine months old. He served as captain in the Civil War. Clausen, "An Immigrant Shipload of 1840," in *Norwegian-American Studies and Records*, 14 (1944), 63; Hans C. Brandt, "Letter to Friends, June 22, 1841," in Blegen, ed., *Land of Their Choice* (St. Paul, Minnesota, 1955), 80; J.A. Johnson, *Det Skandinaviske Regiments Historie* (La Crosse, Wisconsin, 1869), 121.

[46]Heg subscribed to three Wisconsin newspapers which he received regularly: *Emigranten, State Journal,* and *Racine Advocate.* Blegen, *The Civil War Letters,* 209.

[47]In a letter dated June 23, 1863, Heg discusses plans for a store building to be put up for Ole and himself in partnership or for himself alone. Blegen, *The Civil War Letters,* 218, 225.

[48]Even Skofstad, older brother of Anthon Skofstad, set up a "sutler shop" with Christen Hatlestad in March, 1863, at the front. Even Skofstad made several trips to Wisconsin and he was probably in Waterford at this time. Blegen, *The Civil War Letters,* 197–198.

[49]Blegen, *The Civil War Letters,* 228, 230.

# 10

# The Americanization of the Norwegian Pastors' Wives

*by Gracia Grindal*

The world of the pastors' wives in the early Norwegian-American parsonages was a predictable mixture of Norwegian and American traditions and practices. Just exactly what the mixture was still needs to be analyzed. One can learn about the way in which these immigrants adapted to the New World by examining a variety of cultural phenomena, from their press to their art and literature. One of the frequently overlooked perspectives on their acculturation is a close look at the way the women adapted to American life in their kitchens.

This article will focus on a particular drawing by Linka Preus, wife of Herman Amberg Preus, the president of the Norwegian Synod, one of the oldest and, until the 1880s, the largest of the Norwegian Lutheran churches in America. Linka was considered by most of the Synod pastors' wives, who were generally of the upper class, to be their leader; they wrote to her frequently for advice about a variety of problems they met on the new frontier.

Linka not only kept up a long and vigorous correspondence with many of these women, she also was a gifted artist whose sketches of their times together were valued by everyone. It is the sketch she did in October, 1862, of herself and her young companion Henriette Neuberg which will be considered carefully in this article.

Linka (Caroline Dorothea Margrethe) Preus was born in Christiansand, Norway, July 2, 1829, to Agnes Louise Carlsen and Christian Nicolai Keyser, a pastor and later a professor of Sacred Theology at the University of Christiania (Oslo). Her mother died when she was ten and left her to be raised by her father, who died when she was seventeen. As he was in ill health before his death, he sent young Linka from Christiania, where he was teaching, to Askevold, a small parish north of Bergen, to her mother's sister, Mrs. J. Carl Christie, whose husband was also a clergyman. There she was to learn household management and other skills which cultivated young women of the time were expected to possess. She helped instruct the three Christie children for their confirmation and learned to run a household. Her diary from this period indicates that she spent a regular part of each day in reading books such as Sir Walter Scott's *Redgauntlet*, playing the piano, participating in dramatic productions in the home, sewing, spinning, weaving, skating, skiing, gardening, and drawing. Her life as she describes it sounds placid and happy.

The system by which young women learned to be housewives was one of apprenticeship, generally in the home of a close relative or friend of the family. As the century wore on, women began to receive more formal education. This differed markedly from Linka's education, though her social class allowed her the leisure to pursue more of the fine arts and letters than most young girls growing up in Norway at the time. Linka's hunger for a life of the mind grew keener as she grew older, and sometimes she bitterly resented the fact that men had the chance to learn theology while she was expected to darn socks, wondering what, if anything at all, her education was worth. Writing in her diary after her arrival in America, she noted the "advantages a man has over a woman. It is not my opinion that he is more gifted than woman, but that his mind has been developed by many more kinds of knowledge than has woman's. Her intellectual growth is regarded as of secondary importance, as something useless, bringing no benefit to the world. When these thoughts occupy my mind, I frequently become embittered, as it all seems so unjust."[1]

In earlier entries in the diary, one can see the practical kind of education she is getting at the Christies' when she has to decide whether or not to butcher a young calf: "April 1, 1850. Meanwhile, all a housewife's duties have rested on my young shoulders. At first I found it very difficult, but now affairs run as smoothly as though I had been a housewife for years—the food question was especially worrisome, and Mondays were always filled with thoughts of food for the ensuing week. A couple of days ago I was in a great pinch, and we had to butcher a calf, but the old saying, 'Out of season the trolls shall be killed,' indeed came true, for no sooner was the animal slaughtered than Uncle was presented with a hindquarter of beef, and the selfsame day other gifts arrived, a great number of large flounders and some lobsters. Could anything have been more awkward? If only the meat and fish had arrived half an hour earlier, then all would have been well. Now I had to salt some of the veal and the beef—but of salted meat we have enough. To provide Uncle with fresh meat had been my plan, as he likes that best; and now perhaps I shall merit a scolding from Aunty because her pretty calf no longer frolics about."[2]

One reads here the words of a young woman learning how to manage things for the benefit of the rest of the household. But when she writes that she had to salt some beef and veal, it is certain that she did not slaughter the animal herself or become too intimately involved with the dirtiest part of the butchering process. For that she had a good supply of servants.

The cookbook which Linka and her friends in America swore by was that of Fru Hanna Winsnes, *Lærebog i de forskellige grene af huusholdningen* (A Textbook on the Various Branches of Household Economy), which was first published in 1845 and went through twelve editions by 1878. Mrs. Winsnes wrote the book, she said later, to help those young women whose education had been mostly frivolous to cope with the staggering business of managing a large household.

In the preface to the first edition, reprinted in subsequent editions, she marveled that men received so much training for their work, while women received almost none. Her book assumes that women will grow up to be housewives: "I am convinced that each young wife and engaged girl wants to manage her husband's household to his advantage and satisfaction, but the new educational methods keep young women away from home management. The inexperienced young woman is troubled by her uncertainty in this unknown area. Therefore, I am writing this book to help her overcome her anxieties."[3]

The criticism Mrs. Winsnes made of the new educational system is worth considering. She was a writer of romantic novels which she published under the name of Hugo Schwarz. A pastor's wife herself, she was from the official class and continued in the venerable tradition of "parsonage" literature. So she was very much like those women of the nineteenth century who were beginning to participate formally in the masculine life of letters even as she lamented the loss of the peculiarly feminine kind of education which would have kept her from her books. She was, in her career, an example of the very problem which she sought to address.

Her book is filled with practical and helpful instructions on the working of the kitchen: how to care for animals before and during slaughter, the preservation of food, the making of wine and beer. Though she did not develop anything like the full rationale for keeping women in the home that Catharine Beecher did in America, her sense that something had changed was strong. Both Mrs. Winsnes and Miss Beecher feared that the smattering of male education which women were beginning to get as the century wore on only taught women they were too good to work in the kitchen. Mrs. Winsnes did not fill her book, as Catharine Beecher did, with pious references to the sacred duty women have to maintain hearth and home, nor did she try to glorify housekeeping as a science as Miss Beecher did with her paeans of praise for the woman who understands that her work as housewife requires a good bit of formal scientific knowledge, like chemistry and physics.[4]

Mrs. Winsnes has more of the eighteenth century about

her. She was writing for young women of the upper class whose work in the household would be to make the home completely self-sufficient. It was her book which Linka, as the bride of a newly ordained pastor, brought with her to America in 1851 when she and Herman arrived in Spring Prairie, Wisconsin, ready to begin a ministry there which lasted until Herman's death in 1894. The young couple came in response to a call from the Norwegian-American church. Because of their romantic approval of the hearty and fiercely democratic Norwegian peasants and of American ways, they were prepared to adapt to the New World.

Linka describes her first glimpse of the future parsonage, without too much dismay, as merely a hole with water in it. Her youth and hopefulness were great supports at this time, though life must have seemed exceedingly difficult and primitive. When their cabin was finished she wrote that it was so cramped that when they had three people at table, the third, generally she, would have to sit on the bed. But, in general, her tone is more one of hearty accommodation than of despair.

Not long after the Preuses were established, they were visited by another young couple, Vilhelm and Elisabeth Koren, who were on their way to Washington Prairie congregation near Decorah, Iowa. Mrs. Koren also had to adapt to the rugged life of the frontier after being raised in the home of a teacher in Larvik, Norway. Her letters to Linka reveal her to be confident about many things, but still a trifle worried about how, exactly, one goes about the many tasks of raising and preserving food for the long winters. Though both of these women were able to call on the services of young confirmands, teenagers who would work for the pastor as they learned the Lutheran catechism, they never could expect the loyal and longtime help from a family servant that they had known in Norway. Mrs. Koren writes frequently about the lack of good servants in America and allows, in one of her more exasperated moments, that the only reason she would return to Norway to live would be for decent household help. In America conditions were not the same and the women

adapted more or less successfully. That they did adapt is good evidence that they understood quite well the difference between America and Norway.

This sketch which Linka made of herself and her longtime companion and friend, Henriette Neuberg, cleaning an animal's intestines is good evidence of that adaptability.

Mrs. Winsnes wrote in her book that before slaughtering an animal one should make certain there was enough help: at least two boys to cut and hang the carcass, and at least two girls to clean the intestines. "Two girls have enough to do the first day with cleaning the intestines and the stomach, and a third would be helpful."[5]

Such instructions must have amused Linka as she was working. It would almost seem as if she had drawn this picture to say that in America things were quite different. The heading for the picture says, "Fruen og Frøkenen maa selv rense Tarmen i denne Slagten" ("the lady of the house and the young lady must themselves clean the intestines in this slaughter"). The sentence by itself is ironic, but set against the language of Mrs. Winsnes, which Linka had undoubtedly just read, it shows exactly how inappropriate these instructions were to the American situation.

In this self-portrait, Linka is on the left, holding the knife Mrs. Winsnes suggested in her book. One would not describe the portrait as flattering; in fact, that is part of the fun of the drawing: she seems to have enjoyed setting herself into the picture almost like the hefty peasant which she was not. The woman portrayed here is one accustomed to work. And yet, that it is a self-portrait shows her self-awareness and maturity. The woman on the right is Henriette Neuberg, who lived with the Preus family for years. She was a sister of the first wife of Laur. Larsen, the first president of Luther College. Henriette was no servant. As a member of the upper class she doubtless expected to marry well.[6] Her beauty is frequently spoken of in letters from Elisabeth Koren and other pastors' wives, and her endearing warmth as a governess and a companion to the women and children made her a sought-after guest and helper. Though sometimes both she and her younger sister, Karine, were unhappy in a system which simply did not allow either of them the opportunity to work or to be "their own masters," as Karine wished to be, they were very much a part of it until their deaths.

Dependent on their brother-in-law, Laur. Larsen, for money and legal protection, they lived for several years with either the Preuses or the Larsens. They helped in the house and with the education of the children, which wearied the wives, who followed their mothers' example and sent their girls to other parsonages where they could learn the skills of domestic economy from the "aunts" as they had thirty years before.

Once Karine wrote Henriette, not long after this drawing was completed, and said, "Oh, Henriette, I can tell you are weary of working for Preus!" It is not too far-fetched to imagine that Henriette had expressed some disgust at having to clean the intestines of the animal. Still, in this picture, one can see the frank look of pleasure and amusement in the faces of the two women, not so much from their work as from their awareness of its incongruity. Their sophistication does not make them shrink from a scene like this, it allows them to endure it. In America the wife and the governess must do such things.

Though both of these women have been trained to be very like the decorative ladies of the nineteenth-century drawing room, there is still much that is of the eighteenth century about their cool view of themselves. Linka was no coquette; she laughed when the conductor of the train they were riding through Michigan would not allow her into the "ladies' car" because she was not wearing hoops.

As a frontier wife, Linka was independent and productive. She liked managing the farm which she and Herman bought in Spring Prairie and she was successful at it, receiving little help from her husband, whose work kept him away from home a good part of the time. Perhaps one could argue that it was the frontier which gave Linka the chance to develop her talent as a manager to its fullest and gave her a rich sense of being a productive partner in the marriage. If she had lived in the East, an entirely different pattern of acculturation might have obtained.

Given the frontier, however, she and other pastors' wives were able to maintain some of the traditions of the old country, even as they understood that certain of the old ways would clearly have to change. Those pastors' wives such as Caja Munch and others who could not adapt to the New World and its more democratic ways were defeated by the crudity of the frontier and returned to Norway.[7] Much too much has been made of the social superiority of the leaders of the Norwegian Synod by historians looking at them from the point of view of their enemies. To be sure, the Preuses, Larsens, Hjorts, and Korens were "bedrefolk"and not of a class with the cotters (*husmand*) who immigrated in such large numbers. Both the Korens and the Preuses lived on the frontier in the most primitive of conditions and survived well, not because of their rank in society but because they were strong enough to survive. Caja Munch's demand to be treated as a woman of privilege only brought her disaster. Linka Preus and Elisabeth Koren survived happily and well because of their hearty sense for what was possible and their ability to adapt to the new situation with good humor. This drawing shows as well as anything the intelligence and amusement with which at least one pastor's wife adapted to the new land.

## Notes

[1]Linka Preus, *Linka's Diary: On Land and Sea*, trans. and ed. by Johan Carl Keyser Preus and Diderikke Margrethe Brandt Preus (Minneapolis, 1952), 198.

[2]Preus, *Linka's Diary*, 83–84.

[3]Hanna Winsnes, *Lærebog i de forskellige grene af huusholdningen* (Christiania, 1845), iv.

[4]Catharine Beecher, *A Treatise on Domestic Economy* (New York, 1841).

[5]Winsnes, *Lærebog*, 61.

[6]Henriette Neuberg left America for Norway in 1866. In 1875 she married Pastor O. J. Hjort and returned to America. She died in childbirth in 1879.

[7]Caja Munch's letters home are filled with sentiments about America which seldom escaped the pens of either Elisabeth Koren or Linka Preus. See Helene and Peter A. Munch, trans. and ed., *The Strange American Way: Letters of Caja Munch from Wiota, Wisconsin, 1855–1859* (Carbondale, Illinois, 1970).

# 11

## Rølvaag's Lost Novel

*by Einar Haugen*

Of all that Ole Edvart Rølvaag wrote the least read work is surely the story on which he lavished the most time, his apprentice work titled "Nils og Astri." It exists in a neatly handwritten author's copy, presumably his last redaction of 1910, in the Norwegian-American Historical Association archives at St. Olaf College. The present author's recent survey of Rølvaag's life and work characterized it briefly, and there are fuller accounts in the monumental studies by Jorgenson and Solum, in English, and by Gvåle in Norwegian.[1] Rølvaag began writing it while still a senior at St. Olaf College, in 1904–1905, less than ten years out of Norway. He dreamed of selling it to finance his first trip back home, but Aschehoug, which would later publish his world-famous novels in Norway, rejected it out of hand, and he had no better luck in later years with Norwegian-American publishers. By 1912 he had finally thrown it overboard and embarked on his true literary career with his first printed novel, *Amerika-breve* (America-letters), which enjoyed a modest success.[2]

"Nils og Astri" is written in copybooks with numbered pages: Part One in 232 pages, Part Two in 201 pages. There is reason to believe that it was completed in the year 1910, as the preface is dated July of that year. Part One was probably composed in his senior year at St. Olaf; its content bears the mark of Rølvaag's parochial school teaching during the summers of 1903 and 1904. Part Two gives the impression of being hastily written in order to round off the story. By this time he had come to realize that his publishing-house critics were right. In a letter to his friend Ole Farseth dated October 26, 1910, he wrote that Waldemar Ager's novel *Kristus for Pilatus* (Christ before Pilate) had set a standard for Norwegian-American literature that he had not yet equaled.[3.] Even so, this youthful novel has much to interest the student of Rølvaag's career. It reveals a great deal of his background in both life and letters, while at the same time pointing forward to themes that would be more successfully integrated into his later work.

First of all there is his choice of setting: the entire story takes place in a rural South Dakota community such as the one Rølvaag had experienced during his first years in America. He did not choose to describe the Norwegian scene, as did many other immigrant writers, and as he would do in one later novel, *Længselens baat* (Boat of Longing, 1921). He calls the community "Greenfield." The name, like the one he chose in *Amerika-breve* and *Paa glemte veie* (On Forgotten Paths), is reminiscent of the Northfield in which his college was located. The name of his hero Nils would be used again in *Længselens baat* about a dreamer with musical talent. His last name, Haugen, would recur in *Paa glemte veie* for the pastor who is to become the heroine's husband. Nil's father Ole is of course named for the author himself, and he is in fact the spokesman for many of Rølvaag's ideas about the failings of the American environment and the importance of preserving the Norwegian heritage. His querulous criticism of society is unlike Rølvaag's more balanced temper, but Rølvaag may have felt a certain unpopularity and suspicion not unlike that which Ole and after him Nils have to endure from an uncomprehending environment, The heroine's name, Astri, may come from a well-known Norwegian folk song about love, called "Astri, mi Astri." The noble schoolteacher, later pastor, is called Aasmundsen, possibly suggested by the first name of Aasmund Vinje, a well-known poet. The villain, Per Ammandus Skogen, bears a first name much used in Rølvaag's family, that of his father and a brother, but his second name suggests something foreign, ironically a name that means "one who is to be loved," since the character in this story is just the opposite.

The story is all too obviously modeled on Bjørnson's peasant tales from the mid-century, widely admired and imitated by folksy authors: *Synnøve Solbakken* (1857), *Arne* (1858–1859), *En glad gut* (A Happy Boy, 1860), and *Fiskerjenten* (The Fisher Maiden, 1868). The subtitle, *Fragments of Norwegian-American Folk Life*, is suggestive of these books. He dedicated it to "the Norwegian-reading Norwegian-American young people," a departure from the pattern, but one that places it in the mainstream of Rølvaag's work as a professor of Norwegian in America. Norwegian-American schools were still being conducted in Norwegian, although the first signs of language shift were appearing, signs that would become a flood before Rølvaag's death.[4]

In a short preface he disclaimed any intention of writing a "literary work" and called it "mainly short pieces" grouped around Nils and Astri. "It is not a thrilling novel, in which exciting events follow one another in sequence." "Still I have the belief that the book may provide entertainment in an idle hour." These statements are a measure of the naiveté, but also the understated modesty of the author at this time. In fact the novel is cast entirely in the traditional mode of the romantic tale. Boy meets girl, they are separated by sinister forces, but in the end boy wins girl and they live happily ever after. There is an abundance of "exciting events," especially in Part Two, and the reader's patience is sorely tried by the hindrances which this amateur author places in the way of the happy ending.

Although Part One takes place on a South Dakota farm, the atmosphere is saturated with Norwegian sentiment. Not only is Ole Haugen, the father, vehemently Norwegian, but the hired girl Lina, whom he has imported to bring up the motherless Nils, is from Nordland, Rølvaag's Norwegian home. She is an early version of Rølvaag's backward-looking women, his Magdalena in *Paa glemte veie*, Kristine in *Længselens baat*, and above all Beret in *Giants in the Earth* and its sequels. She embodies one aspect of Rølvaag's own "divided heart," which he first presented in the Per Smevik of *Amerika-breve*. Like Per, Lina is the "newcomer" who is out of tune with the Norwegian-American environment in which she has landed: "one of the many pieces of flotsam that the stream of emigration took hold of and carried far, far away to a foreign land." She finds the young people, who speak English, strange; and even those who speak Norwegian do so with a mixture of unfamiliar English words and expressions. She finds some solace in spoiling the child Nils, and fills him with tales from the rich folklore of Nordland. Like Per Smevik's preacher, she climbs to the top of the nearest bluff and gazes on the prairie as if it were the sea, a comparison that Rølvaag was to carry into *Giants in the Earth* as well. To Nils's astonishment, Lina weeps from longing for the sea. Later on, the reader learns her story in more detail: she emigrated because she lost her fiancé on a fishing expedition in the great storm of 1893, which nearly took Rølvaag's own life and led to his emigration in 1896. Like Kristine's in *Længselens baat*, her fiancé's name is Johan, a name that may come from Rølvaag's oldest brother.

Nils as a child is already a mixture of willfulness and artistic talent, very much like his Bjørnsonian models, Thorbjørn and Arne. Like these as well as Bjørnson's Øivind and Petra, the "Fisher Maiden," he grows up in a relatively poor family, since his father has been crippled and has had to rent his farm out. Nils's talent is musical, and he follows his father in a passion for the violin. Lina buys him a cheap fiddle, and he learns readily to play anything he hears.

Most of Part One is devoted to Nils's schooling, chiefly in the Norwegian summer school. The American common school is referred to only in passing and with some contempt. This section begins with an essay that compares children to colts that need careful handling for their successful training. Nils's first teacher goads him into competition with Per Ammandus Skogen, resulting in their becoming enemies for life. Per has "crafty eyes" and bribes the teacher with gifts of fruit and flowers. Eventually Nils meets Astri Bjarne, who becomes his first friend. At length Nils comes under the guidance of a competent teacher, Torger Aasmundsen, who knows how "to break in colts." Coincidentally, one of Per Ammandus's first exploits is to shoot and maim Nils's colt; the teacher compels him to apologize. Nils has a hideout by a "fairy rock" on the river, where he is joined by his friend Olaf Gilbertson and sometimes by Astri. Aasmundsen seeks him out and wins his confidence by joining him in fishing and playing tunes on his violin. He also tells his own life story, which is reminiscent of the schoolmaster's tale in Bjørnson's *En glad gut*. It is the story of two friends whose friendship is destroyed by rivalry over a girl; in a driving accident one of them is killed, which results in the other, Aasmundsen, leaving the community and going off to school.

Aasmundsen is asked to enforce a ban on swimming in the nearby river, but the pupils secretly defy him. The result is the near drowning of Lars, Astri's brother, but he is saved by Nils. When Aasmundsen learns of their disobedience, he is about to punish Nils until Astri informs him of the facts. Nils tries to express his love for Astri in melody, but because of her mother's distaste for Nils, she only half admits her fondness for him. Aasmundsen's problems in teaching are the topic of a discussion which obviously reflects Rølvaag's philosophy: that each pupil needs his or her special approach, and that the class is like a garden in which each plant needs his care.

On the way home from school Astri and her brother Lars are caught in a storm and Astri falls seriously ill. Nils brings flowers, and in spite of the reluctance of her parents, he prays for her recovery. There follows a passage about his father Ole, who has lost a lawsuit against the Skogens and is bitter about the American legal system. He becomes a relentless opponent of "Yankeedom," his name for all things American. At a party he and Skogen get into a bitter argument about the relative merits of Norway and America. In this discussion the author clearly sides with the father in his Norwegian advocacy, foreshadowing one of Rølvaag's major themes.

Astri recovers and the Skogens put on a party in her honor. It is "a dreamy, lovely summer night." Young people are enjoying themselves, dancing, flirting, playing last couple out. Per Ammandus manages to catch Astri, but she laughs at him and rejects his advances when he is bold enough to propose to her. She laughs, but accepts a package which proves to contain a gold watch, with a rather illiterate love letter. It is hinted that Per Ammandus has bought the watch with money stolen from his father's wallet. He devises a scheme to start a fight between Aasmundsen's pupils and those from another school, primarily in order to discredit Aasmundsen. But Aasmundsen smells out the plot and appears on the scene in time to stop the fight and lecture Per Ammandus on the principle that happiness in life can only result from goodness.

On the last day of school the pupils are sad at parting, and only Nils and Astri stay behind. He strokes her hair and cheek, and they part. So ends Part One: it is almost entirely a story of schooling and the teacher's role in inculcating religion and preventing strife. Much of it is in dialogue form. Rølvaag clearly put a great deal of his own experience as a teacher into the novel. Two major themes occupied him: the pedagogical problem, involving the "breaking" of colts or the cultivation of plants; and the conflict of Norwegian with English.

Part Two begins eight years later. Astri has studied music in Minneapolis for four years, after which Nils has studied in Chicago for three years. They have not corresponded, and in the meanwhile Astri has resignedly accepted Per Ammandus as her escort. He is back in Greenfield as a lawyer but with a dubious practice, defending a prisoner and the owner of a "blind pig," a legally outlawed saloon. His parents are proud of his eloquence. They are described as concerned only with making money, and the mother, Elizabeth, is such a hard bargainer that she has won the nickname "for little money" from the mixed-language phrase she uses when bargaining. The father subscribes to the Norwegian Chicago newspaper *Skandinaven* but reads only the farm prices. In this way the contrast is pointed up between these materialistic parents and the Haugens with their poverty but their higher standard of culture. Per Ammandus gets into poker games with a group of gamblers, three Jews and an Irishman, loses all his money, and decides he has to marry Astri to recoup his fortunes.

Aasmundsen has returned to Greenfield as a pastor. He invites the young people's society to his parsonage. The program goes well, including music by the pastor and Nils. The pastor senses that the classical music is not too popular and suggests that Nils play a Norwegian dance tune. He is also urged to play a composition of his own, in which he declares his love and longing for Astri. After the party they stay, while Nils pours out his experiences at the conservatory and expounds on the difference between surface beauty and true inward beauty. He compares the pain of original composition to the pangs of giving birth, a whole little essay expressing Rølvaag's own views on art. Lars comments to his sister that Nils actually "grew with every stroke of the bow," an idea reminiscent of Ibsen's description of Brand in the play of that name. Astri feels inadequate, though she dreams of sharing "his longing and melancholy and the wild flight of his thoughts."

The next scene is the annual Old Settlers' picnic in Greenfield, a festival for the pioneers. Here we find the germ of Rølvaag's *Giants in the Earth*, for he says of the pioneers that "all had performed miracles." They tell stories of "those days" (*i de dage*, the title of *Giants in the Earth* in Norwegian), "a long vanished time . . . when there lived giants on the earth," a quotation that became the motto of his later masterpiece. But now the picnic has "degenerated" into a dancing party. Per Ammandus trips and falls, blames Nils, and the two come to blows. The next day Nils is arrested for mayhem, and in the succeeding trial is sentenced to a fine and a 25-day jail term.

Aasmundsen steps into the case at Astri's request and accuses Per Ammandus of perjury. The villain then draws a revolver and threatens the pastor. But Aasmundsen disarms him and promises to take up the case on behalf of Nils.

Meanwhile Per Ammandus returns to his poker friends and is fleeced of a quarter section of land worth $30,000. Heavily intoxicated and befuddled, he falls into the grass and dies of heart failure. The scene is long-drawn-out and boring.

It is followed by another scene almost as bad, in which the members of the Ladies' Aid meeting at the Bjarnes sympathize with Per Ammandus and criticize the pastor.

Nils has served his term and is back on the farm, now much closer to his father than before, listening eagerly to him telling about his life in Norway. One day he advises his father to sell the farm, because he is planning to leave for good. Lina is dismayed to hear this and decides to go and talk with Astri. She shows Astri a poem Nils has written to express his love for her. It is a long, romantic poem in four-line rhymed stanzas, much in the style of similar inserted poems in Bjørnson's novels. She pleads with the now weeping Astri to go and see Nils and, to emphasize her plea, tells the story of her own love affair with Johan. In both cases the young man was too embarrassed to speak out, and the result was a nearly tragic misunderstanding between the lovers.

The outcome of Lina's matchmaking is that Astri goes to meet Nils at their trysting place on the river. They finally manage to say what needs to be said, he takes her in his arms, and all is well. But Nils wants the consent of her parents and comes to see them; he has been officially cleared of the charge for which he was jailed, and he manages to overcome the parents', especially the mother's, objections. Nils decides that they should be married as soon as possible. He plans to take over the farm, but only after he has completed his musical education. He assures Lina that she will be treated as his mother and have a home for life. At the end we see the newlyweds happily aboard the train for Chicago, where they sit "gazing into fairy tale and dream and the future."

It is clear that there are glints and glimpses here of the author that Rølvaag would become, but as a whole the story is intolerably dragged out, and especially in Part Two one is annoyed at the wordiness that envelopes the dramatic episodes. In contrast, the main characters are themselves tongue-tied, unable to express their emotions, an exaggerated form of what Rølvaag evidently felt was a Norwegian trait. The only point at which the American world impinges on the community is in the absurd scenes of Per Ammandus's poker games. The best one can say for the book is that it served Rølvaag well as an exercise, a warm-up for what would be his real career.

Rølvaag uses the latest form of Dano-Norwegian spelling here, the orthography of 1907, but he is still bound by the phrasing of nineteenth-century Danish. In some cases he has mechanically transposed the Danish forms into erroneous Norwegian, for example, "ingen *brøt* sig," "no one cared" (Danish *brød*, Norwegian *brydde*). There are obsolete German-influenced syntactic constructions, like *det glatdansede gulv*, "the smooth-danced floor," *den av støv opfyldte stue*, "the dust-filled room," *der sat de som der taltes om og som av nogen misundtes*, "there sat the ones who were being spoken of and who were by some envied." There are pastiches drawn from Bjørnson: *Av ham blir det en kjæk kar*, "He will turn into a fine fellow." But one also recognizes some of what would be special for Rølvaag: his emphasis on "following the call" and his esthetic sensibility: *Denne tonen gjemte i sig alt det deiligste i verden*, "This melody embodied all that was most beautiful in the world." It is reminiscent of *Længselens baat* when Lina relates that she and her lover *sat bare og saa paa solen danse nord i havet*, "just sat watching the sun dance in the northern seas."

Rølvaag also followed Bjørnson in mingling his Dano-Norwegian with dialect expressions, especially in dialogue. Some of them he even furnishes with footnotes, as was often the custom in a time when they were still new and startling, for example, the dialect work *rusle* (*drage avsted*, leave, set out), *piskantull* (*sandelig, saamen*, indeed), *fankeren saa godt* (*pokkeren*, a mild profanity), *hele vasen* (*skaren, flokken*, crowd), *stengælen* (*aldeles gal*, completely mad). This is especially characteristic of Lina, who speaks Rølvaag's own Nordland dialect, though only moderately, as Per Hansa and Beret would in the later novels.

The most striking feature of his language, no doubt intended to provide verisimilitude, is his liberal use of Americanisms. This, too, became a feature of his later writing, though one no doubt restrained by his Norwegian publishers. Most of the words are incorporated grammatically into his Norwegian, with the definite article attached at the end, but then are usually underlined to be set in italics in the printed text, for example, *quilt*'en, "the quilt," *bluff*'en "the bluff," *colt*'en, "the colt" (also en *colt*, and plural *colt*'er), *buggy*'en, "the buggy" (en *buggy*, plural *buggy*'er), *teacher*'n, "the teacher" (en *teacher*, definite plural *teacher*'ne). A few nouns are feminine, such as *døst*'a, "the dust," *fil*'a, "the field," and others are neuter: *team*'et, "the team" (et *team*, to *teams*), *county*'et, "the county," *party*'et, "the party," et *basement*, "a basement," et *store*, "a store," *settlement*'et, "the settlement," *court*'et, "the court," *corn*'et, "the corn." As with *team* above, English plurals are sometimes retained, for example, *bronchoes, chores, lovers, cowards, skunks, dollars, settlers*. Compounds are frequent, such as en *safety pin*; some of them are bilingual, for example, *commonskolen*, "the common school," en *skog-claim* "a forest claim," *overalls*buksen, "the overalls trousers," *court*huset, "the court house," *corncob*-pipen, "the corncob pipe," and *brake*manden, "the brakeman."

Adjectives are less common, though *alright* [sic] is frequent: *queer* (also *rar*), *smart*'ere, "smarter," *independent, crazy, bashful*, den *inscreened*'de *porch*'en, "the screened-in porch." Verbs are not frequent, but they do occur: *spænde*, "spend," *meka*, "make," *catch'a* "caught," at *hurt*'e, "to hurt," *settle* (den sak), "settle (the case)," *shake hands*, at *kipa hus*, "to keep house," *leksjonerte*, "electioneered."

There are also numerous exclamations and fixed phrases, such as "bye-bye," *hello, come on, no Sir, that's right, by Jiminy, Great Scott, blame it all, you bet you, never you mind, too bad*, and *yes-siree*. While all the characters and the author can use some of these expressions, they are used especially to characterize Per Ammandus, who is portrayed as *yankeefisert*, that is, yankified, and his family and friends. An oddity is the regular use among the young people of *Miss* in addressing even good friends. There are also some Norwegian phrases that seem like translations from English and may be oversights on Rølvaag's part: *jeg skal ha til at*, "I'll have to," *underskog*, "underbrush," *vaarfeberen*, "spring fever," *blodrosen*, "bloodroot." English loans average about one to a page, and nearly all of them are such as one might expect in the environment Rølvaag was describing.[5]

Some of the best writing in the book is found in two

chapters that interrupt the narrative in Part Two. One is placed at its opening and is a lyrical description of the coming of spring on the prairie. The other follows the first poker game and precedes the pastor's housewarming; it is a similar description of summer. These were later expanded and slightly rewritten to cover all four seasons and published in Rølvaag's first reader (*Norsk læsebok* I, 193–202), after publication in the Christmas annual, *Jul i Vesterheimen*, in 1913.[6] At least so much was salvaged from Rølvaag's first novel.

It is characteristic of Rølvaag's stage of development at this time that he sought his models in the folk classics of Norway's great century, chiefly Bjørnson, but also Jonas Lie. There is no trace of the neo-romanticism of the 1890s or of the great new star on the firmament, Knut Hamsun. Rølvaag probably still regarded him as decadent, an irreligious and irreverent upstart. He would change his mind in time. But when he wrote *Amerika-breve* he tapped the richest possible vein of immigrant writing, with a long tradition of folk practice. From being an imitator he became an innovator.

## Notes

[1]Einar Haugen, *Ole Edvart Rölvaag* (Boston, 1984), 9; Theodore Jorgenson and Nora Solum, *Ole Edvart Rölvaag: A biography* (New York, 1939), 74–79, 89–90, 141–145; Gudrun Hovde Gvåle, *O. E. Rølvaag. Nordmann og amerikanar* (Oslo, 1962), 108–110, 290–292. Special thanks to Lloyd Hustvedt for a Xerox copy of the "Nils og Astri" manuscript.

[2]Translated by Ella Valborg Tweet and Solveig Zempel as *The Third Life of Per Smevik* (Minneapolis, 1971).

[3]Ager's novel was published in Eau Claire in 1910; it was reprinted under the title *Presten Konrad Walter Welde* (Kristiania, 1912). Farseth's letter is here cited from Gvåle, *O. E. Rølvaag*, 290.

[4]See Einar Haugen, *The Norwegian Language in America* (2nd ed., Bloomington, Indiana, 1969), 233–294.

[5]Haugen, *The Norwegian Language*, 383–411.

[6]O. E. Rølvaag and P. J. Eikeland, *Norsk læsebok, bind I, For barneskolen og hjemmet* (Minneapolis, 1919), 193–202; O. E. Rølvaag, "Stemninger fra Prærien," in *Jul I Vesterheimen* (Minneapolis, 1913), reprinted also in O. E. Rølvaag, *Fortællinger og skildringer* (Minneapolis, [1932]), 42–57.

# 12

# A Cappella Choirs in the Scandinavian-American Lutheran Colleges

*by Paul Benson*

Bringing America the beauty of mixed a cappella choral singing is the undisputed contribution to American culture of a small band of Scandinavian-American Lutheran college choirs on the midwestern prairies. They are the American progenitors of an art form which, though a transplant from Europe, took root in the culture of the Scandinavian-American pioneers. Although unaccompanied choral singing was featured in the cathedrals and churches of Europe prior to the Reformation, it was in America and among these Scandinavian-American Lutheran colleges that the a cappella choir was transformed into a concert instrument, the touring mixed choral ensemble. The significance of this new type and approach should not be underestimated, for it has influenced American choral development in every quarter.

The existence of a rich tradition in choral singing at a number of the Scandinavian-American Lutheran colleges is clearly linked to a chain of historical events at several of these institutions, including Augsburg College, Minneapolis; Concordia College, Moorhead; and St. Olaf College, Northfield, all in Minnesota; Augustana College, Rock Island, Illinois; Luther College, Decorah, Iowa; and Pacific Lutheran University, Tacoma, Washington. The specific historical circumstances which allowed for the creation of so many choral ensembles at the various Lutheran colleges are complex, but one event forms the essential starting point for all discussions of Lutheran college choral music. That event was, of course, the founding of the St. Olaf Lutheran Choir in 1911 by F. Melius Christiansen at St. Olaf College, then a small Norwegian Lutheran coeducational institution.

The St. Olaf Lutheran Choir burst onto the national scene in the spring of 1920 with a notable tour of the important music centers on the east coast, in particular Carnegie Hall in New York City. It was the first American collegiate choir to sing there. For a tiny midwestern college of 700 students to send its choir of some fifty voices to the acropolis of American musical life and expect to receive serious consideration was an audacious act. Yet New York critics and a discriminating audience gave the choir a rousing reception. This outpouring of praise reassured the midwesterners and more than justified their boldness. To this day, few American choirs have found such immediate acceptance.

The creation of the St. Olaf Lutheran Choir and its success came about through the vision of two gifted men, F. Melius Christiansen and Paul G. Schmidt. From its inception, the choir's unparalleled success was the result of the combined talents of these two very different individuals. F. Melius Christiansen was a choral perfectionist *par excellence* and a romantic devotee who had a special instinct for the dramatic and a deeply spiritual nature. Christiansen's frequently quoted statement that his art was his religion and religion was his art perfectly reflects the importance he placed on the choir's singing.[1] For Christiansen, the choir was much more than a vehicle for entertainment; it was always his goal to move the audience to a higher spiritual consciousness. He wanted to create a choir on the pattern of the St. Thomas Boys' Choir of Leipzig, Germany, where he had spent several years. But he had in mind a mixed-voice touring ensemble.

Christiansen's early life in Larvik, Norway, was filled with music. Playing the violin and the church organ, and trading music lessons for English lessons from American Mormon missionaries, young F. Melius decided to immigrate to the

United States in the late 1880s in the footsteps of his brother Karl. Becoming director of the Marinette, Wisconsin, Scandinavian Band in 1890, he was encouraged by Theodore Reimestad to enroll at Augsburg College, which he did in 1892. Christiansen's facility with the violin caused him to receive the moniker of the "Ole Bull of Augsburg." After his work at Augsburg and an additional stint at Northwestern Conservatory in Minneapolis, he and his new wife, Edith Lindem, traveled to the Royal Conservatory in Leipzig where he received a diploma in 1897. Returning to Minnesota, he took a position at Northwestern Conservatory, where he taught from 1899 to 1903. While directing the Kjerulf Male Chorus in Minneapolis, Christiansen met a member of the bass section named Paul G. Schmidt who encouraged him to come to St. Olaf College where Schmidt had been teaching since 1902.[2]

Schmidt's connection to St. Olaf through his father is a interesting one. During its first year of operation in 1861, Luther College, then located at Halfway Creek, Wisconsin, had only one faculty member, a young German by the name of Frederick Schmidt, Paul's father. Schmidt had immigrated from Saxony with his mother in 1842 and had attended Concordia Seminary in St. Louis, Missouri, from 1853 to 1857. He became fast friends with a group of young Norwegian Americans who were studying there because their synod lacked a seminary.[3] Schmidt, in fact, became so close to the Norwegians that he learned their language in order to communicate with them and minister to their needs. Later, during a chance meeting in Baltimore with Norwegian Synod president H. A. Preus, Schmidt surprised him with his facility in Norwegian. When Preus offered Schmidt the first faculty position at Luther College in Wisconsin, Schmidt accepted, leaving his pastorate in Baltimore for the West.[4] Schmidt thus became the first music teacher in a Scandinavian-American Lutheran college, and equally important, later taught at St. Olaf College, where his son Paul would eventually become associated with F. Melius Christiansen and the St. Olaf Lutheran Choir.

Paul G. Schmidt became the choir's tireless impresario

and detail man, performing the public relations work so crucial to the choir's success. Schmidt was also the mainstay of the choir's bass section for over forty years. It was Schmidt who got the choir engagements at all the best concert halls and then worked out the complicated logistics necessary for making the extensive tours successful. In fact, Christiansen and Schmidt were so successful that they were able to contribute about half the cost of an impressive new music building, named the Christiansen Music Hall, from the proceeds of choir tours, over and above expenses.[5]

This talented team achieved a coup for choral music by bringing the St. Olaf Lutheran Choir onto the national scene at a time when most American colleges and high schools were proud if their singing groups could perform such works as "Polly Wolly Doodle All the Day."[6] However, the mediocre, if not inferior, quality of American school choral music was forever altered by that 1920 tour. College, university, and particularly high school choir directors began emulating the style and technique of F. Melius Christiansen and performing his choral works. By the late 1920s and early 1930s many American secondary and post-secondary schools and congregations had a cappella choral ensembles which tried to follow the St. Olaf example. This growth was fostered not only by those who heard the choir, but by a cadre of St. Olaf-trained directors who practiced many of Christiansen's ideas in the field.[7]

The choir's tour of 1920 marked the beginning of a golden age of Lutheran choral music in America which existed between the two world wars. This period, in which the influence of Christiansen's theories about choral singing reached its zenith, might with justification be called the Christiansen Era. Christiansen made St. Olaf College, for a time, the capital of a choral tradition from which the new doctrines and dogmas spread quickly into many of the colleges, universities, high schools, and churches of America. In creating the nation's pioneer a cappella collegiate touring choir, Christiansen established a unique type of college choir at a new level of excellence.

Christiansen's choir was not America's first mixed a cappella collegiate choir, even though St. Olaf may have had the first one. The St. Olaf College Sangkor, founded in the year 1875, had little continuity in terms of leadership or membership, however, and did not tour.[8] Another early a cappella choir was created in 1906 by Peter Lutkin at Northwestern University, but it was also a nontouring choir.[9] The difference at St. Olaf is that Christiansen's choir was established as a touring choir, with the avowed purpose of bringing sacred choral music of the highest standard to every part of the United States.

It was unusual in the early years of the twentieth century for a college or university singing ensemble to be of mixed voices. All-male or all-female choruses were much more common because co-education was a relatively new phenomenon on the American scene. In Scandinavia also, the all-male or all-female chorus was well established, whereas the mixed a cappella choir was relatively unknown.[10] Singing without accompaniment was reserved for only the best choirs. That the St. Olaf Lutheran Choir sang its whole concert of two hours and more without accompaniment and from memory was unprecedented.

Within a few years Northfield, Minnesota, became the unlikely mecca for those choral devotees who wanted to study Christiansen's techniques. A whole generation of choir directors traveled either to St. Olaf or to one of the many summer Christiansen Choral Schools to learn his methods. Yet to suggest that the St. Olaf success was a spontaneous happening or that there was not already a fine Scandinavian-American choral tradition in existence is to obscure history. St. Olaf's principal contribution was to bring high caliber a cappella choral singing to the larger American scene on the concert stage, but it was itself the product of several generations of Scandinavian-American singing.

One must try to visualize the spirited a cappella singing of numberless isolated Lutheran congregations in Minnesota, Wisconsin, the Dakotas, Iowa, and the Pacific Northwest. These years of singing the old Lutheran chorales through bleak blizzards and searing summers fostered a love of choral music. Without the state-church trained musicians and the great organs of the European cathedrals, the pioneers developed a feeling for the sound of human voices blending together in choral and congregational singing. In 1943 Paul Glasoe recalled, "The pioneer generation of parents, now almost gone, knew many hymns by heart. Many a mother could accompany her daily round of routine duties with an almost endless series of hymns."[11]

The movement toward fine choral ensembles among the Scandinavian Lutherans started well before the American Civil War with the first wave of Scandinavian immigrant farmers. As early as 1847, the Reverend J. W. C. Dietrichson of Koshkonong, Wisconsin, reported the existence of a "singing school" in his congregation. Soon after the Civil War, Norwegian congregations established parochial schools in which choral singing was a basic part of the curriculum. Another cultural carryover from the Norwegian homeland was the singing societies (*sangerforbund*). These societies eventually developed into large choral unions which brought together the scattered congregational choirs into a single regional, or even national, choir on festive occasions.[12]

Following the pattern of American Protestant denominations, the Scandinavian Lutherans soon began to establish normal schools, academies, and colleges. The earliest of these colleges, which emphasized the training of young adults in music and religion, were Augustana College in Rock Island, Illinois, and Luther College in Decorah, Iowa. Augustana College, founded in 1860, is the oldest Scandinavian Lutheran college, though this statement is somewhat misleading because the original school actually split into three colleges. The Swedish Augustanians remained at Rock Island, Illinois, while the Norwegians eventually founded Augustana College in Sioux Falls, South Dakota, and Augsburg College in Minneapolis, Minnesota. All three of these colleges developed choral programs, but none before the 1880s.[13] The distinction of having the earliest organized choral group among the Scandinavian-American colleges goes to Luther College, which offered music classes at its founding in 1861 and established the Idun Quartette in 1869.[14]

One of the key personalities in the creation of Lutheran collegiate choral music was a teacher at Augsburg Seminary in Minneapolis named Theodore S. Reimestad. Professor Reimestad helped determine much of the future of Scandinavian-American choral singing by co-founding the Norwegian Lutheran Singers Choral Union in 1892.[15] This organization served as the prototype for many such groups. Also significant, Reimestad encouraged F. Melius Christiansen to enter Augsburg as a student, and when he came, put him into the Augsburg Quartet. The Quartet was the first musical organization to tour Norwegian settlements in America and the first American collegiate choral group to visit Scandinavia—in 1895, but without Christiansen.[16]

However, the search for the roots of a cappella singing among Scandinavian Lutheran colleges inevitably centers on St. Olaf, despite the fact that it was not the oldest Lutheran college. It was St. Olaf College, coeducational from its founding, that first experimented with a cappella singing, beginning in 1875. The St. Olaf Sangkor shows St. Olaf's commitment to creating a mixed a cappella choir immediately after the founding of the college.[17] When F. Melius Christiansen launched the St. Olaf Lutheran Choir some thirty-seven years later, in 1911, he was using the earlier choir's constitution, although with some modifications.[18]

The reign of the St. Olaf Lutheran Choir was not disturbed within the Scandinavian-American community for an entire generation. During this period, several non-Lutheran choirs arose to challenge St. Olaf's supremacy, including those of Northwestern University and the Westminster Choir College. However, among the Lutheran college choirs, none owned national prominence to equal St. Olaf's until the 1920s. Yet virtually every Scandinavian-American college in the United States and Canada did at some point create a choir following the St. Olaf model. Among these, five colleges besides St. Olaf would eventually create touring choral organizations of national and sometimes international reputation.[20]

St. Olaf's international choral leadership has remained constant. In 1941 Olaf Christiansen stepped into the immensely difficult situation of following his father as director of the choir. While initially attending St. Olaf, he had dreamed of a career in commercial design or athletic coaching, and for a time he even considered a religious vocation, possibly as a missionary. But what he chose was music. In 1920, at age nineteen, he took over the positions of band director, athletic director, and dean of men at Mayville Normal Teachers' College in Mayville, North Dakota.[21] After Mayville, Olaf Christiansen returned to St. Olaf College from 1921 to 1925 to finish his Bachelor of Music degree. Now he started seriously planning for a career in music. Upon graduation from St. Olaf, he studied opera with Paul Parks in New York City. From 1926 to 1929 he taught music in the Flint, Michigan, public schools, and then in 1929 went to Oberlin College, where he founded the Oberlin A Cappella Choir and edited the Oberlin Choir Series.[22]

The opportunity to direct the St. Olaf Lutheran Choir — the "Lutheran" was dropped in the 1950s — was too great a temptation for Olaf Christiansen to turn down; in 1941 he returned to St. Olaf to share the baton with his father, and in 1942 took over the choir on his own.[23] Two principal elements which he brought to the choir were rhythmic precision and textual intelligibility. Christiansen's stress on enunciation and articulation meant that American audiences could usually understand every word of English text, a noteworthy accomplishment for any choir. Also, like his father, he composed for the choir many distinctive works with religious themes. His early interest in missionary work was not lost but came to fruition in his frequent choir-practice homilies which invariably came back to the theme of the worth and value of each individual.

The replacement of Olaf Christiansen as the St. Olaf Choir director in 1968 was a significant occasion. There was considerable fear that the tradition could not be maintained, but that fear has proved unfounded under the leadership of Kenneth Jennings. Jennings, a Connecticut Yankee who had never heard of St. Olaf, came to the college as a student through a chance Army friendship with a St. Olaf graduate named Luther Onerheim. Onerheim's choral directing skills left such an impression on Jennings that he decided to investigate St. Olaf on his way to Colorado College, where he had planned to study music.[24]

Jennings graduated from St. Olaf in 1950 and returned as a member of the music faculty in 1953. His success with the choir has been widely acknowledged. While maintaining the standards of the choir, he has added his own stamp. In 1970, only two years after he took over the choir, it was invited to sing at the International Strasbourg Music Festival in France. The choir was asked to return in 1972, and one French critic wrote, "One would look in vain for the slightest criticism to make of this international-class group."[25]

The next addition to the ranks of Lutheran collegiate choirs after St. Olaf was the Concordia Choir of Concordia College, Moorhead, Minnesota, founded by Agnes Skartvedt in 1920. It became a fine choral organization under the leadership of Herman Monson, who directed it from 1923 to 1937. Monson, a Luther College graduate who had conducted the Concordia Band from 1915 to 1917 and served as a band director in the Army in 1917–1918, returned to Concordia in the fall of 1923 to take over the choir. Monson had a solid musical background, having taken his undergraduate musical training under the charismatic tutelage of Carlo Sperati of Luther College. Later, as a disabled veteran, he studied at the Louisville Conservatory and at Minneapolis' MacPhail School of Music. Monson was not only well qualified, but very energetic in his devotion to choral music. At Concordia, he compiled 450 pieces of music and revised and adapted them for choral singing.[26] The main body of this work was published by Belwin in New York City as the Concordia Choir Series.[27]

From the beginning, the Concordia Choir under Monson received uniform praise. A critical reviewer of Monson's first-year choir says that it "took the audience by storm in the opening number 'O Sacred Head Now Wounded' sung with dignity and an organ-like beauty of tone. Well-balanced parts, precision of detail and unity of effect were notable achievements."[28] Although, at first, one might discount such a review as friendly and uninformed hyperbole, the yearly tours brought many such statements. For example, a 1926 critique in a Minot, North Dakota, newspaper was typical: "These forty singers from Concordia, trained so effectually by Herman W. Monson, the director, sing as one voice and achieve the beautifully colored shading and effect possible on an organ. The singers respond with such instant unity to the baton that a delightful finish and clear-cut phrasing are made possible."[29]

During the late 1920s, the choir received the appellation "Pride of the Northwest," which, if nothing else, hints at a certain regional acknowledgement.[30]

In 1937 the Christiansen era began at Concordia, an era unprecedented in length in American choral music history. Few if any American conductors have led the same choir for nearly a half century, and Paul J. Christiansen's Concordia Choir was always among the top collegiate choirs in the country. To many, Christiansen symbolized the Concordia Choir. Only a few remember that he inherited a fine choral program intact.

Despite the fact that Paul J. Christiansen was born with one of the most famous names in American choral music, his success in the field was anything but a foregone conclusion. In fact, as a student at St. Olaf, Christiansen had little interest in choral music, though he did sing in his father's choir. Instead, he devoted himself to piano, composition, and orchestra. His early lack of interest in choir work paralleled that of his father, who was a violinist, organist, band and orchestra director long before he became involved in choral music. Paul Christiansen got the choral position at Concordia, then a small college with a tiny music faculty, in 1937, by virtue of his taking the chairmanship of the department and the directorship of the choir in the same package. As with his father before him, his significant gifts as a choral director were revealed over time and were not immediately manifested.

Though Paul Christiansen at age twenty-two had had

pitifully little experience with choral groups, he was well equipped aesthetically. He knew the sound he wanted, and he started to develop it in his choirs. Perhaps the foremost quality he was after was a certain type of color. Not a uniform color or even the same color on different songs, but a richness that came from individual voices blending their own particular tonal qualities. "Color has been a great interest to me and a joy" was the way Christiansen described his fascination with this aspect of choral music.[31]

It is interesting to read Christiansen's reflections on his father's St. Olaf Lutheran Choir: "In 1938, I heard the [St. Olaf Lutheran] Choir which I had not heard for a few years. I was surprised by the lush, rich alto section. Earlier my father was interested in the boys' choir sound, particularly in the sopranos, from his Leipzig years. By '38 he had forgotten about the boys' choir sound."[32]

The impact his brother's St. Olaf Choir had on him reveals much about Paul Christiansen's choral views. "I admired Olaf's St. Olaf Choir very much. It was always clean singing and that is an ideal that one should have in front of him all the time. The St. Olaf sound under Olaf was very unified like an orchestra with the uniform sectional sound coming through whereas F. Melius' choir had less of the sectional alikeness. Olaf was very much for the high overtones like the oboe whereas F. Melius had low overtones like French horns for richness. It is like comparing the Cleveland Symphony under Szell and the Philadelphia Orchestra under Ormandy. Szell's sound was always very clean and no one had better intonation, but Philadelphia had a sensuous, warm sound under Ormandy."[33]

In this comparison Paul Christiansen sees himself as much closer to his father, leaning as he does toward low overtones and vowel richness. There is a more sensuous sound, especially in the alto and bass sections.

The catalog of critical acclaim given to the Concordia Choir under Christiansen since 1937 is voluminous. However, one particular article written during the 1958 European tour might be representative of many which critics have written after hearing the choir for the first time. During that 1958 tour, the choir sang at the Vienna Music Festival with 117 other choirs from eight countries. After it received a surprising foot-stomping ovation, the critic wrote: "The first day of the music festival in Vienna brought us a sensation we shall especially remember. Never before in Vienna have we heard a choir sing in such a musical way. Very sonorous and homogeneous. Seldom before have we heard a concert that from the first to the last tone was so perfectly sung. There was nothing more to wish. It is impossible to sing more artistically."[34]

In the spring of 1986, Dr. Christiansen retired after forty-nine years as director of the Concordia Choir.

The third Lutheran college to develop a nationally touring a cappella choir was Pacific Lutheran College in Parkland, now a part of Tacoma, Washington. In the fall of 1925, Pacific Lutheran College, by then grown to nearly 150 students, hired a young St. Olaf College graduate, Joseph Edwards, to head the music department. Edwards was very much a product of the Norwegian-American community. His pastor father had served Lutheran parishes in Minnesota and South Dakota and later in Everett and Tacoma, Washington. Joseph had been a member of the St. Olaf Lutheran Choir at the time of its famous 1920 tour, and even roomed with another well-known member of that choir, Olaf Christiansen. The influence of F. Melius Christiansen on Edwards was pronounced. It was the elder Christiansen who recommended Edwards for his first job, as organist at the First Lutheran Church in Toledo, Ohio.[35]

During the opening weeks of the 1926–1927 school year, Edwards started trying out voices for an a cappella choir at Pacific Lutheran College along the lines of the St. Olaf Lutheran Choir. From the beginning the title "Choir of the West" was used, a name suggested by Victor Elvestrom, an early tour manager of the choir.[36] Despite a shortage of qualified singers, Edwards started building a choir which became respectable and even excellent in time. Although there were short tours, the choir did not make a major tour until

1932, when it traveled as far east as Chicago. According to a *Lutheran Herald* article written about the choir's performance at the Luther League convention, the choir was well received. "The 'Choir of the West' came from Tacoma to take part in the convention, and surprised all by its wonderful singing under the directorship of Professor Joseph O. Edwards."[37]

Edwards' tenure at Pacific Lutheran College was cut short by the Great Depression. Since the college was barely able to pay even its meager salaries to teachers, Edwards felt he had no choice but to leave Parkland. He was replaced by Gunnar Malmin, who had a background similar to Edwards'. Son of a midwestern Norwegian Lutheran pastor, Malmin attended Luther College, played in the Carlo Sperati band for five years, and received his B.A. degree there in 1923. In 1924 he decided to enroll in St. Olaf College to work on a Bachelor of Music degree and sing in the St. Olaf Lutheran Choir. This experience made an impression on Malmin which would influence his future work at Pacific Lutheran. After brief teaching stints at Drake University, Des Moines, Iowa, where he directed the Men's Glee Club and the University Band, and Dana College, Blair, Nebraska, where he directed the choir and took it on a tour of Denmark in 1935, he came to Pacific Lutheran College in the fall of 1937.[38]

At first Malmin's efforts to keep the Choir of the West going were something of a struggle. During the war years of 1941–1945, the male student body was reduced at one point to nine, yet the choir never stopped singing. Also, during this period, Malmin, along with other faculty members, worked in the Tacoma Shipyards to help in the war effort and to supplement his income.

The postwar years were a time of strong development for the Choir of the West. The choir made its yearly tours to large and enthusiastic audiences, mainly on the West Coast, and it was well loved by the college's constituents. The choir under Malmin was essentially a church choir, with an exclusively religious purpose, as distinct from a concert choir. Malmin said of it, "I have always believed that the a cappella choir singing sacred music expresses the highest ideals of Christian higher

education culturally and spiritually."[39] It was also a fine singing organization which profited greatly from Malmin's flair
for programming. Gunnar Malmin knew his audience and
what they wanted to hear.

The choir's 1963 tour of Norway marked its peak of artistic attainment, as demonstrated by the reviews in many
Scandinavian and German newspapers. No fewer than fifteen
Norwegian newspapers reviewed the various concerts and the
comments were universally favorable.

In the fall of 1964, Maurice Skones came to Pacific Lutheran University, as it had become in 1960, as chairman of
the Music Department and director of the Choir of the West.
Skones was well prepared for his new role, having studied
choral directing under Paul J. Christiansen at Concordia College, directed an award-winning high school choir at Cut
Bank, Montana, and created a good collegiate choir at Adams
State College in Colorado. When Skones took over the Choir
of the West, he immediately put his own stamp on it. Although he was well within the historical tradition of Lutheran
college choirs, he wanted to emphasize the choir as a concert
ensemble rather than strictly as a church-choir training group.

Skones was raised in Turner, Montana, where his earliest
musical influence besides his brother and father, both amateur
musicians, was a St. Olaf graduate named Hazel Hansen, the
pastor's wife, who directed the local church choir. It was
through Mrs. Hansen that he first heard about the St. Olaf
choral tradition. After a short period in the Navy, Skones entered Concordia College in the fall of 1944 to prepare for a career in medicine. When he got to the campus, after the term
had begun, he went to a chapel service and heard the Concordia Choir, directed by Paul Christiansen, for the first time. He
was overwhelmed by the experience. Later that week Skones
was in an ear-training class with Christiansen, who asked him
to try out for the choir. From that point on he sang in the
Concordia Choir, though it was not until the end of his junior
year that he decided on a career in music education.[40]

At Pacific Lutheran University Skones developed an entirely new type of choral sound which departed in some ways

from the Lutheran choral tradition of emphasis on sectional unity. In its place he created a "heterogenous" choral formation in which the choir is organized not by sections but by quartets. The problem, as Skones saw it, was that the individual voice, its color and beauty, was often lost in the section because, surrounded by others singing the same part, the individual singers could not tell if it was their own sound they were hearing. So Skones started developing a choir of quartets, with each quartet containing soprano, alto, tenor, and bass voices. Skones gives his wife Pat credit for this musical idea, tracing it to her comments about his Adams State Choir in the early 1960s. Mrs. Skones felt that the choir's sound was too thin and that individual choir members were blending only with their section rather than with the choir as a whole.[41]

Skones' new approach to a cappella choir singing paid good dividends. Seattle music critic R. M. Campbell commented enthusiastically on a 1981 concert by saying, "One of the hallmarks of the group is its evenly produced sound. . . . so perfectly molded are its phraseology and formulation of choral sonorities."[42] Skones retired in 1983 and his place as choir director was taken by Richard Sparks, the founder of the Seattle Pro Musica.[43]

Credit for developing the a cappella choir program at Augsburg College belongs to Henry P. Opseth. Opseth came to Augsburg in the early 1920s from St. Olaf College on the recommendation of F. Melius Christiansen. Opseth had been a tuba virtuoso in the St. Olaf Band under Christiansen's baton; he came to Augsburg, however, as director of the Men's Glee Club and a women's ensemble called the Choral Society formed when Augsburg introduced coeducation in 1922. The Glee Club and the Choral Society functioned and toured as independent units from 1922 to 1933. In 1924 there was a mixed choral ensemble identified in the yearbook as "The Augsburg Choir." This organization did not survive, however, and it was not until the fall of 1933 that the Glee Club and the Choral Society merged to create a permanent Augsburg Choir under Opseth.[44] In addition to his choral work, Opseth was particularly good at encouraging students to develop their latent talents. Leland B. Sateren, an Augsburg alumnus who eventually took Opseth's place, made this observation: "Opseth was absolutely selfless in his encouragement of many of us. In my case, he gave me many opportunities to direct the choir — even in public appearances, and finally in my senior year appointed me assistant director. And he performed — as regular program — compositions of both [Norman] Myrvik and myself."[45]

The Augsburg Choir was similar to most Lutheran college choirs of the 1930s and 1940s whose repertoire was exclusively religious and whose concerts were aimed at Lutheran congregations. The choir sang well under Opseth's leadership, with a passion which reflected Opseth's intense personality. His training as a bandsman, as in the case of Christiansen, aided him in his work as a choral director. Opseth built a choir with distinctive choral tone and, with only limited vocal resources, accomplished the task of producing a quality choir year after year.

Upon his death in December, 1950, the choir was taken over by Sateren, who had joined the Augsburg music faculty in 1946 and had been directing the second choir known as the Choral Club. Sateren's years at Augsburg were to be the richest period in the college's choral history; it was he who raised the Augsburg Choir into the top rank of Lutheran college choirs.

Sateren was born in Everett, Washington, where his father, the Reverend Lawrence Sateren, was president of Bethania College, a small Lutheran Free Church junior college. Sateren graduated from Augsburg in 1935. After World War II, he was asked to return to Augsburg as a teacher. Taking the good choral tradition already established there, Sateren began building and expanding the choir with a view to creating a first-rate choral organization. He also saw the need for the choir to expand its audience by singing not only in church sanctuaries, but also in concert halls.[46]

Music critics, both in Europe and in America, suggest the artistic stature and the particular character of Sateren's choir. *Dagbladet* (Oslo) commented on the choir's "extraordinarily pure sound" while Oslo's *Aftenposten* noted its "exquisite pianissimos and truly full-toned singing with power and body." In Germany, the Stuttgart *Nachrichten* remarked that Sateren was "a virtuoso 'playing' on the choir as one would on a precious instrument." In the American press, the *Capitol Times* (Madison, Wisconsin) called the singing of the Augsburg Choir "magnificent"; and perhaps the most generous praise came from the National Broadcasting Company's music supervisor who wrote, "I can remember no better choral performance on the air in all the years I have been with NBC."[47]

Sateren took early retirement in 1979 to allow more time for creative work as a composer and writer, as well as guest conducting and choral workshop engagements both here and abroad. "As both the Choir and the Music Department had reached a fairly reasonable degree of excellence, it seemed like the right time to move on."[48] Larry Fleming, who had earlier developed the choir at Valparaiso University, succeeded Sateren, and thus was presented with the opportunity of carrying forward a strong and influential choral tradition.

Although Augustana College, Rock Island, Illinois, did not have an a cappella touring choir until 1934, the Augustana Choir was actually created in 1931 by Henry Veld when he combined the male Wennerberg Chorus with the female Oriole (later Jenny Lind) Chorus for a concert in Chicago's Orchestra Hall on March 18, 1931. Within a very few years Henry Veld, who spent thirty-seven years at Augustana, created from this fusion a choir of national stature.[49]

Veld, of Dutch extraction, was an Augustana product, having studied both at Augustana and at the Chicago Musical College, where he was influenced by his vocal teacher, Richard DeYoung. Veld was also choirmaster at St. Mark's Episcopal Church in Chicago. Starting his career as an organist, he came to Augustana in 1929 to teach singing and direct the Oriole Chorus. Veld said about the choral situation at Augustana, "They had no male chorus then — it disintegrated the year before — and had 22 girls in what they called the Oriole Chorus. I don't know why they called it that; the female oriole doesn't sing."[50]

A strict disciplinarian, Veld insisted on regular rehearsals and was always concerned with the religious importance of the music the choir sang. His often stated theory was that the enunciation of the words affects the tone and that both tone and words were essential to his primary goal of conveying the religious meaning.[51]

One of the key influences on Veld's concept of a cappella singing was dramatically demonstrated when he took his choir to St. Olaf College to start its first tour. This concert was performed as a tribute to F. Melius Christiansen, whom Veld greatly admired.[52]

Honors and attention came early to the choir, as when it was asked to sing at both the Music Educators National Conference and the Music Teachers National Convention in 1934. In 1936 the American Council on Education described the Augustana Choir as one of the four leading collegiate choirs in the United States, together with the St. Olaf Lutheran Choir, the Northwestern University A Cappella Choir, and the Harvard University Glee Club.[53]

The choir has toured extensively since 1934. In 1936 it made its first east coast tour. During World War II, the choir's tours were curtailed for lack of singers, and for a time Veld was in the service, training choruses of military personnel at army centers in Europe. Veld's American Army University Chorus appeared with the London Symphony Orchestra at Albert Hall, London, and later made a series of recordings of part songs for male voices under the sponsorship of Boosey and Hawkes, music publishers.[54] Veld's chorus also made an extensive tour of British towns and cities.

Veld returned to Augustana in 1946, and in the spring of 1949 the choir made its first tour to the west coast. In June of that year the choir sang for 20,000 people in the Chicago Stadium to celebrate the 100th anniversary of Swedish migration to the Midwest. In 1950 it gave concerts at Symphony Hall in Boston, Constitution Hall in Philadelphia, and in New York's Carnegie Hall with the Swedish tenor Jussi Björling. Veld was named conductor of the 2,000 voice choir of the World Council of Churches Assembly held at Soldier's Field,

Chicago, in 1954. He was also conductor of the Apollo Musical Club, a 200-voice mixed choir which was Chicago's oldest musical group.[55]

The critical comments that follow suggest the enthusiastic response to the choir's tours: "Unquestionably the top college choral group in the United States"*Reading* (Pennsylvania) *Eagle-Times*; "The most impressive undergraduate choral body in the United States," *Detroit News*; and "One of America's truly great choral organizations," *Los Angeles Times*.[56]

Veld had a talent for getting recognition. No other Lutheran college choir has had anything like the media attention of the Veld Augustana Choir, which made more than ninety nationwide broadcasts over the major radio networks, including a broadcast from Radio City in New York over NBC in 1939 and a three-month series of weekly concerts for the Mutual Network called "Concerts in Miniature." The series was repeated annually from 1940 through 1944.[57]

During the early days of television, the choir was seen on ABC for an hour's program in 1952 and in 1955 the choir appeared on the *Ed Sullivan Show*. In addition to this, in 1938 the Augustana Choir was the only choir recording on the RCA Red Seal label, and eleven recordings were made in succeeding years. A long-playing record was made for RCA in 1953. During this period the Augustana Choir was the only collegiate choral group in America receiving royalties for recordings simultaneously from two different companies, since they had another contract with Key Records of New York City.[58]

Veld was succeeded in 1966 by Donald Morrison, Morrison, quite different in temperament, nevertheless maintained the level of musicality established by Veld. A Stuart, Iowa, native, Morrison received a Bachelor of Music degree from Drake University and a master's degree in sacred music from Union Theological Seminary in New York City.[59] He has combined his background in voice, organ, and conducting to achieve noteworthy results. Morrison puts great emphasis on the religious work of the choir; it is more a church choir than Veld's, singing mostly in churches or cathedrals on tour.

Morrison's choir has received its own set of accolades, including this in 1970 from a *New York Times*critic: "The Augustana Choir has the reputation of being one of the finest in the country and yesterday at Carnegie Hall they quite lived up to it. The seventy singers displayed remarkable finesse in matters of diction, phrasing, balance and intonation. Performing without music, under the deftly controlling direction of Donald Morrison, their vocal blend had a silken sheen, and their stylistic perception ranged unfailingly over 350 years of music."[60]

Development of a touring a cappella choir at Luther College was relatively late because the school was all-male until the middle 1930s. In June of 1934, two years prior to Luther's adoption of coeducation, Theodor Hoelty-Nickel organized a mixed choir, with women from Decorah College for Women, which was the forerunner of Luther's later mixed a cappella chorus.[61] Unfortunately, Hoelty-Nickel's outstanding work at Luther was shortened by the war. Because of his German background, he did not feel welcome in Decorah at that time and so took a job at the Lutheran Church — Missouri Synod's radio station KFUD and Concordia Theological Seminary in St. Louis. He later became the head of the Music Department at Valparaiso University.[61]

Hoelty-Nickel's departure from Luther in 1941 left a vacancy in the directorship of the choir. This void was filled for the remainder of the year by Sigvart Hofland, who was much more talented as a composer than as a director. Hofland's interim duties ended with the return to Luther of another Sigvart, Sigvart Steen. Steen had studied music at St. Olaf College under F. Melius Christiansen and had been a member of the St. Olaf Lutheran Choir. He and Hofland had joined the Luther faculty together in 1942, but Steen had served in the Navy from 1942 to 1946. During this period, Hofland did nothing with Hoelty-Nickel's mixed choir.[62]

Upon his return, Steen reinvigorated the choir, named it the Nordic Cathedral Choir and took it on tour for the first time in 1946.[63] History professor Chellis Evanson had suggested the name Nordic Cathedral Choir because Luther College was Norwegian in background, the choir sang sacred music, and it was to represent the highest type of choral singing. Later the name was changed to the Luther College Choir and finally to the Nordic Choir of Luther College.[64]

Steen's choir was Luther's first attempt to produce a first-class mixed a cappella ensemble. The previous and short-lived mixed choir did not tour, but Steen's group traveled extensively during his brief tenure as director. Steen might very well have led the choir for many years had not his wife, a professional singer who sang under her maiden name of Margery Mayer, been given an opportunity to join the New York City Opera. This was too good an offer for her to pass by, and so Steen left Luther and took a position at Wagner College on Staten Island.[65]

Weston Noble's association with Luther started as a student. The Riceville, Iowa, native had already paid his room deposit at the University of Iowa when he was visited by a Luther College admissions officer. After a two-hour visit, the man left, and Noble and his father decided he should try Luther. Of English and Methodist heritage, Noble was not the typical Luther student. In fact, when he first attended a Lutheran church service, he thought "it was the weirdest thing I ever attended."

Gradually, Noble became involved in Lutheran choral music through his Luther years. He had, in fact, had a strong interest in choral music from his boyhood. One of his heroes was Fred Waring, and he never failed to listen to the "Pennsylvanians" on the radio.

After leaving Luther, Noble spent three years in the Army, as well as some time at the University of Michigan working on a Master of Music degree. In the fall of 1948, he was called to Luther on a one-year contract to direct the band and the choir. The contract was extended, however, and during the next twenty-five years both the Luther band and the choir achieved national and international distinction under Noble's direction. Finally, in 1972, he decided to relinquish the band and concentrate his energies on the choir.[67]

The Nordic Choir under Weston Noble has been known for its sensitive performances of sacred choral music, and particularly for performances of Romantic works. A vital part of the Luther College Choir tradition, Noble's interpretations occasionally are marked by a distinctively personal and at times a more than usually emotional approach to standard repertoire. The distinctive sound of the choir is a product of Noble's quest for lyricism which stems primarily from his soprano and tenor sections. The alto-bass forces tend not to be quite so deep and rich as some others among the Lutheran college choirs.

The praise which the Nordic Choir received under Weston Noble has been plentiful. One of its highest honors was to be chosen to sing on the internationally televised program "The Joy of Bach." Paul Salamonovitch, assistant conductor of the Roger Wagner Chorale, perhaps best summarized the choir's finest achievement when he said, "The sensitivity to the musical phrase attained by this group is seldom equaled by professionals."[68]

The six choirs discussed in this article make up the core of a larger group of Scandinavian college choirs in the United States and Canada which have together had an impact on American choral music. For over sixty years these church-related college choirs have established and maintained a reputation and standard for excellence in choral singing which is one of America's musical treasures.

## Notes

[1] Albert Johnson, "The Christiansen Choral Tradition: F. Melius Christiansen, Olaf C. Christiansen and Paul J. Christiansen" (Ph.D. dissertation, University of Iowa, 1973), 142.

[2] Robert Jennings, "A Study of the Historical Development of Choral Ensembles at Selected Lutheran Liberal Arts Colleges in the United States" (Ph.D. dissertation, Michigan State University, 1969), 67.

[3] Edel Ytterboe Ayers, "The Old Main" (Anniston, Alabama, 1969), 101.

[4] Richard Irl Kegerreis, "The A Cappella Ideal," in *The Choral Journal*, 9 (April, 1971), 19.

[5] William Benson, *High on Manitou: A History of St. Olaf College, 1874–1949* (Northfield, Minnesota, 1949), 250–251, records that the total

cost of the building, dedicated in 1926, was $102,928.77, of which the choir and other musical organizations of the college raised about $50,000.

[6]Leonard Van Camp, "The Formation of A Cappella Choirs at Northwestern University, St. Olaf College, and Westminster Choir," in *Journal of Research in Music Education*, 13/4 (February, 1968), 228–230.

[7]Paul Glasoe, "A Singing Church," in *Norwegian-American Studies and Records*, 13 (Northfield, Minnesota, 1943), 103.

[8]Glasoe, "A Singing Church," 97.

[9]J.C.K. Preus, *The History of the Choral Union of the Evangelical Lutheran Church, 1847–1960* (Minneapolis, 1961), 3–7.

[10]Preus, *History of the Choral Union*, 3.

[11]Jennings, "Historical Development of Choral Ensembles," 326.

[12]Jennings, "Historical Development of Choral Ensembles," 220.

[13]Paul G. Schmidt, *My Years at St. Olaf* (Northfield, Minnesota, 1964), 2.

[14]Schmidt, *My Years*, 2–3.

[15]Interview with Frederick Schmidt, July 14, 1982, Northfield, Minnesota.

[16]Glasoe, "A Singing Church," 107.

[17]Glasoe, "A Singing Church," 102.

[18]Benson, *High on Manitou*, 27.

[19]Jennings, "Historical Development of Choral Ensembles," 80.

[20]Other Lutheran colleges with noteworthy choral programs include: Augustana College, Sioux Falls, South Dakota; Bethany College, Lindsborg, Kansas; California Lutheran University, Thousand Oaks, California; Camrose College, Camrose, Alberta; Dana College, Blair, Nebraska; Gustavus Adolphus College, St. Peter, Minnesota; Midland College, Fremont, Nebraska; Texas Lutheran College, Seguin, Texas; Upsala College, East Orange, New Jersey; and Waldorf College, Forest City, Iowa.

[21]Interview with Olaf C. Christiansen, July 9, 1982, Little Sister Bay, Wisconsin.

[22]Interview with Olaf Christiansen.

[23]Interview with Olaf Christiansen.

[24]Interview with Kenneth Jennings, July 14, 1982, Northfield, Minnesota.

[25]"The Ultimate Accolade" in *Saint Olaf*, 20 (Northfield, Minnesota, 1972), 12.

[26]Ariel Molldrem and Kenneth Halvorson, "A History of the Concordia Choir, 1920–1931" (Moorhead, Minnesota, 1931), 15.

[27]Erling Rolfsrud, *Cobber Chronicle* (Moorhead, Minnesota, 1966), 193.

[28]Molldrem and Halvorson, "History of the Concordia Choir," 21.

[29]Molldrem and Halvorson, "History of the Concordia Choir," 21.

[30]Jennings, "Historical Development of Choral Ensembles," 165.

[31]Interview with Paul J. Christiansen, July 12, 1982, Moorhead, Minnesota.

[32]Interview with Paul J. Christiansen.

[33]Interview with Paul J. Christiansen.

[34]Jennings, "Historical Development of Choral Ensembles," 171.

[35]Interview with Joseph Edwards, July 26, 1983, Fresno, California.

[36]Letter from Joseph Edwards, April 9, 1983, Fresno, California.

[37]Preus, *History of the Choral Union*, 84–85.

[38]Letter from Gunnar Malmin, October 28, 1982, Sioux Falls, South Dakota.

[39]Interview with Gunnar Malmin, August, 1984, Sioux Falls, South Dakota.

[40]Interview with Maurice Skones, July 28, 1982, Parkland, Washington.

[41]Interview with Maurice Skones.

[42]R. M. Campbell, "PLU's First-rate Choir," in *Seattle Post-Intelligencer* (Seattle, Washington), February 23, 1981, 86.

[43]Jim Peterson, "The Awesome Oneness of Many," in *Scene*, 63 (Parkland, Washington, 1983), 5.

[44]Leland Sateren, "A Brief History of Augsburg College and Its Choral Music" (Edina, Minnesota, 1983), 4.

[45]Sateren, "Brief History," 4.

[46]Interview with Leland Sateren, July 12, 1982, Moose Lake, Minnesota.

[47]Michael Walgren, "Reviews of the Augsburg Choir" (Minneapolis, Minnesota, 1978), 1.

[48]Interview with Leland Sateren.

[49]Jennings, "Historical Development of Choral Ensembles," 343–344.

[50]Don Clasen, "Many Faces of Veld," in *The Argus Roundup* (Rock Island, Illinois), December 4, 1965.

[51]Jennings, "Historical Development of Choral Ensembles," 342–343.

[52]Jennings, "Historical Development of Choral Ensembles," 344.

[53]Jennings, "Historical Development of Choral Ensembles," 344–345.

[54]*The Argus Roundup*, June 16, 1976.

[55]Jennings, "Historical Development of Choral Ensembles," 348–351.

[56]"Press Comments," a publicity brochure published by Augustana College (Rock Island, Illinois, 1942).

[57]Jennings, "Historical Development of Choral Ensembles," 351.

[58]Jennings, "Historical Development of Choral Ensembles," 352.

[59]"Augustana Choir 1984 Press Book" (Rock Island, Illinois, 1984), 3.

[60]"Augustana Press Book," 8.

[61]Jennings, "Historical Development of Choral Ensembles," 273.

[62]Jennings, "Historical Development of Choral Ensembles," 266.

[63]Jennings, "Historical Development of Choral Ensembles," 234.

[64]David Nelson, *Luther College, 1861–1961* (Decorah, Iowa, 1961), 295.
[65]Jennings, "Historical Development of Choral Ensembles," 171.
[66]Interview with Weston Noble, May 1, 1982, Dallas, Texas.
[67]Interview with Weston Noble.
[68]Jennings, "Historical Development of Choral Ensembles," 245.

# Some Recent Publications*

*compiled by Rolf H. Erickson*
*with Norwegian listings by Johanna Barstad*

BOOKS AND PAMPHLETS

Alba, Richard D. *Italian Americans: Into the Twilight of Ethnicity*. Englewood Cliffs, New Jersey, 1985. ix, 182 pp.

Almås, Reidar. *Norwegian Farmers in the USA: A Contemporary Report Based on the Stories of 36 Midwestern Families*. Santa Cruz, California, 1988. 71 pp.

*And All Our Yesterdays. Book 2*. Beldenville, Wisconsin, 1987. 62 pp.
   A collection of essays on the history of Spring Valley, Wisconsin, many of which are about Norwegian Americans.

Anderson, John Louis. *Scandinavian Humor & Other Myths*. Minneapolis, 1986. 219 pp.
   Presented as humor, this is also a perceptive look at an often neglected aspect of immigrant culture.

Anderson, Philip J., ed. *Amicus Dei: Essays on Faith and Friendship Presented to Karl A. Olsson on His 75th Birthday*. Chicago, 1988. xviii, 293 pp.
   A festschrift for a Swedish American who was president of North Park College, Chicago. Includes fourteen essays and a seventy-nine page bibliography titled "Published and Unpublished Writings of Karl A. Olsson," by Timothy J. Johnson.

*The compiler is grateful to Roger D. Sween, Multitype Library Cooperation Specialist, Library Development and Services, Minnesota Department of Education, for his invaluable assistance in checking information and for adding a number of items to the bibliography.

*Årsskrift*, Etne sogelang. 63, 1986. 103 pp.

> This yearbook contains articles on emigration from Sunnhordland and Nord-Rogaland to America by Nils Kolle, Ståle Dryvik, Martin Gjersvik, Olaf Holen, Loren Osman, and Ingvald Skålnes.

Beijbom, Ulf. *Utvandrarna och Svensk-Amerika*. Stockholm, 1986. 253 pp.

> The emigration and Swedish America. A collection of essays by a leading scholar in the field.

Betsinger, Signe T. Nielsen. *Danish Immigrant Homes: Glimpses from Southwestern Minnesota*. St. Paul, Minnesota, 1986. 56 pp.

> A well-illustrated catalog for an exhibition held March 9–April 25, 1986, at the University of Minnesota.

Bjerke, Robert A. *Manitowoc County 1872 Plat Map Index: An Index of the Names on E. M. Harney's Map of Manitowoc County Wisconsin 1872*. Manitowoc, Wisconsin, 1985. 145 pp.

> A useful tool for the local historian or genealogist studying the large Norwegian settlements in this Wisconsin county.

Bliss, Patricia Lounsbury. *Christian Petersen Remembered*. Ames, Iowa, 1986. 217 pp.

> Reminiscences of students, colleagues, and family of a sculptor who emigrated with his parents from Denmark in 1894. Illustrated with 100 photographs of Petersen's sculptures.

Bodnar, John E. *The Transplanted: A History of Immigrants in Urban America*. Bloomington, Indiana, 1985. xxi, 294 pp.

*The Bridge*. 10, 2, 1987. 82 pp.

> This issue consists of ten articles about Enok Mortensen, the well-known authority on Danish-American history and life.

Browning, Harley L. and Rodolfo O. de la Garza, eds. *Mexican Immigrants and Mexican Americans: An Evolving Relation*. Austin, Texas, 1986. 256 pp.

> A collection of twelve essays, "written principally by sociologists from the University of Texas at Austin," which "focuses on distinctions and differences between individuals of Mexican origin who were born in the United States and Mexican-born legal and illegal immigrants."

Christensen, Elisabeth Riber and John Pedersen, compilers. *Bibliografi over dansk-amerikansk Udvandrerhistorie*. Aalborg Denmark, 1986. 243 pp.

> A bibliography on Danish emigration from 1840 to 1920 and Danish-American history to 1983.

Christianson, Erik, compiler. *Symra Index 1905–1914*. [Decorah, Iowa, 1987]. 12 pp.

Clark, Dennis. *Hibernia America: The Irish and Regional Cultures*. Westport, Connecticut, 1986. xix, 213 pp.

> "A major contribution to Irish-American and ethnic historiography. Clark is primarily concerned with how the Irish adapted to America and how the American experience influenced their character."

Damm, Jens and Anette, and Stig Thornsohn, eds. *The Dream of America*. Translated by Hanne Ejsing Jørgensen and Daniel McCarthy. Viborg, Denmark, 1986. 140 pp.

The exhibit by this name about Danish-American life was the inspiration and basis for this book of seventeen essays.

Daniels, Roger, Sandra C. Taylor, and Harry H. L. Kitano, eds. *Japanese Americans: From Relocation to Redress*. Salt Lake City, 1986. 216 pp.

Some thirty essays on Japanese Americans, "focusing on their wartime relocation."

Draxten, Nina. *The Testing of M. Falk Gjertsen*. Northfield, Minnesota, 1988. 134 pp.

The involvement of a Minneapolis Lutheran minister in a sexual scandal which threatened to destroy his career. Published as volume four in the Topical Studies series by the Norwegian-American Historical Association.

Dyrvik, Ståle and Nils Kolle, eds. *Eit blidare tilvere? Drivkrefter og motiv i den tidlegaste utvandringa frå Hordaland og Sogn og Fjordane*. Voss, 1986. 215 pp.

Motivational forces in the earliest emigration from Hordland and Sogn and Fjordane. Twelve papers about emigration from Hordaland and Sogn and Fjordane given at a seminar in conjunction with the 150th anniversary of emigration from Voss held in Voss, April 18–20, 1986.

Eide, Harald. *The Norwegian: A Rollicking Tale of Wild Trails and the Lure of Gold*. Edmonds, Washington, 1982. 128 pp.

Fiction first published in 1975 under the title *The Alaska Adventures of a Norwegian Cheechako*.

*Fåberg og Lillehammer*. 7, 1986. 178 pp.

This issue, with the title "Utvandringen," deals with emigration from Fåberg and Lillehammer to America.

Gerrard, Nelson S. *The Icelandic Heritage*. Arborg, Manitoba, Canada, 1986. 127 pp.

A general history of the Icelandic people with a chapter on emigration to America.

Gilseth, Margaret Chrislock. *Julia's Children: A Norwegian Immigrant Family in Minnesota*. St. Charles, Minnesota, 1987. 443 pp.

"Although the focus is on the second generation, we become involved in three generations from the 1870s to World War II." Foreword by Carl H. Chrislock.

Greene, Victor R. *American Immigrant Leaders, 1800–1910: Marginality and Identity*. Baltimore, 1987. xii, 181 pp.

"The chapter on the Norwegians and Swedes invites the reader to revise some old ideas."

Hale, Frederick. *Their Own Saga*. Minneapolis, 1986. 183 pp.

Letters written by Scandinavian immigrants in the United States, Canada, Australia, South Africa, and several other countries in the years from the 1880s until the 1930s.

Hamre, James S. *Georg Sverdrup: Educator, Theologian, Churchman*. Northfield, Minnesota, 1986. 218 pp.

Published as volume one in the Biographical Series of the Norwegian-American Historical Association.

Hasund, Knut J. and Asbjørn Waage. *Ulstein og Hareid i Amerika*. Ulsteinvik, Norway, 1986. 271 pp.
Summary in English.

Hernt, William R. *Stef: A Biography of Vilhjalmur Stefansson, Canadian Arctic Explorer*. Vancouver, 1986. 317 pp.

Hoerder, Dirk, ed. *Labor Migration in the Atlantic Economies: The European and North American Working Classes During the Period of Industrialization*. Westport, Connecticut, 1985. 491 pp.

Hong, Margot Höjfors. *Ölänningar över haven. Utvandring från Öland 1840–1930*. Uppsala, 1986. 276 pp.
Emigration from the island of Öland, Sweden, 1840–1930. Published as number 143 of the series, Studia Historica Upsaliensis.

Hought, Anna Guttormsen with Florence Ekstrand. *Anna*. Seattle, Washington, 1986. 142 pp.
Autobiography of a girl from Oslo who settled in northern Montana.

Johansson, Anders. *Amerika. Dröm eller mardröm*. Stockholm, 1985. 235 pp.
America—dream or nightmare? A series of interviews with Swedish immigrants to America, largely after World War I. The book has come under criticism for its biases.

Jonassen, Christen T. *Value Systems and Personality in a Western Civilization: Norwegians in Europe and America*. Columbus, Ohio, 1983. xvii, 357 pp.

Jordan, Terry G. *American Log Buildings: An Old World Heritage*. Chapel Hill, North Carolina, 1985. x, 193 pp.
An attempt to resolve the debate over the European antecedents of American log technology with field research in the Alps and southwestern Germany, southern Finland, Soviet Karelia, Sweden, and Norway.

Jordahl, Leigh and Harris Kaasa. *Stability and Change: Luther College in its Second Century*. Decorah, Iowa, 1986. 263 pp.

Kaplan, Anne R., Marjorie A. Hoover, and Willard B. Moore. *The Minnesota Ethnic Food Book*. St. Paul, Minnesota, 1986. 449 pp.
Fourteen essays and more than 150 authentic recipes documenting traditional foods and foodways of fourteen ethnic groups.

Keillor, Garrison. *Lake Wobegon Days*. New York, 1985. 337 pp.
Fiction featuring an imaginary town peopled with German and Norwegian immigrants, much of which was first heard on Minnesota Public Radio's program, "A Prairie Home Companion."

Keillor, Garrison. *Leaving Home*. New York, 1987. 244 pp.
A collection of Lake Wobegon stories.

Keillor, Steven J. *Hjalmar Petersen of Minnesota: The Politics of Provincial Independence*. St. Paul, Minnesota, 1987. xii, 342 pp.
A biography of a politician who rose to prominence in Minnesota's Farmer-

Labor Party and served briefly as governor following the death in office of Floyd B. Olson.

Kirn, Mary Em and Sherry Case Maurer. *Härute—Out Here: Swedish Immigrant Artists in Midwest America: An Exhibition of Works from Augustana College and the Quad Cities Community.* Rock Island, Illinois, 1985. 144 pp.

A well-illustrated exhibition catalog with eight essays.

Kolltveit, Bård. *Amerikabåtene.* Oslo, 1984, 112 pp.

The passenger ships of the Norwegian America Line brought immigrants from Norway to America.

Knudsen, Knud. *Beretning om en reise fra Drammen i Norge til New York i Nord-Amerika.* Drammen, 1986. xxi, 27 pp.

Facsimile edition of a work originally published in Drammen in 1840.

Kongslien, Ingeborg Ragnhild. *Draumen om fridom og jord. Ein studie i skandinaviske emigrantromaner.* Oslo, 1986. 446 pp.

A study of Scandinavian emigrant novels by Johan Bojer, Ole E. Rølvaag, Wilhelm Moberg, and Alfred Hauge.

Kvelstad, Ragnvald, ed. *Poulsbo: Its First Hundred Years.* Poulsbo, Washington, 1986. 300 pp.

Kverndal, Roald. *Seamen's Missions: Their Origin and Early Growth.* Pasadena, California, 1986. 936 pp.

Includes information about Norwegian merchant seamen's missions in the United States.

Laird, Helen. *Carl Oscar Borg & the Magic Region: Artist of the American West.* Salt Lake City, 1986. xvi, 248 pp.

Includes 125 illustrations, 40 in color.

Lee, Robert Lloyd. *Fever Saga.* Minneapolis, 1985. 160 pp.

A fictionalized account of the life of Thrond Helgeson Opdahl (1847–1898), a Norwegian-American pioneer from Valdres.

Leiren, Terje I. *Marcus Thrane: A Norwegian Radical in America.* Northfield, Minnesota, 1987. 167 pp.

Published as volume two in the Biographical Series of the Norwegian-American Historical Association.

Leirfall, Jon. *Old Times in Norway.* Translated by C. A. Clausen. Oslo, 1986. 126 pp. Introduction by Odd S. Lovoll.

Lindahl, Sharon L. *Through Norwegian Eyes: Paintings by Christian Midjo 1880–1973.* Ithaca, New York, 1986. [24 pp.]

An exhibition catalog with a biography of an artist from Trondheim who taught at Cornell University. 17 illustrations.

Lovoll, Odd S. *A Century of Urban Life: The Norwegians in Chicago before 1930.* Northfield, Minnesota, 1988. 367 pp.

Lovoll, Odd S., ed. *Norwegian-American Studies.* Vol. 31. Northfield, Minnesota, 1986. 347 pp.

Published by the Norwegian-American Historical Association. The contents are listed individually by authors in the following section on articles. The volume contains twelve articles largely devoted to immigrant life in America's great cities and published "In Honor of C. A. Clausen on His Ninetieth Birthday."

Lowell, Briant Lindsay. *Scandinavian Exodus: Demography and Social Development of 19th-Century Rural Communities.* Boulder, Colorado, 1987. xxiii, 262 pp.

Magee, Joan. *A Scandinavian Heritage: 200 Years of Scandinavian Presence in the Windsor-Detroit Border Region.* Toronto, 1985. 128 pp.

Published as volume three in the Dundurn Local History Series.

Mayer, George H. *The Political Career of Floyd B. Olson.* St. Paul, Minnesota, 1987. 329 pp.

A Minnesota politician who forged Minnesota's successful Farmer-Labor coalition during the 1920s and became the state's governor from 1931 to 1936. First issued in 1951, this edition has an introduction by Russell W. Fridley.

McCree, Barbro Persson. *John Sjolander: The Poet of Cedar Bayou.* Austin, Texas, 1987. xi, 185 pp.

A biography and anthology of the poetry of John Sjolander (1851–1939), who came to Texas from Sweden in 1871 and worked as a truck gardener while writing poetry.

Miller, Sally M., ed. *The Ethnic Press in the United States.* New York, 1987. 459 pp.

Twenty-seven ethnic presses are described: included are "The Norwegian-American Press" by Arlow W. Andersen; "The Swedish Press" by Ulf A. Beijbom; "The Finnish Press" by William Hoglund; and "The Danish Press" by Marion Tuttle Marzolf.

*Mission of Mercy . . . Women of Action.* Park Ridge, Illinois, 1985. 39 pp.

A brief history of the deaconess movement in Chicago and the Norwegian Lutheran Deaconess Society of Chicago established in 1896.

Mohl, Raymond A. and Neil Betten. *Steel City: Urban and Ethnic Patterns in Gary, Indiana, 1906–1950.* New York, 1986. 227 pp.

Mormino, Gary Ross. *Immigrants on the Hill: Italian-Americans in St. Louis, 1882–1982.* Urbana, Illinois, 1986. xi, 289 pp.

Natvik, Hallvard. *Frå husmann til borgar: To slekter frå Nadvik i Sogn. Utvandrarar 1845–1976/From dependence to freedom: Two family groups from Nadvik in the district of Sogn. Emigrants 1845–1976.* Volda, Norway [1986]. 203 pp.

*New Sweden: the 350th Anniversary of the Settlement of the Swedes and Finns in Delaware.* Newark, Delaware, 1988. 32 pp.

"An Exhibition Catalog with an Introduction by John A. Monroe; Entries Compiled by Gary E. Yela." Published by the University of Delaware Library for an exhibition March 1–July 15, 1988.

Nordstrom, Byron J., ed. *Dictionary of Scandinavian History*. Westport, Connecticut, 1986. xix, 703 pp.

A work "intended for the entrance level historian."

Norman, Hans and Harald Rundblom. *Transatlantic Connections: Nordic Migration to the New World after 1800*. Oslo [1988]. 335 pp.

Nygaard, Kaare. *Knife, Life and Bronzes: Sculpture and Vignettes*. Scarsdale, New York, 1986. 192 pp.

Autobiographical writing by a Norwegian-American sculptor, surgeon, and humanist born in Lillehammer. Illustrations and background on 44 sculptures.

Prouty, Andrew Mason. *More Deadly Than War! Pacific Coast Logging, 1827–1981*. New York, 1985. 252 pp.

Rasmussen, Rasmus Elias. *"Viking" from Norway to America*. Translated by Helen Fletre. Chicago, 1984. 95 pp.

A partial translation of *"Viking" fra Norge til Amerika*, an account of the sailing of the *Viking* from Norway to the Columbian Exposition in Chicago in 1893, which was published in 1894.

Rockaway, Robert A. *The Jews of Detroit: From the Beginning, 1762–1914*. Detroit, 1986. xi, 162 pp.

Rølvaag, Ole E. *I de dage. Riket grunnlegges. Peder Seier. Den signede dag*. Oslo, 1987. 836 pp.

A new Norwegian edition of Rølvaag's immigrant trilogy. Four volumes published in one in the series Gigantbøkene.

Rosendahl, Peter. *More Han Ola og Han Per*. Edited by Einar Haugen and Joan N. Buckley. Iowa City, 1988. xxvi, 167 pp.

The remaining comic strips not included in the first collection published in 1984. A bilingual edition.

Rosholt, Malcolm. *From the Indian Land: First-Hand Account of Central Wisconsin's Pioneer Life*. Iola, Wisconsin, 1985. iv, 348 pp.

A history of the Scandinavian settlements in Waupaca county with a translation by Rosholt of pertinent stories from the second volume of Thor Helgesen's *Fra "Indianernes Lande" og andre steder i Wisconsin*.

Rundblom, Harald and Dag Blanck, eds. *Scandinavia Overseas: Patterns of Cultural Transformation in North America and Australia*. Uppsala, 1986. 145 pp.

Published as number seven of the series Uppsala Multiethnic Papers, it contains the papers delivered at a seminar at Uppsala University, October 18, 1984.

Rutzebeck, Hjalmar. *Alaska Man's Luck and Other Works*. Compiled and edited by Clark Branson. Santa Barbara, California, 1988. 610 pp.

Rutzebeck (1889–1980) was a Danish immigrant and adventurer who became a legend in his own time in Alaska.

Sande, Lars Chr., ed. *De som dro ut*. Stavanger, 1986. 160 pp.

An abridged edition of the same title published in 1975. Articles about the Norwegian migration to America with an emphasis on Rogaland.

Sande, Lars Chr. *Norsemen Follow the Trail.* Translated by Rosalie Rayburn. Stavanger, 1986. 160 pp.

A translation of *De som dro ut* listed above.

*Scandinavian Literature in a Transcultural Context.* Edited by Sven H. Rossel and Birgitta Steene. Seattle, 1986. 285 pp.

Papers from the XV IASS Conference, University of Washington, August 12–18, 1984.

Sherman, William C. and Playford V. Thorson, eds. *Plains Folk: North Dakota's Ethnic History,* Fargo, 1988. 419 pp.

Simonson, Harold P. *Prairies Within: The Tragic Trilogy of Ole Rölvaag.* Seattle, 1987. vii, 103 pp.

Beret, the central figure of *Giants in the Earth, Peder Victorious,* and *Their Fathers' God,* is examined in establishing Rölvaag's portrayal of the immigrant experience.

Skårdal, Dorothy Burton and Ingeborg R. Kongslien. *Essays on Norwegian-American Literature and History.* Oslo, 1986. 375 pp.

Twenty-six papers given at a seminar held in Oslo, June 26–30, 1984, published by NAHA-Norway, the American Institute, University of Oslo, and the International Summer School, the University of Oslo.

Skuggevik, Dordi Glærum. *Utvandringshistorie fra Nordmøre. Stangvik og Surnadal prestegjeld.* Surnadal, Norway, 1986. 460 pp.

Emigration history from Nordmøre. Summary in English.

Steiner, Dale R. *Of Thee We Sing: Immigrants and American History.* San Diego, 1987. 259 pp.

The life of Norwegian-American Gro Svendsen is presented in chapter 8.

Strøm, Elin and Wenche Herwig. *Norwegians to America.* Oslo, 1984. 80 pp.

Book prepared for the "Promise of America" exhibit when it opened in Oslo in June, 1984.

Swierenga, Robert P., ed. *The Dutch in America: Immigration, Settlement, and Cultural Change.* New Brunswick, New Jersey, 1985. xv, 303 pp.

Thirteen papers on Dutch immigration presented at the Balch Institute for Ethnic Studies in the fall of 1982.

Thompson, Harry F., Arthur R. Huseboe, and Sandra Olsen Looney, eds. *A Common Land, a Diverse People: Ethnic Identity on the Prairie Plains.* Sioux Falls, South Dakota, 1987. 190 pp.

Upton, Dell, ed. *America's Architectural Roots: Ethnic Groups That Built America.* Washington, D.C., 1986. 193 pp.

Included are essays on the Danes by Thomas Carter, the Finns by Matti Kaups, the Norwegians by Darrell D. Henning, and the Swedes by Lena Andersson-Palmquist.

von Holt, Ida Elizabeth Knudsen. *Stories of Long Ago: Niihua, Kauai, Oahu.* Honolulu, Hawaii, 1985. 158 pp.

A revised edition of the stories of Mrs. von Holt (1868–1941). Included is an essay on Valdemar Knudsen, the author's father, who emigrated from Oslo to the United States in the 1850s and later settled in the kingdom of Hawaii.

Weatherford, Doris. *Foreign and Female: Immigrant Women in America, 1840–1930.* New York, 1986. 288 pp.

Contains numerous references to Danish, Norwegian, and Swedish immigrants.

Wefald, Knud. *Dikt i Samling: Selected Poetry.* Edited by Øyvind Tveitereid Gulliksen. [Porsgrunn], Norway, 1987. 120 pp.

Twenty-nine poems by a noted Norwegian-American poet (1869–1936), five in English.

Wheeler, Wayne. *An Analysis of Social Change in a Swedish-Immigrant Community: The Case of Lindsborg, Kansas.* New York, 1986. 386 pp.

Wretlind, Eric. *A Swedish City Directory of Boston 1881.* Translated and edited with notes by Nils William Olsson. Winter Park, Florida, 1985. 78 pp.

ARTICLES

Andersen, Arlow W. "Danish Methodists in the United States." *The Bridge,* 10,1: 20–38 (1987).

Andersen, Arlow W. "The Haymarket Affair and the Norwegian Immigrant Press." *Norwegian-American Studies,* 31: 97–112 (1986).

A survey of contemporary Norwegian-American press opinion on a significant event in the American labor movement.

Andersen, Arlow W. "Reflections on Denmark As It Was, and Emigration to America." *The Bridge,* 9,1: 17–35 (1986).

Anderson, Alan B. "Scandinavian Settlements in Saskatchewan: Migration History and Changing Ethnocultural Identity." *Scandinavian-Canadian Studies: Études Scandinaves au Canada,* 2: 89–113 (1986).

Anderson, Lorna. "Telelaget i USA." *Telemark Historie,* 8: 54–60 (1987).

The society of emigrants and their descendants from Telemark in the United States.

Andersson-Palmquist, Lena. "Buildings on Swedish-American Farms in Two Minnesota Communities." *The Swedish-American Historical Quarterly,* 38, 1: 13–28 (January, 1987).

Bakken, Reidar. "Grøneriet ved Teksle-bottomen; eksempel på norsk-amerikansk bygningshistorie i Iowa." *Norveg,* 30: 127–147 (1987).

With English summary. The granary at Teksle-bottom. An example of Norwegian-American building in Iowa. The granary is now at the Norwegian Emigrant Museum, Hamar, Norway.

Bakken, Reidar. "En solungs amerikanske hus; tilpasninger til kultur og naturmiljø." *Nytt om gammalt. Glomdalsmuseets årbok,* 1986, 69–87.

The article is based on a study of a timber house now at the Norwegian Emigrant Museum, Hamar, which was built in Norman, North Dakota, in 1871 by Peder Borderud, an emigrant from Grue in Solør.

Barton, H. Arnold. "Bibliography of Articles Published, 1950–1985." *The Swedish-American Historical Quarterly*, 37, 1: 3–33 (January, 1986).

Barton, H. Arnold. "Måns Jakob's Grindstone, or Documentary Sources and the Transference of Swedish Material Culture to North America." *The Swedish-American Historical Quarterly*, 38, 1: 29–40 (January, 1987).

Beatty, William K. "The Jens Nyholm Papers." *The Bridge*, 8, 2: 60–68 (1985).

   Jens Nyholm from Denmark was Northwestern's University Librarian from 1944–1968 and his extensive papers are preserved in the University Archives.

Beijbom, Ulf A. "From Sweden to America." *Scandinavian Review*, 73, 4: 93–103 (Winter, 1985).

Beijbom, Ulf A. "The Swedish Emigrants' Liverpool." *The Swedish-American Historical Quarterly*, 38, 3: 97–116 (July, 1987).

Betsinger, Signe Nielsen. "The Danish Immigrant." *The Bridge*, 9, 1: 5–16 (1986).

   A recounting of the establishment of the Danish Immigrant Museum Committee and the decision not to establish a central Danish-American Archives but to rely on the Danish Immigrant Archival Listing (DIAL).

Bjaaland, Pat. "Meet Dik Browne the Wonderful, Creator of Hägar the Horrible." *The Norseman*, 27, 6: 22–25 (November, 1987).

   An American cartoonist has created a comic strip about a Norwegian Viking which has proved popular with Norwegians and Norwegian Americans alike.

Björnson, Valdimar. "Preserving Tradition: The Icelandic-Americans." *Scandinavian Review*, 73, 4: 73–79 (Winter, 1985).

Blanck, Dag. "History at Work: The 1888 New Sweden Jubilee." *The Swedish-American Historical Quarterly*, 39, 2: 5–20 (April, 1988).

Cartwright, Carol Lohry. "Rock Island: The Personification of Chester H. Thordarson." *Wisconsin Magazine of History*, 69, 3: 211–227 (Spring, 1986).

   A wealthy Chicago electrical inventor and businessman, born in Iceland, designed and supervised the construction of six unusual stone buildings on his estate on Rock Island, Door county, Wisconsin. His book collection was acquired by the University of Wisconsin after his death and forms part of the library's history of science collection.

Chrislock, Carl H. "Profile of a Ward Boss: The Political Career of Lars M. Rand." *Norwegian-American Studies*, 31: 35–72 (1986).

   Rand, a Norwegian-American Minneapolis politician, was able to advance politically by responding to the divisions, needs, and interests within his constituency, the sixth ward.

Christensen, Carl Christian Anton. "By Handcart to Utah." Translated by Richard L. Jensen. *Nebraska History*, 66, 4: 333–348 (Winter, 1985).

Reminiscences by a Danish immigrant artist who made the trek to Salt Lake City in 1857.

Christianson, J. R. "Early Landscape Mimics European Model." *Luther*, 21, 2: 5 (April, 1986); "Luther Campus: monument to prairie school." *Luther*, 21, 3: 7–8 (August, 1986); "Recultivating Luther's 'Symbolic Prairies'." *Luther*, 22, 1: 10 (January, 1987).

A history of Danish-American Jens Jensen's landscaping work on the Luther College campus, Decorah, Iowa, with a proposal to restore the original plan and extend it.

Christianson, J. R. "Jens Jensen and the Prairie School Campus of Luther College." *The Palimpsest*, 67, 4: 130–140 (July/August, 1988).

Christianson, J. R. "Marcus Lee Hansen Returns to his Roots." *The Bridge*, 10, 1: 67–81 (1987).

Clausen, C. A. "Some Recent Publications." *Norwegian-American Studies*, 31: 305–316 (1986).

A listing of books and articles, published largely during the years 1982–1985, dealing with immigration history.

Cleven, Harry T. "A. B. Wilse: Immigrant With a Camera." *The Norseman*, 26, 3: 19 (July, 1986).

Anders Beers Wilse (1865–1949) of Flekkefjord learned the photography trade in the United States between 1884 and 1900 and returned to Norway to become a successful photographer.

Daniels, Roger. "Japanese America, 1930–1941: An Ethnic Community in the Great Depression." *Journal of the West*, 24, 4: 35–49 (October, 1985).

Draxten, Nina. "Laurits Stavnheim." *The Sons of Norway Viking*, 82, 12: 434–435, 456 (December, 1985).

A biographical sketch of one of the early officers of the Sons of Norway in Minneapolis.

Erickson, Rolf H. "Norwegian-American Artists' Exhibitions Described in Checklists and Catalogs." *Norwegian-American Studies*, 31: 283–304 (1986).

Art exhibitions were urban phenomena in Norwegian-American life. Six illustrations.

Erickson, Rolf H. and Nils William Olsson. "Scandinavian Physicians in Chicago 1887–1912." *Swedish American Genealogist*, 6, 1: 1–12 (March, 1986).

Ericson, Kathryn. "Triple Jeopardy: The Muus vs. Muus Case in Three Forums." *Minnesota History*, 50, 8: 298–308 (Winter, 1987).

The divorce case of Pastor B. J. Muus and his wife, Oline, gained wide attention.

Fagerhaug, Tore. "Ola J. Rise." *Bøgda vår. Årsskrift for lokalhistorie*, 1987, 4–10.

During his stay in America, 1899–1909, Rise published a book and wrote poems for Norwegian-American periodicals and newspapers.

Fink, Deborah. "Anna Oleson: Rural Family and Community in Iowa, 1880–1920." *Annals of Iowa*, 48: 5–6, 251–263 (Summer/Fall, 1986).

Anna Ravnaas Oleson of Strand, Norway, became a central figure in a Friends settlement in O'Brien county, Iowa.

Fløystad, Ingeborg. "Kvinnene i (det ville) Vesten: En gren av amerikanske kvinners historie og norske immigrantkvinners plass i den." *Historisk Tidsskrift*, 66, 2: 209–222 (1987).

Women in the (wild) West. A survey of literature about this part of the history of American women and about the role Norwegian immigrant women played in it.

Foss, Hans A. "The Pioneer's Christmas." Translated by Sigvald Stoylen. *The Sons of Norway Viking*, 83, 12: 484–485 (December, 1986).

Friedman, Philip S. "The Danish Community of Chicago." *The Bridge*, 8, 1: 5–95 (1985).

Furman, Anastasia. "What Was the Yeppo of Yesteryear?" *Winchester Academy Round Table*, 1986, 25–28.

An account of a Norwegian-American outdoor game.

Gaukstad, Even. "Utvandrerne og det Norge de forlot." *Maihaugen*, 1980–1985: 9–37.

The exhibit by this name about the emigrants and the country they left is described in text and pictures.

Gilbertson, Donald E. "Norwegian Antiques: Recognition of a Rich Wisconsin Heritage." *Antique Review*, September, 1987, 37–41.

A well-illustrated article discussing items brought from Norway by immigrants, articles constructed by immigrants to furnish their homes, and articles imported for commercial purposes.

Gjerde, Jon. "Conflict and Community: a Case Study of the Immigrant Church in the United States." *Journal of Social History*, 19, 4: 681–697 (Summer, 1986).

Gjersvik, Martin. "Karmøys rolle i utvandringen til Amerika." *Ætt og heim. Lokalhistorisk årbok for Rogaland*, 1986, 153–164.

The island of Karmøy's impact on emigration to America.

Gladhaug, Ole A. "Fra Valdres til Alaska—Historien om Mikkel Gladhaug." *Sagn og Soge i Søndre Ourdahl*, 1986, 50–56.

An emigrant from South Aurdal, Valdres, first settled in Wisconsin in 1866, later explored in the West, went on to seek gold in Alaska in the 1890s, and died in Wyoming in 1901.

Grindal, Gracia. "Linka Preus' Sketches of Iowa." *The Palimpsest*, 67, 4: 118–129 (July/August, 1986).

The wife of Herman Preus, pioneer pastor of the Norwegian Lutheran Synod, sketched for her own amusement between 1858 and 1866 and left a remarkable record of her life. Thirteen illustrations.

Gulliksen, Øyvind T. "Amerikabrev i Telemark." *Telemark Historie*, 8: 7–23 (1987).

Gulliksen, Øyvind T. "In Defense of a Norwegian-American Culture: Waldemar Ager's *Sons of the Old Country.*" *American Studies in Scandinavia*, 19, 1: 39–52 (1987).

Gulliksen, Øyvind T. "Rui-folket frå Kilen i Kviteseid reiser til Amerika." *Årbok for Telemark*, 32: 21–41 (1986).

Gullikson, Øyvind T. and Carla R. Waal. "Peder Kristoffersen Waal; En utvandrer fra Notodden." *Notodden historielag årsskrift*, 4: 66–77 (1986).

Gunderson, Ida. "Dagbok fra en reise med prærievogn fra Mitchell County i Iowa till Chippewa County i Minnesota høsten 1899." *Solør-Odal*, 9, 6, no. 2: 237–244 (1986).

Hallberg, Carl V. "Nineteenth-Century Colorado Through Swedish Eyes." *The Swedish-American Historical Quarterly*, 36, 2: 112–132 (April, 1985).

Hanson, Henry. "Yankee from Småland: An Immigrant Saga." *The Swedish-American Historical Quarterly*, 36, 2: 133–144.
A biography of the senior Henry Hanson, the author's father, who emigrated to Middletown, Connecticut, where he worked as a machinist and took an active part in church and community affairs.

Harvey, Anne-Charlotte and Richard H. Hulan. " 'Teater, Visafton och Bal': The Swedish-American Road Show in Its Heyday." *The Swedish-American Historical Quarterly*, 37, 3: 126–141 (July, 1986).

Haugen, Einar. " 'Dear Sara Alelia': An Episode in Rølvaag's Life." *Norwegian-American Studies*, 31: 269–282 (1986).
Hitherto unknown correspondence between the Norwegian-American novelist and Marie Halling Swensen of Norway.

Heyerdahl, Johan Fr. "Arley Bjella: Norsk ess i Minneapolis." *The Norseman*, 27, 5: N–4–5 (September, 1987).
An interview with the retiring president of Lutheran Brotherhood.

Higham, John. "The Mobilization of Immigrants in Urban America." *Norwegian-American Studies*, 31: 3–33 (1986).
A review of the scholarly debate about the immigrant's impact of urban America.

"History of the Leif Erikson Statue in Boston." *Norway Times/Nordisk Tidende*, October 8, 1987, 5, 7.
The statue, the first of Leif Ericson to be erected in the United States, is 100 years old.

Hoglund, A. William. "Finnish-Americans and Their Disappearing Immigrant Generation." *Scandinavian Review*, 73, 4: 62–71 (Winter, 1985).

Jacobson, Charlotte. "From the Archives." *Norwegian-American Studies*, 31: 317–323 (1986).
A listing, with brief analyses, of recent acquisitions by the Archives of the Norwegian-American Historical Association, Northfield, Minnesota.

Jensen, Karl. "Karl Jensen's Diary." *Winchester Academy Round Table*, 1986, 3–23.
A translation of a diary written by a Dane from Jutland during his journey to America in 1903.

Jenswold, John R. " 'I Live Well, But . . . ': Letters from Norwegians in Industrial America." *Norwegian-American Studies*, 31: 113–129 (1986).
Documentation of the experiences of Norwegian immigrant workers in the 1890s.

Jenswold, John R. "In Search of a Norwegian-American Working Class." *Minnesota History*, 50, 2: 63–70 (Summer, 1986).
Originally published in Norwegian in *Samtiden*, 93, 3: 9–17 (1985).

Jenswold, John R. "The Missing Dimension: The Historiography of the Urban Norwegian Immigrants." *The Immigration History Newsletter*, 18, 1: 4–7 (May, 1986).

Jonassen, Christen T. "The Norwegian Heritage in Urban America: Conflict and Cooperation in a Norwegian Immigrant Community." *Norwegian-American Studies*, 31: 73–95 (1986).
Transplanted ethnic value systems and attitudes, as well as American patterns, influenced behavior and produced both conflict and cooperation in the Norwegian Brooklyn community.

Johnson, Emeroy, "Early History of Chisago Lake Reexamined." *The Swedish-American Historical Quarterly*, 39, 1: 215–225 (January, 1988).

Klevstrand, Rolf. "Norske farmasøyter i USA." *Norges apotekerforenings tidsskrift*, 90: 303–305 (1982); 92: 233–236 (1984); 93: 257–262 (1985); 94: 244–247 (1986); 95: 218–221 (1987).
A series of five articles on Norwegian immigrant pharmacists in the United States, with summaries in English: (1) Albert Bellerud (1849–1921); (2) Peter Olivarius Bugge (1875–1970); (3) Norwegian pharmacists in Chicago; (4) Norwegian pharmacists in Minneapolis; (5) views on American pharmacy.

Kongslien, Ingeborg R. "Fiction as Interpretation of the Emigrant Experience: The Novels of Johan Bojer, O. E. Rølvaag, Vilhelm Moberg and Alfred Hauge." *American Studies in Scandinavia*, 18, 2: 83–92 (1986).

Kongslien, Ingeborg R. " 'Härborta—därhemma': The Emigration Process as Depicted by O. E. Rølvaag, Vilhelm Moberg, and Alfred Hauge." *Scandinavian Literature in a Transcultural Context*, Rossel and Steene, eds. 267–270.

[Langton, Charles.] "Minnekirken, a Norwegian Landmark." *Norwegian-American Museum Newsletter*, 22, 1: [1, 8] (Spring, 1987).
Minnekirken is the last surviving Norwegian-language church in Chicago.

Larsen, Karl. "Sketches of My Life." *The Bridge*, 9, 2: 29–42 (1986).
A Danish immigrant worked as a commercial artist in Detroit.

Larsson, Evert A. "Pastor Eric Biörck and the Revival of Swedish Religious Life in the Delaware Valley." *The Swedish-American Historical Quarterly*, 36, 2: 83–92 (April, 1985).
An account of the efforts of a Swedish pastor in the 1690s.

Liestman, Daniel. "The Chinese in the Black Hills, 1876–1932." *Journal of the West*, 27, 1: 74–83 (January, 1988).
A small but significant number of Chinese were lured by the gold rush in the Black Hills of the Dakota Territory but, because of white resentment against their mining of gold, instead provided services to the miners with laundries and restaurants.

Lindquist, Emory. "Sweden's Search for Answers: *The Emigration Survey*, Then and Now." *The Swedish-American Historical Quarterly*, 37, 4: 159–173 (October, 1986).
A reflection on the impact of the study authorized by the Swedish Parliament and issued between 1907–1913.

Lovoll, Odd S. "On Being a Norwegian-American in the 1980s." *Scandinavian Review*, 73, 4: 80–91 (Winter, 1985).

Lovoll, Odd S. "*Washington Posten*: A Window on a Norwegian-American Urban Community." *Norwegian-American Studies*, 31: 163–186 (1986).
The role of the immigrant press in the Norwegian community of Seattle.

MacLeish, William H. "New England fishermen battle the winter ocean on Georges Bank." *Smithsonian*, 16, 2: 105–116 (May, 1985).
Adapted from *Oil and Water: The Struggle for Georges Bank* (Boston, 1985). Norwegian-American fishermen from New Bedford, Massachusetts, give interviews.

Magnusson, Brian. "Olof Grafström: An Immigrant Artist Portrays the Early Pacific Northwest, 1886–1890." *The Swedish-American Historical Quarterly*, 37, 2: 42–59 (April, 1986).

Mamen, Hans Christian. "Fra Vestfold til Vesterheimen i litt om Amerika-emigrasjonen fra Jarlsberg og Larvik Amt." *Vestfoldminne*, 1987, 24–31.

Metcalf, Michael F. "Letters from the Delaware, I: The Rev. Erick Björck, March 22, 1698." *The Swedish-American Historical Quarterly*, 39, 1: 195–214 (January, 1988).

Miller, Deborah L. "Minneapolis Picture Album, 1870–1935: Images of Norwegians in the City." *Norwegian-American Studies*, 31: 131–162 (1986).
Thirty-one illustrations.

Moen, Per. "Norsk språk i USA idag — fins det?" *The Norseman*, 28, 1: N-6 (January, 1988).
Article on Norwegian language in the United States today, based on interviews in Iowa, Minnesota, North Dakota, and Wisconsin.

Mørner, Magnus. "The Swedish Migrants to Texas." *The Swedish-American Historical Quarterly*, 38, 2: 49–74 (April, 1987).

Mosbæk, Ludvig. "A Transplanted Dane Looks Back on 80 Years." Translated by Edith Kilgren, abridged and edited by Olga S. Opfell. *The Bridge*, 10, 1: 39–66 (1987).

Muehlberg, Julie. "Round Robin Celebrates Centennial Flight." *The Sons of Norway Viking*, 82, 7: 221–223 (July, 1985).
The descendants of Abel and Cathrine Anderson's nine children (Rasmus Bjørn Anderson of Madison was one) keep alive a round-robin letter begun in 1885.

Nelson, Marion J. "American Woodcarvers from Telemark," in *Telemark Historie*, 8: 24–53 (1987).

Nelson, Marion J. "J. Theodore Sohner 1906–1962." *Norwegian-American Museum Newsletter*, 21, 3: [1–6] (Fall, 1986).
A catalog of the work of a Norwegian-American artist from St. Paul, Minnesota, for exhibits held in Decorah, Iowa, and Minneapolis.

Nelson, Marion J. "Land and Sea; the Art of William Torjesen 1897–1971." *Norwegian-American Museum Newsletter*, 21, 1: 1–6 (Spring, 1986).
Illustrated catalog of an exhibition of paintings by a Norwegian immigrant painter from Kristiansand held in Decorah, Iowa.

Nøkkentved, Christian D. "Migration in Nineteenth-Century Rural Denmark: The Case of Magleby Parish." *Scandinavian Studies*, 59, 4: 389–403 (Autumn, 1987).

Oberg, Elmer B. "The Farm Life of a Swedish Immigrant in Illinois, circa 1900–1925." *The Swedish-American Historical Quarterly*, 36, 3: 168–185 (July, 1985).

O'Connor, David E. "The Swedish Element in America: Confirming the Trends—the 1980 Census." *The Swedish-American Historical Quarterly*, 37, 3: 111–125 (July, 1986).

Ohnstad, Åsmund. "Emigrantane frå Voss 1847–1849: kvifor drog dei ut?" *Gamalt frå Voss*, 18: 22–34 (1986).

Ohnstad, Åsmund. "Koshkonong, Dane County, Wisconsin, eit framgangsrikt nybyggje." *Gamalt frå Voss*, 19: 106–116 (1987).

Opfell, Olga Strandvold. "The Dancing Danes in America." *The Bridge*, 9, 1: 36–54 (1986).

Osberg, Edward E. "Reminiscences of Chicago and Englewood." *The Swedish-American Historical Quarterly*, 36, 3: 200–207 (July, 1985).

Øverland, Orm. "Da embetsmannsklassen tok seg til rette i Vesterheimen." *Nytt norsk tidsskrift*, 3, 2: 49–61 (1986).

Øverland, Orm. "The Fiction of Hans A. Foss: From Norwegian to American Populism." *Scandinavian Literature in a Transcultural Context*, Rossel and Steene, eds., 271–276.

Øverland, Orm. "Norwegian-American Theater and Drama 1865–1885." *Essays in Honour of Kristian Smidt*, Peter Bilton et al, eds. (Oslo, 1986), 189–200.

Øverland, Orm. "*Skandinaven* and the Beginnings of Professional Publishing." *Norwegian-American Studies*, 31: 187–214 (1986).

The Chicago newspaper *Skandinaven* fostered Norwegian immigrant literature in the 1860s and 1870s.

Petterson, Lucille, translator and editor. "Ephraim Is My Home Now: Letters of Anna and Anders Petterson, 1884–1889 (Part I)." *Wisconsin Magazine of History*, 69, 3: 187–210 (Spring, 1986); (Part II) 69, 4: 284–304 (Summer, 1986); (Part III) 70, 1: 32–56 (Autumn, 1986); (Part IV) 70, 2: 107–131 (Winter, 1986–1987).

Anders, a Swede, and Anna, a Dane, were both educated in Moravian schools in Germany, he as a missionary and she as a music teacher. After they were married they emigrated to the United States, arriving in Door county, Wisconsin, in October, 1884, to serve the Moravians settled there. These are their letters "home."

Pfeffer, Paula F. "Homeless Children, Childless Homes." *Chicago History*, 16, 1: 51–65 (Spring, 1987).

The Cradle Society of Evanston, Illinois, and the Illinois Children's Home and Aid Society (ICHAS) were two agencies devoted to the welfare of orphaned and illegitimate children established in the Chicago area with divergent philosophies of adoption. The Cradle was founded by Florence Walrath, a Norwegian American.

Rasmussen, Janet E. " 'The Best Place on Earth for Women': The American Experience of Aasta Hansteen." *Norwegian-American Studies*, 31: 245–267 (1986).

This Norwegian feminist lived in America from 1880 to 1889 and was greatly affected by the more advanced American feminist movement.

Ravenholt, Reimert T. "Hanne Ravnholt — Pioneer Wisconsin Buttermaker." *The Bridge*, 10, 1: 5–19 (1987).

"Restored 1856 Homestead." *Country Living*, 10, 1: 70–76 (January, 1987).

Photographic essay about Little Norway, a privately-owned open-air museum in Blue Mounds, Wisconsin.

Richtik, James M. "Chain Migration Among Icelandic Settlers in Canada to 1891." *Scandinavian-Canadian Studies: Études Scandinaves au Canada*, 2: 73–88 (1986).

Seland, Per. "Hvordan oppspore slektninger i Amerika?" *Norsk slekts-historisk tidsskrift*, 30, 3: 265–270 (1986).

How do you trace your relatives in America?

Semmingsen, Ingrid. " 'Det norske Amerika' — i fortid og nåtid." *Kirke og kultur*, 92, 6: 321–345 (1984).

Semmingsen, Ingrid. "The Norwegian Immigrant Woman in America — Some Glimpses Through Her Letters." *The Sons of Norway Viking*, 84, 4: 140–141, 156–157 (April, 1987).

Semmingsen, Ingrid. "Who was Herm. Wang?" *Norwegian-American Studies*, 31: 215–243 (1986).

A recounting of the life and career of a Norwegian-American humorist and dissident, Ole S. Hervin, who wrote under the pseudonym Herm. Wang.

Setterdahl, Lily. "Adjusting to America." *The Palimpsest*, 68, 5: 136–144 (Fall, 1987).

Ida Jensen Hansen of Ringsaker, Norway, eased the transition to American society for thousands of Scandinavian-American women with her *Kvinnen og Hjemmet* (Woman and the Home), published in both Norwegian and Swedish editions.

Seyersted, Per. "Hjalmar Hjorth Boyesen: Norwegian-American Writer." *The Norway-America Association Yearbook*, 1985, 9–14.

Skårdal, Dorothy Burton. "Danes in America." *Scandinavian Review*, 73, 4: 50–59 (Winter, 1985).

Skårdal, Dorothy Burton. "Danish-American Literature in Transition." *The Bridge*, 9, 1: 55–69 (1986).

Stang, Cæcilie. "Mønstringsprotokoller som kilde til utvandringshistorien." *Heimen*, 24, 2: 96–100 (1987).

Patterns of enlistment and occupation among Norwegian seamen which give insight into emigration history.

Stang, Cæcilie. "Utvandring og arbeidsvandring fra Feda til USA ca. 1850–1950." *Årsskrift. Agder historielag*, 62: 52–59 (1986).

Strickon, Arnold. "Norwegians and Tobacco in Wisconsin." *The Norseman*, 25, 5: 4–7 (September, 1985).

Sunde, Arne. "Jon Norstog—telemarking, norskdomsforkjempar, bladmann og diktar i det norske Amerika." *Telemark Historie*, 8: 61–70 (1987).

Sween, Roger and Rolf Erickson. "Between the Lines: Family Profile Revealed Through Manuscripts." *Manuscripts*, 37, 1: 33–40 (Winter, 1985).

The reassembled archives of a Norwegian-American family are examined.

Trägårdh, Kurt G. "Sven Mattisson Trägårdh, Swedish Labor Leader and Emigrant." *Swedish American Genealogist*, 7, 4: 145–158 (December, 1987).

Vaage, Jakob. "Legendary Herman Smith-Johannsen died at the age of 111 years, 6 months and 20 days." *The Norway-America Association Yearbook*, 1987, 13–15.

Van der Kloot, Robert. "Right Place, Right Time—The William S. Knudsen Story." *The Bridge*, 9, 2: 5–28 (1986).

This Danish American became president of General Motors. During World War II he was called on by President Roosevelt to head the Office of Production

Management and later commissioned a Lieutenant General to supervise production for the United States Army.

Vasaasen, Ole K. "Ole K. Vasaasens reisedagbok: Afreisen fra hjemmet." *Gammalt frå Stange og Romedal*, 1985, 104–117.

Diary of his journey from Stange in Norway to Otter Tail county, Minnesota, in 1883.

Vickery, Jim Dale. "With deep Norwegian roots, cross-country skiing flourishes in the Midwest." *Cross Country Skier*, January, 1987, 44–50.

Volkel, Lowell M., ed. "Genealogical Collections in Illinois." *Illinois Libraries*, 68: 243–284 (April, 1986).

A special issue with articles describing the genealogical resources of the Swenson Swedish Immigration Center, Rock Island; the Newberry Library, Chicago; the University of Illinois Library at Urbana-Champaign; the Shawnee Library System, the Peoria Public Library, the Chicago Branch of the National Archives, the Illinois State Historical Library, the Illinois State Library, the Illinois Regional Archives, and the Illinois State Archives. A useful article on using Illinois' death records is included.

Webb, Anne B. "Forgotten Persephones—Women Farmers on the Frontier." *Minnesota History*, 50, 4: 134–148 (Winter, 1986).

A large percentage of homesteads and other farm acquisitions were taken by single women. Among them were Scandinavian immigrants such as Pauline Auzjon from Norway in Grant county, Minnesota, and Emma Satterlund from Sweden in Traverse county, Minnesota.

Wendelius, Lars. "Fredrika Bremer and the Woman Question in America." *Scandinavian Literature in a Transcultural Context*, Rossel and Steene, eds., 263–266.

Wiehl, Inga W. "Jens Munk: The Story of a Sailor Who Embraced His Fate." *The Bridge*, 8, 2: 16–32 (1985).

A history of the seventeenth-century Danish explorer who sought the Northwest Passage and died at Hudson Bay in 1619.

Winsberg, Morton D. "The Changing Relative Location of the Swedish-Born in the United States, 1850–1980." *The Swedish-American Historical Quarterly*, 38, 4: 160–166 (October, 1987).

# From the Archives

*by Charlotte Jacobson*

*Balchen, Bernt*

Tributes, clippings, correspondence, information about honors and decorations, and photographs of the Norwegian-born aviator and polar explorer who became world-renowned for his career which included rescue missions, transatlantic flights, South Pole expeditions with Byrd and with Ellsworth, and service in the Second World War to the Scandinavian countries. He came to the United States in 1926 and was made an American citizen by a special act of Congress in 1930.

*Bergeim, Ingeborg Olsdatter*

A 3500-page collection of fifty-two notebooks, which constitute the daily records of a woman from Surnadal who emigrated to the United States in 1880, married Peter Bergeim, and settled with him in Watertown, Dakota Territory.

The first diaries are written in Norwegian, but beginning in 1903 they are in English. They cover her thoughts, personal and family life, and everyday happenings. There are accounts of the Atlantic crossing and of an attempt at homesteading.

Her son Joseph discovered the diaries and translated the story of her early married life into a manuscript called "Ingeborg's Story." This volume also includes genealogy, chronology of important events, her husband's autobiography, and family pictures, as well as a summary of the diaries.

*Bjork, Kenneth O.*

Papers relating to the Norwegian-American interests of a professor of history at St. Olaf College, 1937–1974. A graduate of

St. Olaf College in 1930, he earned his doctorate at the University of Wisconsin in 1935. His publications dealing with the immigrant experience include a great many articles published in *Norwegian-American Studies* and in other journals and books. His two books, *Saga in Steel and Concrete*, 1947, and *West of the Great Divide*, 1958, are landmarks in the field of immigration studies.

He served as editor for the publications of the Norwegian-American Historical Association from 1960 to 1980, during which time twenty-four books were published. On the occasion of his retirement as editor, he was presented with a book of essays in his honor: *Makers of an American Immigrant Legacy*. The opening essay, "Kenneth O. Bjork: Teacher, Scholar, and Editor," by Odd S. Lovoll, is an assessment of his career which reflects "a consistent view of the nature and goal of historical investigation, planted securely in a broad interest in human endeavor." His own statement of purpose was to tell "the whole story of a transplanted people that is now deeply rooted in America."

In Norway his work was recognized with the award of the Knight's Cross, First Class, Order of St. Olav, in 1962, and with the presentation of an honorary Doctor of Philosophy degree at the University of Oslo in 1976.

Papers relating to his career as teacher of history at St. Olaf College and as a political activist are filed in the St. Olaf College Archives.

*Djupedal, Jakob*

"Ei Amerikaferd," the memoirs of an emigrant who helped build a railway, the Grand Trunk Line, in Canada, 1907–1909. The memoirs were edited by Reidar Djupedal and published in *Jul i Nordfjord*, 1982–1984. The accounts cover the trip across the Atlantic to a place near Kenora, Ontario, as well as life and working conditions on the railway and in a new country.

*Fedde, Gabriel Anensen*

"Pennestrøg—Oplevelser," the reminiscences of an emigrant from Feda to Brooklyn in 1880. In Norway he had been a teacher and sea captain; in Brooklyn he established himself as a ship chandler and ship builder. He was influential in the religious life of the community as a lay preacher and Sunday School teacher. He was one of the founders of Trinity Lutheran Church in Brooklyn and also of the Norwegian Deaconess Hospital there.

*Fosholt, Sanford K.*

Notes for a speech given by Fosholt when he made a donation of $50,000 to establish an Archives Fund at the Norwegian-American Historical Association in 1985. In it he explained how he became aware of the need for the preservation of records from our heritage.

Also included is a pamphlet, "A Visit to Dunvegan," an account of his trip in 1983 to the Island of Skye where some of his ancestors had belonged to the Clan MacLeod of Dunvegan.

*Gunnersen, Elise Margrethe Cammermeyer Welhaven*

Xerox copy of pages 135–270 of the handwritten reminiscences of the wife of Professor Sven Rud Gunnersen, who taught at Augsburg College, Minneapolis, 1874–1883.

The memoir is a lively account of the interrelated lives of the Sverdrups, the Oftedals, and the Gunnersens, who occupied three apartments in the same house near the Augsburg campus. Elise Gunnersen found it difficult to adapt to life in Minneapolis, and her husband was not happy in his work at Augsburg. After leaving Augsburg the family spent a year at the Hauge Seminary in Red Wing, where August Weenaas was president. The Gunnersens returned to Norway in 1884, where Elise settled into a life that was more in accord with her background.

*Hagen, Ole Erikson*

Scattered papers of a Norwegian immigrant from Skjåk, Gudbrandsdalen, who came to the United States in 1881, and who spent much of his life at Crookston, Minnesota, where he worked as a stonemason and contractor. In 1896 he became Judge of Probate Court in Polk county.

He was also a journalist who established the popular weekly *Rodhuggeren* in Fergus Falls, Minnesota, in 1893, editing it for the next three years. Eventually this paper consolidated with others to become *Fram*, which he edited from 1899 to 1902. In 1904–1905 he was editor of *Normanden* in Grand Forks, North Dakota.

His other publications include a novel *Tilfjelds*, a summary of which is in the papers; a number of pamphlets published in Crookston; and a biography: *Erik O. Hagen, kort omrids af hans liv og virksomhet i Norge og Amerika* (A brief sketch of his life and activities in Norway and in America). There is also one issue (1/9, August, 1896) of *Frisind*, a periodical which he published together with Halvor Shirley in Fergus Falls, Minnesota.

*Haslerud, Peter Peterson*

"Petersen fra Peterson," a pamphlet containing translations of an article about and letters to and from Peter Peterson Haslerud, an 1843 emigrant from Rollag, Numedal, who founded Peterson, Fillmore county, Minnesota. The translation is by Karl Pedersen, edited by John Erickson.

The story of Peter K. Haslerud, a nephew of Peter Peterson Haslerud, is also included in the pamphlet.

*Hjelmeseth, Eilert*

Correspondence and records dealing chiefly with Landsforbundet for Norsk Ungdom i Amerika, the national union of Norwegian youth societies. Hjelmeseth, who was born in Nordfjordeid, was the editor for the Landsforbundet publication *Norsk Ungdom*. He was also associated with other Norwegian-American publications.

*Kilde, Clarence*

Correspondence and other materials collected by a retired Norwegian-American Episcopal priest in connection with his interest in Waldemar Ager. This interest began when he was growing up in Eau Claire, Wisconsin, and learned to know members of Ager's family and led eventually to his receiving a master's degree at the University of Minnesota in 1978 on the completion of a thesis, *Tragedy in the Life and Writings of Waldemar Ager: Immigrant, Author and Editor*, a copy of which is in the St. Olaf College Library.

This collection supplements and in part duplicates papers previously contributed by Kilde to the Ager Papers.

*Larson, Harold*

Chiefly letters from Norway to the family of a Norwegian-American educator. Included also are the citizenship papers of Michael Larsen, 1885, and three letters from N. J. Thomasberg, then a student at Augsburg Seminary, to members of the Larson family. Letters from 1928 to 1937 are to Harold Larson from his mother.

Larson was born in Sioux City, Iowa, and received his B.A. degree from Morningside College, Sioux City, in 1927, and his M.A. and Ph.D. degrees from Columbia University. In 1929–1930 he was a Lydia C. Roberts Traveling Scholar to the University of Oslo. The King's College Press published his doctoral dissertation, *Bjørnstjerne Bjørnson: A Study in Nationalism*, in 1944.

Larson taught history at McKendree College, Lebanon, Illinois; at the Municipal University of Omaha; at the University of Maryland; and at the Pentagon. He was an archivist at the United States National Archives and served as an historian for the United States Army and the United States Air Force. Complete details of his professional career are covered in a letter from the Rare Book and Manuscript Library at Columbia University, where the bulk of his papers are kept.

*Lindley, Lester G.*

"To Fulfill This Mission: A History of Kendall College, 1934–1984," written by a teacher at Kendall College, Evanston, Illinois, to commmemorate its fiftieth anniversary. Kendall was originally a two-year college, called Evanston Collegiate Institute; it had been the recipient of property from the Swedish Methodist Episcopal Theological Seminary and the Norwegian-Danish Theological Seminary. The name was changed to Kendall College in 1950, and the school became a four-year college in 1976.

The building that was originally constructed for the Norwegian-Danish Theological Seminary and later turned over to the Evanston Collegiate Institute was made into an office building by Frank Wheby. His notes on the building are in the file.

*Logan Square First Baptist Church, Chicago*

A church register listing membership, officers, chronology, and statistics of the Logan Square Norske Baptist Menighet. Minutes of the meetings, written in Norwegian, cover the period 1908–1918. Some of the other listings continue until 1956.

*Lundeberg, Knut Olafson*

"Glimt fra mit liv" (Glimpses from my life), an eighty-one page memoir, together with some biographical data, about a prominent Norwegian Lutheran pastor who emigrated from Kviteseid, Telemark, in 1878. He came to Chickasaw county, Iowa, and wrote his first letter to his people in Norway from there. He studied at Luther College in Decorah, Iowa, in 1881–1882. During the years 1886–1889 he attended the seminary which was located at St. Olaf College from 1886 to 1890. This seminary later became part of the Theological Seminary of the newly-formed United Lutheran Church. He was ordained in 1889 and had a varied career as pastor, teacher, and administrator. A founder of a small Lutheran group, Brodersamfundet, he served as editor of their publication, but later returned to the United Lutheran Church. An interesting item in the collection is a brief history of the seminary in Northfield.

*Molde, Jostein*

"Settlement Patterns for Immigrants from Verdal, Norway, a Survey and Analysis," a study prepared by a Norwegian student at St. Olaf College, 1981–1982, as part of a thesis to be completed at the University of Trondheim.

*Øien Family*

A collection of letters, dated from 1907 to 1948, written from Chicago, Eau Claire, Wisconsin, and Kvalshaug, Norway, by siblings, brothers- and sisters-in-law, nieces and nephews of Randi Larsdatter Øien Flatreit. She was the only one of eight children from the last generation to be raised at the Øyegrinde *husmanns* place at Nedre Øien who remained in Norway. An explanatory letter concerning the relationships is included in the file.

*Oyen, Odin J.*

"A Catalog of the Oyen Collection from the University of Wisconsin, La Crosse," which gives the history of the Oyen Interior Design Firm. Oyen came from Trondheim in 1870 with his parents to Chicago and later to Madison, Wisconsin. After having studied art in Chicago, Oyen settled in La Crosse in 1888, where, together with Louis Nelson, he organized an interior decorating firm, working chiefly on public buildings. The firm was dissolved in 1931.

*Peterson, Gerhard Augustine*

Biographical data, clippings, photographs, sermons, and poems of a Norwegian-American Lutheran pastor, a graduate of St. Olaf College in 1916. As a member of the St. Olaf College Band he traveled to Norway and remained there for a year of study at Menighetsfakultetet. After serving in several parishes he became Executive Secretary for the Zion Society for Israel, 1943–1952.

*Scandinavian Young Men's Christian Society, Chicago*

Minutes and financial records of two societies, the first organized in 1872 as De unge Mænds kristelige Forening tilhørende Trefoldigheds Menighed, Chicago, Illinois, and soon disbanded. The second organization was founded in 1876. The purpose of these societies was to foster spiritual, intellectual, and social development among Scandinavians.

*Sohner, Jacob Theodore*

"J. Theodore Sohner, Portrait Painter," by Ione Kadden, the story of a versatile artist who was also a fine musician. Subjects for his portraits were many distinguished Minnesotans: governors, senators, judges, scientists, and musicians. A plea is made in the story for locating the extant Sohner portraits so that this record may be preserved at the Vesterheim Museum in Decorah, Iowa.

*Solwald, Gunnar Olsen*

"Remembrance From My Life," an autobiographical account of an 1875 emigrant from Skien, who tells about his childhood and youth and his career as seaman, soldier, and teacher in Norway. The emigrant journey in 1875 is covered in detail; it finally ended near Rushford, Minnesota, where Solwald was a farmer and teacher. Later he and his family moved to Clay county, Minnesota, and in 1887 went to the state of Washington.

An epilogue by Gertrude Solwold Wells tells the story of the last years of his life in Tacoma, Washington.

A later addition to the collection is "Borghild," a memoir by Borghild Solwold Melbye.

*Stavangeren, Chicago*

Records of a local *bygdelag* organized by immigrants from

Stavanger in Chicago, whose stated purpose was to foster traditions and connections among the members through regular meetings and social gatherings. For a time the group published a newsletter, *Mortepumpen*, for its members. Some of the articles and stories from it are preserved in the papers.

### Tangjerd, Peder

Clippings, naturalization certificate, letters, and other data concerning a Norwegian-born pastor who came from Karmøy in 1888. After serving as a parish pastor, he became editor of *Lutheraneren*, the official organ of the Norwegian Lutheran Church in America. Among the papers is a manuscript "En fiskedag på vestsiden af Karmøi," a memoir of a day in 1880.

### Winger, Bjorn

Poems, stories, and an unpublished novel by a Norwegian-American teacher, folklorist, and writer, a graduate of St. Olaf College in 1914, who received a master's degree from Indiana University in 1930. He taught English in an Indianapolis high school, 1916–1941, and saw army service in France during the First World War.

The papers include information about his father, Anders Winger, who had been an actor in his youth in Norway, but who emigrated to the United States in 1882 and lived in Minnesota the rest of his life. He died in 1928.

### Woodside, Lorence Munson

The papers of an American woman, born in Hamilton county, Iowa, the daughter of Norwegian emigrants Sivert and Mesine Monson. She was a graduate of Highland Park Normal College, Des Moines, Iowa, in 1893, and did further study at the University of Chicago and at Boston University. She was an instructor in elocution at Buena Vista College, Storm Lake, Iowa, and for a short time Director of Physical Culture for the Iowa WCTU. From 1901 to 1927 she was employed by the Redpath Lyceum, the Eastern Lyceum, and the Chautauqua system as a reader, occasionally as a manager. In 1909 she married Alonzo Woodside, a veteran of the Spanish-American War, whose later career included service in the First World War and work in the Boston Post Office.

Lorence Woodside's varied interests led her into many fields in addition to her career in public speaking. She was a gardener, leading school garden projects during the two world wars; she developed a dahlia which was given the name "Mrs. Woodside." Much of her energy was devoted to civic and community service and to clubs and organizations.

Her trips to Norway in 1906, 1913, and 1926, the last as an

Honorary Fellow of the American–Scandinavian Foundation, brought her into contact with many Norwegian writers. Her major achievements in this regard were the translation of Sverre Brandt's play, *Sonja and the Christmas Star*, produced by the New York Junior League Players in December, 1929, and the translation of Barbara Ring's short story, *Peik*, published by Little Brown in Boston, 1932.

# Contributors

Robert A. Ibarra is an anthropologist at the University of Wisconsin in Madison with special research interests in Mexican-American migrant farm workers and economic elites in Latin America, and also in ethnicity and the farm culture of Norwegian Americans in rural Wisconsin. He is currently involved together with Professor Arnold Strickon in a project to investigate the impact of the contemporary farm crisis on patterns of ethnicity in Vernon county, Wisconsin, as these relate to agriculture.

Arnold Strickon is professor of anthropology at the University of Wisconsin in Madison. During his early academic career he studied cattle-ranching communities in Argentina and became interested in rural communities established primarily by European immigrants and in the role of ethnicity, which led to his later examination of multi-ethnic farming communities in Wisconsin.

Aage Engesæter is on the faculty of Sogn og Fjordane Regional College at Sogndal. His professional interests include Norwegian social history and migrational forces; he is the author of *"Rift om brødet"? Befolkning, ressursar og økonomi i Sogn 1801–1855*, published in 1985, and a recent history of the county of Sogn og Fjordane for its sesquicentennial anniversary.

C.A. Clausen, a member of the Association's Board of Publications and professor emeritus of Norwegian and history at St. Olaf College, has contributed regularly to the series.

B. Lindsay Lowell earned a doctoral degree in sociology from Brown University in 1985; his thesis *Scandinavian Exodus: Demography and Social Development of 19th-Century Rural Communities* was published two years later.

Janet E. Rasmussen is Humanities Dean at Pacific Lutheran University in Tacoma and a professor in the Scandinavian Area Studies Program. She has contributed earlier to this series.

Steven L. Johnson is assistant curator and manager of the Jacobson farmstead at Vesterheim, the Norwegian-American Museum, and is extensively involved in local preservation and history.

Marion J. Nelson, professor of art history at the University of Minnesota and director of Vesterheim, the Norwegian-American Museum, has a special interest in the folk and fine arts of Norwegians in America. He has lectured and published widely in this field.

J.R. Christianson is professor of history at Luther College. He has contributed numerous articles and translations to journals and collective works in the fields of Scandinavian studies and Scandinavian immigration history. He is presently completing a study of the sixteenth-century Danish astronomer Tycho Brahe.

Øyvind T. Gulliksen teaches American literature and culture at Telemark Regional College in Bø. He contributes regularly to popular and professional publications on topics relating to Norwegian emigration and immigrant life in America. In 1988 he published *Ole Helgesens dagbok, 1872–1878. Tinn, Telemark, Calmar, Iowa*, the diary of a Norwegian Synod schoolteacher in Iowa from Tinn in Telemark.

E. Biddle Heg is a great grandson of Colonel Hans Christian Heg of Civil War fame. He is retired from a career in university teaching and administration and is actively pursuing research interests in the Norwegian pioneer settlement at Muskego.

Gracia Grindal, associate professor of pastoral theology and ministry at Luther Northwestern Theological Seminary, has a special interest in hymnology, and has published poetry, as well as articles on Scandinavian folk songs and in her area of teaching.

Einar Haugen, emeritus Victor S. Thomas Professor of Scandinavian and linguistics in Harvard University and a member of the Association's board of publications, has published and lectured extensively within his field and the related areas of Norwegian-American history and literature. The Association's next publication will be his study of the Norwegian-American author Waldemar Ager.

Paul Benson acquired an interest in choral music when he was a student at St. Olaf College. While teaching in the fields of English and religion at Mountain View College in Dallas, Texas, he completed his doctoral degree in English at the University of North Texas.

Rolf H. Erickson is the Circulation Services Librarian at Northwestern University Library and Second Vice President of the Norwegian-American Historical Association. Since 1981 he has served as chairman of the Chicago History Committee. Erickson has agreed to compile "Some Recent Publications" for forthcoming volumes in this series.

Johanna Barstad is a librarian at the university library in Oslo. She has published a list of holdings of the university library pertaining to Norwegian-American subjects, *Litteratur om utvandringen fra Norge til Nord-Amerika* (Oslo, 1975).

Charlotte Jacobson is the Association's archivist. She continues to receive and process significant documents.

Norwegian-American Historical Association

# Officers

*Executive Board*

Lawrence O. Hauge, Edina, Minnesota, President
Roy N. Thorshov, Minneapolis, Minnesota, First Vice President
Rolf H. Erickson, Evanston, Illinois, Second Vice President
Arthur E. Andersen, Chicago, Illinois, Treasurer
Lloyd Hustvedt, Northfield, Minnesota, Secretary
Ruth Hanold Crane, Northfield, Minnesota, Assistant Secretary
Charlotte Jacobson, Northfield, Minnesota, Archivist
Odd S. Lovoll, Northfield, Minnesota, Editor
Mary R. Hove, Northfield, Minnesota, Editorial Assistant
Jostein Molde, Trondheim, Norway, Research Assistant
Samuel Abrahamsen, New York, New York
Oscar A. Anderson, Plymouth, Minnesota
Arley R. Bjella, Edina, Minnesota
Henning C. Boe, Seattle, Washington
J. R. Christianson, Decorah, Iowa
Karen F. Davidson, Hanover, New Hampshire
Russell W. Fridley, St. Paul, Minnesota
Arthur R. Huseboe, Sioux Falls, South Dakota
Derwood Johnson, Waco, Texas
Alf Lunder Knudsen, Seattle, Washington
William J. Korsvik, Wilmette, Illinois
Robert L. Lillestrand, Edina, Minnesota
Elsie M. Melby, Duluth, Minnesota
Marion J. Nelson, Minneapolis, Minnesota
Lois M. Rand, Minneapolis, Minnesota
Dorothy Burton Skårdal, Oslo, Norway
Harry J. Williams, Chicago, Illinois

280

# Publications

*Studies and Records*

**Volume I.** Minneapolis, 1926. 175 pp. Illustrations. Health Conditions and the Practice of Medicine among the Early Norwegian Settlers, 1825–1865, by Knut Gjerset and Ludvig Hektoen; The Norwegian Quakers of 1825, by Henry J. Cadbury; Bishop Jacob Neumann's Word of Admonition to the Peasants, translated and edited by Gunnar J. Malmin; Norwegians in the West in 1844: A Contemporary Account, by Johan R. Reiersen, translated and edited by Theodore C. Blegen; An Emigrant Voyage in the Fifties, by H. Cock-Jensen, translated by Karen Larsen; Reminiscences of a Pioneer Editor, by Carl Fredrik Solberg, edited by Albert O. Barton. ISBN 0-87732-001-2 Out of print

**Volume II.** Northfield, 1927. 137 pp. Norwegian Emigrant Songs, translated and edited by Martin B. Ruud; Four Immigrant Shiploads of 1836 and 1837, by Henry J. Cadbury; Immigration As Viewed by a Norwegian-American Farmer in 1869, a letter translated and edited by Jacob Hodnefield; The Norwegian Pioneer in the Field of American Scholarship, by Laurence M. Larson; Norwegian Language and Literature in American Universities, by George T. Flom; Norwegian-American Church History, by George M. Stephenson. ISBN 0-87732-003-9 Out of print

**Volume III.** Northfield, 1928. 133 pp. The Disillusionment of an Immigrant: Sjur Jørgensen Haaeim's "Information on Conditions in North America," translated and edited by Gunnar J. Malmin; A Doctrinaire Idealist: Hans Barlien, by D. G. Ristad; Norwegian-American Emigration Societies of the Forties and Fifties, by Albert

O. Barton; Emigration As Viewed by a Norwegian Student of Agriculture in 1850: A. Budde's "From a Letter about America," translated by A. Sophie Bøe, with an introduction by Theodore C. Blegen; An Immigration Journey to America in 1854, a letter translated and edited by Henrietta Larson; Chicago As Viewed by a Norwegian Immigrant in 1864, a letter translated and edited by Brynjolf J. Hovde; The Historical Value of Church Records, by J. Magnus Rohne; A Norwegian-American Landnamsman: Ole S. Gjerset, by Knut Gjerset; The Icelandic Communities in America: Cultural Backgrounds and Early Settlements, by Thorstina Jackson.
ISBN 0-87732-006-3                                    Out of print

**Volume IV.** Northfield, 1929. 159 pp. A Contribution to the Study of the Adjustment of a Pioneer Pastor to American Conditions: Laur. Larsen, 1857–1880, by Karen Larsen; Report of the Annual Meeting of the Haugean Churches Held at Lisbon, Illinois, in June, 1854, translated and edited by J. Magnus Rohne; The Attitude of the United States toward Norway in the Crisis of 1905, by H. Fred Swansen; Immigration and Social Amelioration, by Joseph Schafer; The Mind of the Scandinavian Immigrant, by George M. Stephenson; Three Civil War Letters from 1862, translated and edited by Brynjolf J. Hovde; The Sinking of the "Atlantic" on Lake Erie, a letter translated and edited by Henrietta Larson; An Account of a Journey to California in 1852, by Tosten Kittelsen Stabæk, translated by Einar Haugen.
ISBN 0-87732-008-X                                    Price $8.00

**Volume V.** Northfield, 1930. 152 pp. An Early Norwegian Fur Trader of the Canadian Northwest, by Hjalmar R. Holand; Immigrant Women and the American Frontier, Three Early "America Letters," translated and edited by Theodore C. Blegen; From New York to Wisconsin in 1844, by Johan Gasmann, translated and edited by Carlton C. Qualey; Social and Economic Aspects of Pioneering As Illustrated in Goodhue County, Minnesota, by Theodore Nydahl; Norwegian-American Fiction, 1880–1928, by Aagot D. Hoidahl; Bjørnson and the Norwegian-Americans, 1880–81, by Arthur C. Paulson; The Beginnings of St. Olaf College, by I. F. Grose; Some Recent Publications Relating to Norwegian-American History, compiled by Jacob Hodnefield.
ISBN 0-87732-009-8                                    Price $8.00

**Volume VI.** Northfield, 1931. 191 pp. Illustrations, map. Norwegians in the Selkirk Settlement, by Paul Knaplund; Claus L. Clausen, Pioneer Pastor and Settlement Promoter: Illustrative Documents, translated and edited by Carlton C. Qualey; Lars Davidson Reque: Pioneer, by Sophie A. Bøe; A Pioneer Pastor's

Journey to Dakota in 1861, by Abraham Jacobson, translated by J. N. Jacobson; The Campaign of the Illinois Central Railroad for Norwegian and Swedish Immigrants, by Paul W. Gates; Norwegians at the Indian Forts on the Missouri River during the Seventies, by Einar Haugen; The Convention Riot at Benson Grove, Iowa, in 1876, by Laurence M. Larson; Bjørnson's Reaction to Emigration, by Arne Odd Johnsen; Alexander Corstvet and Anthony M. Rud, Norwegian-American Novelists, by Albert O. Barton; The Norwegian-American Historical Museum, by Knut Gjerset; Norwegian Migration to America before the Civil War, by Brynjolf J. Hovde; Some Recent Publications Relating to Norwegian-American History, II, compiled by Jacob Hodnefield. ISBN 0-87732-10-1                               Price $8.00

**Volume VII.** Northfield, 1933. 139 pp. Illustrations. Social Aspects of Prairie Pioneering: The Reminiscences of a Pioneer Pastor's Wife, by Mrs. R. O. Brandt; The Fraser River Gold Rush: An Immigrant Letter of 1858, translated and edited by C. A. Clausen; O. E. Rølvaag: Norwegian-American, by Einar I. Haugen; Some Recent Publications Relating to Norwegian-American History, III, compiled by Jacob Hodnefield; A Hunt for Norwegian-American Records, by Carlton C. Qualey; Ole Edvart Rølvaag, 1876–1931: In Memoriam, by Julius E. Olson. ISBN 0-87732-13-6                               Out of print

**Volume VIII.** Northfield, 1934, 176 pp. Tellef Grundysen and the Beginnings of Norwegian-American Fiction, by Laurence M. Larson; The Seventeenth of May in Mid-Atlantic: Ole Rynning's Emigrant Song, translated and edited by Theodore C. Blegen and Martin B. Ruud; Johannes Nordboe and Norwegian Immigration: An "America Letter" of 1837, edited by Arne Odd Johnsen; The First Norwegian Migration into Texas: Four "America Letters," translated and edited by Lyder L. Unstad; Norwegian-Americans and Wisconsin Politics in the Forties, by Bayrd Still; The Emigrant Journey in the Fifties, by Karl E. Erickson, edited by Albert O. Barton; The Political Position of *Emigranten* in the Election of 1852: A Documentary Article, by Harold M. Tolo; The Editorial Policy of *Skandinaven*, 1900–1903, by Agnes M. Larson; Some Recent Publications Relating to Norwegian-American History, IV, compiled by Jacob Hodnefield; Fort Thompson in the Eighties: A Communication. ISBN 0-87732-014-4                               Price $8.00

**Volume IX.** Northfield, 1936. 131 pp. Immigration and Puritanism, by Marcus L. Hansen; Svein Nilsson, Pioneer Norwegian-American Historian, by D. G. Ristad; The Sugar Creek Settlement in Iowa, by H. F. Swansen; Pioneer Town Building in the West: An America Letter Written by Frithjof Meidell at Springfield, Illinois, in 1855, translated with a foreword by Clarence A. Clausen; A Typical Norwegian Settlement: Spring Grove, Minnesota, by Carlton C. Qualey; Marcus Thrane in America: Some Unpublished Letters from 1880–1884, translated and edited by Waldemar Westergaard; The Missouri Flood of 1881, by Halvor B. Hustvedt, translated by Katherine Hustvedt; The Collection and Preservation of Sources, by Laurence M. Larson; Some Recent Publications Relating to Norwegian-American History, V, compiled by Jacob Hodnefield.

ISBN 0-87732-017-9                                           Price $8.00

**Volume X.** Northfield, 1938. 202 pp. Language and Immigration, by Einar I. Haugen; Two Early Norwegian Dramatic Societies in Chicago, by Napier Wilt and Henriette C. Koren Naeseth; A School and Language Controversy in 1858: A Documentary Study, translated and edited by Arthur C. Paulson and Kenneth Bjørk; A Newcomer Looks at American Colleges, translated and edited by Karen Larsen; The Norwegian Quakers of Marshall County, Iowa, by H. F. Swansen; The Main Factors in Rølvaag's Authorship, by Theodore Jorgenson; Magnus Swenson, Inventor and Engineer, by Olaf Hougen; Some Recent Publications Relating to Norwegian-American History, VI, compiled by Jacob Hodnefield.

ISBN 0-87732-019-5                                           Price $8.00

**Volume XI.** Northfield, 1940. 183 pp. *A Doll's House* on the Prairie: The First Ibsen Controversy in America, by Arthur C. Paulson and Kenneth Bjørk; Scandinavian Students at Illinois State University, by Henry O. Evjen; Stephen O. Himoe, Civil War Physician, by E. Biddle Heg; A Pioneer Church Library, by H. F. Swansen; Norwegian Emigration to America during the Nineteenth Century, by Ingrid Gaustad Semmingsen; Jørgen Gjerdrum's Letters from America, 1874–75, by Carlton C. Qualey; The Introduction of Domesticated Reindeer into Alaska, by Arthur S. Peterson; The Unknown Rølvaag: Secretary in the Norwegian-American Historical Association, by Kenneth Bjørk; The Sources of the Rølvaag Biography, by Nora O. Solum; Some Recent Publications Relating to Norwegian-American History, VII, compiled by Jacob Hodnefield.

ISBN 0-87732-022-5                                           Price $10.00

**Volume XII.** Northfield, 1941. 203 pp. Norwegian-American Surnames, by Marjorie M. Kimmerle; Norwegian Folk Narrative in America, by Ella Valborg Rølvaag; A Journey to America in the Fifties, by Clara Jacobson; James Denoon Reymert and the Norwegian Press, by Martin L. Reymert; Recollections of a Norwegian Pioneer in Texas, by Knudt Olson Hastvedt, translated and edited by C. A. Clausen; Norwegian Clubs in Chicago, by Birger Osland; Buslett's Editorship of *Normannen* from 1894 to 1896, by Evelyn Nilsen; Ole Edvart Rølvaag, by John Heitmann; Ole Evinrude and the Outboard Motor, by Kenneth Bjørk; Some Recent Publications Relating to Norwegian-American History, VIII, compiled by Jacob Hodnefield. ISBN 0-87732-024-1                                   Out of print

**Volume XIII.** Northfield, 1943. 203 pp. Pioneers in Dakota Territory, 1879–89, edited by Henry H. Bakken; An Official Report on Norwegian and Swedish Immigration, 1870, by A. Lewenhaupt, with a foreword by Theodore C. Blegen; Memories from Little Iowa Parsonage, by Caroline Mathilde Koren Naeseth, translated and edited by Henriette C. K. Naeseth; A Norwegian Schoolmaster Looks at America, an America letter translated and edited by C. A. Clausen; A Singing Church, by Paul Maurice Glasoe; A Norwegian Settlement in Missouri, by A. N. Rygg; Carl G. Barth, 1860–1939: A Sketch, by Florence M. Manning; Pioneering on the Pacific Coast, by John Storseth, with a foreword by Einar Haugen; Materials in the National Archives Relating to the Scandinavian Countries; The Norwegians in America, by Halvdan Koht; Some Recent Publications Relating to Norwegian-American History, IX, compiled by Jacob Hodnefield; Notes and Documents: Norway, Maine, by Halvdan Koht. ISBN 0-87732-025-X                                   Out of print

**Volume XIV.** Northfield, 1944. 264 pp. A Migration of Skills, by Kenneth Bjørk; An Immigrant Exploration of the Middle West in 1839, a letter by Johannes Johansen and Søren Bache, translated by the Verdandi Study Club; An Immigrant Shipload of 1840, by C. A. Clausen; Behind the Scenes of Emigration: A Series of Letters from the 1840's, by Johan R. Reiersen, translated by Carl O. Paulson and the Verdandi Study Club, edited by Theodore C. Blegen; The Ballad of Oleana: A Verse Translation, by Theodore C. Blegen; Knud Langeland: Pioneer Editor, by Arlow W. Andersen; Memories from Perry Parsonage, by Clara Jacobson; When America Called for Immigrants, by Halvdan Koht; The Norwegian Lutheran Academies, by B. H. Narveson; Pioneering on the Technical Front: A Story Told in America Letters, by Kenneth Bjørk; Some Recent Publications Relating to Norwegian-American History, X, by Jacob Hodnefield; Notes and Documents: Karel Hansen Toll, by A. N. Rygg. ISBN 0-87732-026-8                                   Out of print

**Volume XV.** Northfield, 1949. 238 pp. A Norwegian-American Pioneer Ballad, by Einar Haugen; Our Vanguard: A Pioneer Play in

Three Acts, with Prologue and Epilogue, by Aileen Berger Buetow; An Immigrant's Advice on America: Some Letters of Søren Bache, translated and edited by C. A. Clausen; Lincoln and the Union: A Study of the Editorials of *Emigranten* and *Fædrelandet*, by Arlow W. Andersen; Thorstein Veblen and St. Olaf College: A Group of Letters by Thorbjørn N. Mohn, edited by Kenneth Bjork; Kristian Prestgard: An Appreciation, by Henriette C. K. Naeseth; Julius B. Baumann: A Biographical Sketch, by John Heitmann; Erik L. Petersen, by Jacob Hodnefield; Scandinavia, Wisconsin, by Alfred O. Erickson; Some Recent Publications Relating to Norwegian-American History, XI, by Jacob Hodnefield; Notes and Documents: Norway, Maine, by Walter W. Wright.
ISBN 0-87732-030-6                                    Out of print

**Volume XVI.** Northfield, 1950. 218 pp. Hvistendahl's Mission to San Francisco, 1870–75, by Kenneth Bjork; Oregon and Washington Territory in the 1870's as Seen through the Eyes of a Pioneer Pastor, by Nora O. Solum; From the Prairie to Puget Sound, by O. B. Iverson, edited by Sverre Arestad; Life in the Klondike and Alaska Gold Fields, letters translated and edited by C. A. Clausen; From the Klondike to the Kougarok, by Carl L. Lokke; Some Recent Publications Relating to Norwegian-American History, XII, compiled by Jacob Hodnefield.
ISBN 0-87732-033-0                                    Price $10.00

**Volume XVII.** Northfield, 1952. 185 pp. The Struggle over Norwegian, by Einar Haugen; Brother Ebben in His Native Country, by Oystein Ore; Norwegian Gold Seekers in the Rockies, by Kenneth Bjork; Søren Jaabæk, Americanizer in Norway: A Study in Cultural Exchange, by Franklin D. Scott; First Sagas in a New World: A Study of the Beginnings of Norwegian-American Literature, by Gerald H. Thorson; Controlled Scholarship and Productive Nationalism, by Franklin D. Scott; The Second Twenty-five Years, by Theodore C. Blegen; Some Recent Publications Relating to Norwegian-American History, XIII, by Jacob Hodnefield.
ISBN 0-87732-035-7                                    Price $10.00

**Volume XVIII.** Northfield, 1954. 252 pp. Maps. Norwegian Migration to America, by Einar Haugen; Rasmus B. Anderson, Pioneer and Crusader, by Paul Knaplund; Early Norwegian Settlement in the Rockies, by Kenneth Bjork; A Little More Light on the Kendall Colony, by Richard Canuteson; Segregation and Assimilation of Norwegian Settlements in Wisconsin, by Peter A. Munch; The Novels of Peer Strømme, by Gerald Thorson; Norwegian-American *Bygdelags* and Their Publications, by Jacob Hodnefield;

Some Recent Publications Relating to Norwegian-American History, XIV, by Jacob Hodnefield.
ISBN 0-87732-037-3                                   Price $10.00

**Volume XIX.** Northfield, 1956. 218 pp. The Immigrant Image of America, by Theodore C. Blegen; Boyesen and the Norwegian Immigration, by Clarence A. Glasrud; Norwegian Forerunners among the Early Mormons, by William Mulder; "Snowshoe" Thompson: Fact and Legend, by Kenneth Bjork; Norwegian-Danish Methodism on the Pacific Coast, by Arlow William Andersen; A Quest for Norwegian Folk Art in America, by Tora Bøhn; The Trials of an Immigrant: The Journal of Ole K. Trovatten, translated and edited by Clarence A. Clausen; Norwegian Emigrants with University Training, 1830–1880, by Oystein Ore; Some Recent Publications Relating to Norwegian-American History, XV, compiled by Clarence A. Clausen.
ISBN 0-87732-039-X                                   Price $10.00

**Volume XX.** Northfield, 1959. 246 pp. Ibsen in America, by Einar Haugen; Still More Light on the Kendall Colony: A Unique Slooper Letter, by Mario S. De Pillis; A Texas Manifesto: A Letter from Mrs. Elise Wærenskjold, translated and edited by Clarence A. Clausen; History and Sociology, by Peter A. Munch; Beating to Windward, by Otto M. Bratrud, edited by Sverre Arestad; Pioneering in Alaska, by Knute L. Gravem; Marcus Thrane in Christiania: Some Unpublished Letters from 1850–51, translated and edited by Waldemar Westergaard; A Centenary of Norwegian Studies in American Institutions of Learning, by Hedin Bronner; Elizabeth Fedde's Diary, 1883–88, translated and edited by Beulah Folkedahl; The Content of Studies and Records, Volumes 1–20, compiled by Helen Thane Katz; "With Great Price," by John M. Gaus; Some Recent Publications Relating to Norwegian-American History, XVI, compiled by Clarence A. Clausen.
ISBN 0-87732-041-1                                   Price $10.00

**Volume XXI** *(Norwegian-American Studies).* Northfield, 1962. 311 pp. Theodore C. Blegen, by Carlton C. Qualey; The Scandinavian Immigrant Writer in America, by Dorothy Burton Skårdal; Questing for Gold and Furs in Alaska, edited by Sverre Arestad; Norwegians Become Americans, translated and edited by Beulah Folkedahl; Cleng Peerson and the Communitarian Background of Norwegian Immigration, by Mario S. De Pillis; Early Years in Dakota, by Barbara Levorsen; A Pioneer Diary from Wisconsin, by Malcolm Rosholt; A Covenant Folk, with Scandinavian Colorings, by Kenneth O. Bjork; Reiersen's Texas, translated and edited by Derwood Johnson; J. R. Reiersen's "Indiscretions," by Einar Hau-

gen; Some Recent Publications, compiled by Beulah Folkedahl; From the Archives, by Beulah Folkedahl.
ISBN 0-87732-043-8                              Price $10.00

**Volume XXII.** Northfield, 1965. 264 pp. Illustrations. A Pioneer Artist and His Masterpiece, by Marion John Nelson; Kristofer Janson's Lecture Tour, 1879–80, by Nina Draxten; Two Men of Old Waupaca, by Malcolm Rosholt; Pioneering in Montana, edited by Sverre Arestad; Seven America Letters to Valdres, translated and edited by Carlton C. Qualey; Music for Youth in an Emerging Church, by Gerhard M. Cartford; Our Bread and Meat, by Barbara Levorsen; The Independent Historical Society, by Walter Muir Whitehill; Some Recent Publications, compiled by Beulah Folkedahl; From the Archives, by Beulah Folkedahl.
ISBN 0-87732-045-4                              Price $10.00

**Volume XXIII.** Northfield, 1967. 256 pp. The Norwegian Immigrant and His Church, by Eugene L. Fevold; Some Civil War Letters of Knute Nelson, edited by Millard L. Gieske; An Immigrant Boy on the Frontier, by Simon Johnson, translated with an introduction by Nora O. Solum; The Gasmann Brothers Write Home, translated and edited by C. A. Clausen; Knud Knudsen and His America Book, by Beulah Folkedahl; Kristofer Janson's Beginning Ministry, by Nina Draxten; Knut Hamsun's America, by Arlow W. Andersen; The Romantic Spencerian, by Marc L. Ratner; Some Recent Publications, compiled by Beulah Folkedahl; From the Archives, by Beulah Folkedahl.
ISBN 0-87732-048-9                              Price $10.00

**Volume XXIV.** Northfield, 1970. 301 pp. Thor Helgeson: Schoolmaster and Raconteur, by Einar Haugen; The Letters of Mons H. Grinager: Pioneer and Soldier, collected by Per Hvamstad, translated by C. A. Clausen; The Norwegian Press in North Daktota, by Odd Sverre Løvoll; H. Tambs Lyche: Propagandist for America, by Paul Knaplund; The Social Criticism of Ole Edvart Rølvaag, by Neil T. Eckstein; A Thanksgiving Day Address by Georg Sverdrup, by James S. Hamre; Hamsun and America, by Sverre Arestad; Gold, Salt Air, and Callouses, by Thomas L. Benson; Norwegians in New York, by Knight Hoover; Some Recent Publications, compiled by Beulah Folkedahl; From the Archives, by Beulah Folkedahl.
ISBN 0-87732-050-0                              Price $10.00

**Volume XXV.** Northfield, 1972. 293 pp. The *Bygdelag* Movement, by Odd Sverre Løvoll; Knut Gjerset, by David T. Nelson; Norway's Organized Response to Emigration, by Arne Hassing; The Founding of Quatsino Colony, by Kenneth O. Bjork; Norwegian Soldiers in the Confederate Forces, by C. A. Clausen and Derwood Johnson;

Lars and Martha Larson: "We Do What We Can for Them," by Richard L. Canuteson; Ibsen in Seattle, by Sverre Arestad; From Norwegian State Church to American Free Church, by J. C. K. Preus; The 1842 Immigrants from Norway, by Gerhard B. Naeseth; Some Recent Publications, compiled by Beulah Folkedahl and C. A. Clausen; From the Archives, by Beulah Folkedahl and C. A. Clausen.

ISBN 0-87732-052-7                                    Price $10.00

**Volume XXVI.** Northfield, 1974. 271 pp. Scandinavian Migration to the Canadian Prairie Provinces, 1893–1914, by Kenneth O. Bjork; The Story of Peder Anderson, translated and edited by Eva L. Haugen; Emigration from Land Parish to America, 1866–1875, by Arvid Sandaker, translated by C. A. Clausen; The Brothers Week, by Malcolm Rosholt; Rølvaag's Search for Soria Moria, by Raychel A. Haugrud; Notes of a Civil War Soldier, by Bersven Nelson, translated and edited by C. A. Clausen; Farewell to an Old Homestead, by Ethel J. Odegard; Georg Sverdrup and the Augsburg Plan of Education, by James S. Hamre; Factors in Assimilation: A Comparative Study, by Torben Krontoft; The School Controversy among Norwegian Immigrants, by Frank C. Nelsen; Norwegians in "Zion" Teach Themselves English, by Helge Seljaas; Breidablik, by Rodney Nelson; Some Recent Publications, compiled by C. A. Clausen.

ISBN 0-87732-054-3                                    Price $10.00

**Volume XXVII.** Northfield, 1977. 323 pp. Hegra before and after the Emigration Era, by Jon Leirfall, translated and edited by C. A. Clausen; Marcus Hansen, Puritanism and Scandinavian Immigrant Temperance Movements, by Frederick Hale; Three America Letters to Lesja, translated and edited by Carlton C. Qualey; Berdahl Family History and Rølvaag's Immigrant Triology, by Kristoffer F. Paulson; *Decorah-Posten*: The Story of an Immigrant Newspaper, by Odd S. Lovoll; *Symra*: A Memoir, by Einar Haugen; Erik Morstad's Missionary Work Among Wisconsin Indians, by A. E. Morstad; Polygamy among the Norwegian Mormons, by Helge Seljaas; Wisconsin Scandinavians and Progressivism, 1900–1950, by David L. Brye; Name Change and the Church, 1918–1920, by Carl H. Chrislock; American Press Opinion and Norwegian Independence, 1905, by Terje I. Leiren; The Kendall Settlement Survived, by Richard L. Canuteson; The Popcorn Man, by Rodney Nelson; An Outsider's View of the Association, by Rudolph J. Vecoli; Some Recent Publications, compiled by C. A. Clausen; From the Archives, by Charlotte Jacobson.

ISBN 0-87732-058-6                                    Price $10.00

**Volume XXVIII.** Northfield, 1979. 367 pp. Authority and Freedom: Controversy in Norwegian-American Congregatons, by Peter A. Munch; *Skandinaven* and the John Anderson Publishing Company, by Jean Skogerboe Hansen; Martha Ostenso: A Norwegian-American Immigrant Novelist, by Joan N. Buckley; Norwegians, Danes, and the Origins of the Evangelical Free Tradition, by Frederick Hale; Two Immigrants for the Union: Their Civil War Letters, by Lars and Knud Olsen Dokken, translated by Della Kittleson Catuna, edited by Carol Lynn H. Knight and Gerald S. Cowden; Oslo on the Texas High Plains, by Peter L. Petersen; Dark Decade: The Declining Years of Waldemar Ager, by Clarence Kilde; Methodism from America to Norway, by Arne Hassing; Beret and the Prairie in *Giants in the Earth*, by Curtis D. Ruud; The Vossing Correspondence Society and the Report of Adam Løvenskjold, translated and edited by Lars Fletre; The Danish-Language Press in America, by Marion Marzolf; Norwegian-American Pastors in Immigrant Fiction, 1870–1920, by Duane R. Lindberg; Carl L. Boeckmann: Norwegian Artist in the New World, by Marilyn Boeckmann Anderson; Some Recent Publications, compiled by C. A. Clausen; From the Archives, by Charlotte Jacobson.
ISBN 0-87732-063-2                                      Price $10.00

**Volume XXIX.** Northfield, 1983. 402 pp. Haugeans, Rappites, and the Emigration of 1825, by Ingrid Semmingsen, translated by C. A. Clausen; Emigration from the Community of Tinn, 1837–1907: Demographic, Economic, and Social Background, by Andres A. Svalestuen, translated by C. A. Clausen; *Angst* on the Prairie: Reflections on Immigrants, Rølvaag, and Beret, by Harold P. Simonson; Emigration from the District of Sogn, 1839–1915, by Rasmus Sunde, translated by C. A. Clausen; Emigration from Sunnfjord to America Prior to 1885, by Leiv H. Dvergsdal, translated by C. A. Clausen; The Lynching of Hans Jakob Olson, 1889: The Story of a Norwegian-American Crime, by Odin W. Anderson; Emigration from a Fjord District on Norway's West Coast, 1852–1915, by Ragnar Standal, translated by C. A. Clausen; Emigration from Dovre, 1865–1914, by Arnfinn Engen, translated by C. A. Clausen; Sigbjørn Obstfelder and America, by Sverre Arestad; Emigration from Brønnøy and Vik in Helgeland, by Kjell Erik Skaaren, translated by C. A. Clausen; Emigration from Agder to America, 1890–1915, by Sverre Ordahl, translated by C. A. Clausen; Sondre Norheim: Folk Hero to Immigrant, by John Weinstock; Some Recent Publications, compiled by C. A. Clausen; Index to Volumes 1–29 of *Norwegian-American Studies*, compiled by Charlotte Jacobson.
ISBN 0-87732-068-3                                      Price $10.00

**Volume XXX.** Northfield, 1985. 340 pp. O. A. Tveitmoe: Labor Leader, by Lloyd Hustvedt; Scandinavian Settlement in Seattle, "Queen City of the Puget Sound," by Patsy Adams Hegstad; Ole and the Reds: The "Americanism" of Seattle Mayor Ole Hanson, by Terje I. Leiren; Norwegians in the Pacific Coast Fisheries, by Sverre Arestad; Reindeer, Gold, and Scandal, by Kenneth O. Bjork; The Pioneers of Dog Fish Bay, by Rangvald Kvelstad; Three Spokesmen for Norwegian Lutheran Academies: Schools for Church, Heritage, Society, by James S. Hamre; The Domestic Architecture and Cabinetry of Luther Valley, by Claire Selkurt; The Poetry of Agnes Mathilde Wergeland, by Larry Emil Scott; Some Recent Publications, compiled by C. A. Clausen and Johanna Barstad; From the Archives, by Charlotte Jacobson.
ISBN 0-87732-070-5                                     Price $15.00

**Volume XXXI.** Northfield, 1986. 347 pp. The Mobilization of Immigrants in Urban America, by John Higham; Profile of a Ward Boss: The Political Career of Lars M. Rand, by Carl H. Chrislock; The Norwegian Heritage in Urban America: Conflict and Cooperation in a Norwegian Immigrant Community, by Christen T. Jonassen; The Haymarket Affair and the Norwegian Immigrant Press, by Arlow W. Andersen; "I Live Well, But . . . ": Letters from Norwegians in Industrial America, by John R. Jenswold; Minneapolis Picture Album, 1870–1935: Images of Norwegians in the City, by Deborah L. Miller; *Washington Posten*: A Window on a Norwegian-American Urban Community, by Odd S. Lovoll; *Skandinaven* and the Beginnings of Professional Publishing, by Orm Øverland; Who Was Herm. Wang?, by Ingrid Semmingsen; "The Best Place on Earth for Women": The American Experience of Aasta Hansteen, by Janet E. Rasmussen; "Dear Sara Alelia": An Episode in Rølvaag's Life, by Einar Haugen; Norwegian-American Artists' Exhibitions Described in Checklists and Catalogs, by Rolf H. Erickson; Some Recent Publications, compiled by C. A. Clausen and Johanna Barstad; From the Archives, by Charlotte Jacobson.
ISBN 0-87732-072-1                                     Price $15.00

**Volume XXXII.** Northfield, 1989. 298 pp. The Norwegian-American Dairy-Tobacco Strategy in Southwestern Wisconsin, by Robert A. Ibarra and Arnold Strickon; Poverty, Overpopulation, and the Early Emigration from Sogn, by Aage Engesæter, translated by C. A. Clausen; Sociological Theories and the Great Emigration, by B. Lindsay Lowell; "I met him at Normanna Hall": Ethnic Cohesion and Marital Patterns among Scandinavian Immigrant Women, by Janet E. Rasmussen; Immigrant Dynamics — The Jacobson Farmstead, by Steven L. Johnson and Marion J. Nelson; Two Museum Houses: A Microanalysis of Cultural Adaptation in the Upper Midwest in the Late Nineteenth Century, by Reidar Bakken, translated by C. A. Clausen; A Letter of 1852 from Eldorado, translated and edited by J. R. Christianson; Letters to Immigrants in the Midwest from the Telemark Region of Norway, by Øyvind T. Gulliksen; Twelve Civil War Letters of Col. Hans C. Heg to his Son, edited by E. Biddle Heg; The Americanization of the Norwegian Pastors' Wives, by Gracia Grindal; Rølvaag's Lost Novel, by Einar Haugen; A Cappella Choirs in the Scandinavian-American Lutheran Colleges, by Paul Benson; Some Recent Publications, compiled by Rolf H. Erickson and Johanna Barstad; From the Archives, by Charlotte Jacobson.

ISBN 0-87732-076-4                                    Price $15.00

### Travel and Description Series

**Volume I.** *Ole Rynning's True Account of America.* Translated and edited by Theodore C. Blegen. Minneapolis, 1926. 100 pp. Historical introduction; original text of Rynning's book about America as published in Norway in 1838; and a complete English translation.
ISBN 0-87732-002-0                                    Out of print

**Volume II.** *Peter Testman's Account of His Experiences in North America.* Translated and edited by Theodore C. Blegen. Northfield, 1927. 60 pp. Historical introduction; facsimile of Testman's account of America as published in Norway in 1839; and a complete English translation.
ISBN 0-87732-004-7                                    Price $3.00

**Volume III.** *America in the Forties: The Letters of Ole Munch Ræder.* Translated and edited by Gunnar J. Malmin. Published for the Norwegian-American Historical Association by the University of Minnesota Press, Minneapolis, 1929. 244 pp. Historical introduction, frontispiece, index. A series of informal travel letters written 1847–48 by a Norwegian scholar who was sent by his government to America to make a study of the jury system.
ISBN 0-87732-007-1                                    Out of print

**Volume IV.** *Frontier Parsonage: The Letters of Olaus Fredrik Duus, Norwegian Pastor in Wisconsin, 1855–1858.* Translated by the Verdandi Study Club of Minneapolis and edited by Theodore C. Blegen. Northfield, 1947. 120 pp. Historical introduction, index.
ISBN 0-87732-029-2                                    Out of print

**Volume V.** *Frontier Mother: The Letters of Gro Svendsen.* Translated and edited by Pauline Farseth and Theodore C. Blegen. Northfield, 1950. 153 pp. Historical introduction, frontispiece, index.
ISBN 0-87732-031-4                                    Out of print

**Volume VI.** *The Lady with the Pen: Elise Wærenskjold in Texas.* Translated by the Verdandi Study Club of Minneapolis and edited by C. A. Clausen; foreword by Theodore C. Blegen. Northfield, 1961. 183 pp. Historical introduction, illustrations, index.
ISBN 0-87732-042-X                                   Out of print

**Volume VII.** *Klondike Saga: The Chronicle of a Minnesota Gold Mining Company.* by Carl L. Lokke. Preface by Kenneth O. Bjork; foreword by Senator Ernest Gruening. Published for the Norwegian-American Historical Association by the University of Minnesota Press, Minneapolis, 1965. 211 pp. Illustrations, maps, appendices, index.
ISBN 0-87732-046-2                                   Out of print

**Volume VIII.** *A Pioneer Churchman: J. W. C. Dietrichson in Wisconsin, 1844–1850.* Includes Dietrichson's Travel Narrative and Koshkonong Parish Journal. Edited and with an Introduction by E. Clifford Nelson. Translated by Malcolm Rosholt and Harris E. Kaasa. Published for the Norwegian-American Historical Association by Twayne Publishers, Inc., New York. 1973. 265 pp. Introduction, appendices, index, illustration, maps.
ISBN 0-87732-053-5                                   Price $9.00

**Volume IX.** *Pathfinder for Norwegian Emigrants.* By Johan Reinert Reiersen. Translated by Frank G. Nelson. Edited by Kenneth O. Bjork. Northfield, 1981. 239 pp. Historical introduction, frontispieces, appendices, index.
ISBN 0-87732-065-9                                   Price $12.00

**Volume X.** *On Both Sides of the Ocean: A Part of Per Hagen's Journey.* Translated, with Introduction and Notes, by Kate Stafford and Harald Naess. Northfield, 1984. 70 pp.
ISBN 0-87732-069-1                                   Price $8.00

*Special Publications*

*Norwegian Sailors on the Great Lakes: A Study in the History of American Inland Transportation.* By Knut Gjerset. Northfield, 1928. 211 pp. Illustrations, index.
ISBN 0-87732-005-5                                   Out of print

*Norwegian Migration to America, 1825–1860.* By Theodore C. Blegen. Northfield, 1931. 412 pp. Illustrations, maps, appendix, index.
ISBN 0-87732-011-X                                   Out of print

*Norwegian Sailors in American Waters: A Study in the History of Maritime Activity on the Eastern Seaboard.* By Knut Gjerset. Northfield, 1933. 271 pp. Illustrations, index.
ISBN 0-87732-012-8                                   Out of print

*The Civil War Letters of Colonel Hans Christian Heg.* Edited by Theodore C. Blegen. Northfield, 1936. 260 pp. Historical introduction, illustrations, index.
ISBN 0-87732-015-2 Out of print

*Laur. Larsen: Pioneer College President.* By Karen Larsen. Northfield, 1936. 358 pp. Illustrations, bibliographical note, index.
ISBN 0-87732-016-0 Out of print

*The Changing West and Other Essays.* By Laurence M. Larson. Northfield, 1937. 180 pp. Illustrations, index.
ISBN 0-87732-018-7 Price $8.00

*Norwegian Settlement in the United States.* By Carlton C. Qualey. Northfield, 1939. 285 pp. Illustrations, maps, appendix, bibliography, index.
ISBN 0-87732-020-9 Out of print

*The Log Book of a Young Immigrant.* By Laurence M. Larson. Northfield, 1939. 318 pp. Illustrations, selected list of Larson's writings, index.
ISBN 0-87732-021-7 Price $9.00

*Norwegian Migration to America: The American Transition.* By Theodore C. Blegen. Northfield, 1940. 655 pp. Illustrations, appendix, index.
ISBN 0-87732-023-3 Out of print

*A Long Pull from Stavanger: The Reminiscences of a Norwegian Immigrant.* By Birger Osland. Northfield, 1945. 263 pp. Portrait, index.
ISBN 0-87732-027-6 Price $8.00

*Saga in Steel and Concrete: Norwegian Engineers in America.* By Kenneth Bjork. Northfield, 1947. 504 pp. Illustrations, index.
ISBN 0-87732-028-4 Price $10.00

*Grass of the Earth: Immigrant Life in the Dakota Country.* By Aagot Raaen. Northfield, 1950. 238 pp. Index.
ISBN 0-87732-032-2 Out of print

*A Chronicle of Old Muskego: The Dairy of Søren Bache, 1839–1847.* Translated and edited by Clarence A. Clausen and Andreas Elviken. Northfield, 1951. 237 pp. Historical introduction, portrait, appendix, index.
ISBN 0-87732-034-9 Out of print

*The Immigrant Takes His Stand: The Norwegian-American Press and Public Affairs, 1847–1872.* By Arlow William Andersen. Northfield, 1953. 176 pp. Bibliography, index.
ISBN 0-87732-036-5 Out of print

*The Diary of Elisabeth Koren, 1853–1855.* Translated and edited by David T. Nelson. Northfield, 1955. 381 pp. Historical introduction, illustrations, index. Available through Vesterheim, the Norwegian-American Museum, Decorah, Iowa.
ISBN 0-87732-038-1

*West of the Great Divide: Norwegian Migration to the Pacific Coast, 1847–1893.* By Kenneth O. Bjork. Northfield, 1958. 671 pp. Illustrations, maps, index.
ISBN 0-87732-040-3                                             Out of print

*John A. Johnson: An Uncommon American.* By Agnes M. Larson, Northfield, 1969. 312 pp. Illustrations, appendixes, index.
ISBN 0-87732-049-7                                             Price $8.00

*A Folk Epic: The* Bygdelag *in America.* By Odd Sverre Lovoll. Published for the Norwegian-American Historical Association by Twayne Publishers, Inc., Boston, 1975. 326 pp. Illustrations, bibliography, index.
ISBN 0-87732-055-1                                             Price $15.00

*The Norwegian-American Historical Association, 1825–1975.* By Odd Sverre Lovoll and Kenneth O. Bjork. Northfield, 1975. 72 pp. Appendix.
ISBN 0-87732--056-X                                            Price $3.00

*Guide to Manuscripts Collections of the Norwegian-American Historical Association.* Compiled and edited by Lloyd Hustvedt. Northfield, 1979. 158 pp.
ISBN 0-87732-062-4                                             Price $7.50

*Makers of an American Immigrant Legacy: Essays in Honor of Kenneth O. Bjork.* Edited by Odd S. Lovoll. Northfield, 1980. 223 pp. Frontispiece. Tabula Gratulatoria.
ISBN 0-87732-064-0                                             Out of print

*The Promise of America: A History of the Norwegian-American People.* By Odd S. Lovoll. Published in cooperation with the University of Minnesota Press, Minneapolis, 1984. 239 pp. Illustrations, bibliography, index.
ISBN 0-8166-1331-1                                             Price $35.00

*Han Ola og han Per: A Norwegian-American Comic Strip.* By Peter J. Rosendahl. Introduced and edited by Joan N. Buckley and Einar Haugen. Published in cooperation with Universitetsforlaget, Oslo, 1984. 262 pp.
ISBN 82-00-06741-6                                            Price $30.00

*A Century of Urban Life: The Norwegians in Chicago before 1930.* By

Odd S. Lovoll. Northfield, 1988. 367 pp. Illustrations, maps, index.
ISBN 0-87732-075-6                                          Price $29.95

*Authors Series*

**Volume I.** *Hjalmar Hjorth Boyesen.* By Clarence A. Glasrud. Northfield, 1963. 245 pp. Illustrations, bibliography, index.
ISBN 0-87732-044-6                                          Price $8.00

**Volume II.** *Rasmus Bjørn Anderson: Pioneer Scholar.* By Lloyd Hustvedt. Northfield, 1966. 381 pp. Illustrations, bibliography, index.
ISBN 0-87732-047-0                                          Out of print

**Volume III.** *Kristofer Janson in America.* By Nina Draxten. Published for the Norwegian-American Historical Association by Twayne Publishers, Inc., Boston, 1976. 401 pp. Illustrations, bibliography, index.
ISBN 0-87732-057-8                                          Price $12.00

**Volume IV.** *Theodore C. Blegen: A Memoir.* By John T. Flanagan. Northfield, 1977. 181 pp. Bibliography, index.
ISBN 0-87732-060-8                                          Price $8.00

**Volume V.** *Land of the Free: Bjørnstjerne Bjørnson's America Letters.* Edited and translated by Eva Lund Haugen and Einar Haugen. Northfield, 1978. 311 pp. Illustrations, bibliography, index.
ISBN 0-87732-061-6                                          Price $15.00

**Volume VI.** *A Chronicler of Immigrant Life: Svein Nilsson's Articles in Billed-Magazin, 1868–1870.* Translated and introduced by C. A. Clausen. Northfield, 1982. 171 pp. Illustrations, index.
ISBN 0-87732-067-5                                          Price $12.00

*Topical Studies*

**Volume I.** *A Voice of Protest: Norwegians in American Politics, 1890–1917.* By Jon Wefald. Northfield, 1971. 94 pp. Bibliography, index.
ISBN 0-87732-051-9                                          Out of print

**Volume II.** *Cultural Pluralism versus Assimilation: The Views of Waldemar Ager.* Edited by Odd S. Lovoll. Northfield, 1977. 136 pp. Frontispiece.
ISBN 0-87732-059-4                                          Price $6.00

**Volume III** *Ethnicity Challenged: The Upper Midwest Norwegian-American Experience in World War I.* By Carl H. Chrislock. Northfield, 1981. 174 pp. Illustrations, index.
ISBN 0-87732-066-7                                          Price $10.00

**Volume IV.** *The Testing of M. Falk Gjertsen.* By Nina Draxten. Northfield, 1988. 134 pp. Illustrations, index.
ISBN 9-87732-074-8                                    Price $12.00

*Biographical Series*

**Volume I.** *Georg Sverdrup: Educator, Theologian, Churchman.* By James S. Hamre. Northfield, 1986. 218 pp. Illustrations, index.
ISBN 0-87732-071-3                                    Price $15.00

**Volume II.** *Marcus Thrane: A Norwegian Radical in America.* By Terje I. Leiren. Northfield, 1987. 167 pp. Illustrations, index.
ISBN 0-87732-073-X                                    Price $12.00

# A Suggestion

Permanent endowment funds for the Norwegian-American Historical Association are being built up to insure the carrying on of the work that has been started. It is imperative that these funds be increased generously, and it is hoped that in not a few instances gifts and bequests will be made to the Association for this purpose.* The treasurer has suggested the following form of bequest.

Being in sympathy with the movement to preserve the records and make public the historical facts pertaining to the Norwegian-American people, I hereby give and bequeath unto the Norwegian-American Historical Association, incorporated under the laws of Minnesota, the sum of _____ dollars to be paid in due course of the administration of my estate.

Signed

*Persons planning bequests are advised to comply with the laws concerning the preparation of wills in the states in which they reside. In case of doubt, consult an attorney.